K

VOICES OF

VIETNAM

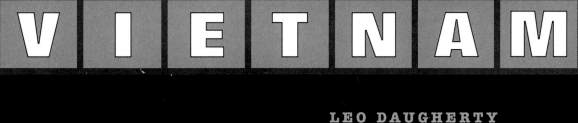

VIETNAM

LEO DAUGHERTY

First published in the United States in 2003 by
Lewis International, Inc.
Copyright © 2003 The Brown Reference Group plc

The right of The Brown Reference Group plc to be
identified as authors of this work has been asserted
by them in accordance with the Copyright,
Designs and Patents Acts, 1988.

Lewis International, Inc.
2201 N.W. 102 Place, #1
Miami, F1 33172 USA

Tel: 305-436-7984 / 800-259-5962
Fax: 305-436-7985 / 800-664-5095

ISBN 1-930983-18-2

Editorial and Design:
The Brown Reference Group plc
8 Chapel Place
Rivington Street
London
EC2A 3DQ
UK
www.brownreference.com

Printed in China

Senior Editor: Peter Darman
Editor: Alan Marshall
Junior Editor: James Murphy
Picture Research: Andrew Webb, Peter Darman
Design: Jerry Udall
Map Artworks: Bob Garwood
Production: Alastair Gourlay

Page 2: A US CH-47 Chinook during Operation
Cedar Falls. (Brown Reference Group/US National
Archives)

CONTENTS

CHAPTER 1
THE FIRST INDO-CHINESE WAR 1946-1954

General Henri Eugène Navarre, who led French forces at the end of the First Indo-Chinese War (1946–54), could have abandoned Laos while under pressure from enemy forces and thus avoided the Battle of Dien Bien Phu. However, to have done so "would have branded me as the man who had betrayed the honour of his country".[1]

The story of France's involvement in the First Indo-Chinese War is one replete with honour won and lost in a war fought in the swamps, jungles and coastal enclaves of Vietnam. It lasted until the start of the Geneva Conference in May 1954, which partitioned Vietnam into two de facto states at the 17th Parallel. Even as the diplomats decided the fate of Indo-China against the backdrop of the Geneva Conference and Cold War in Southeast Asia, French and Vietnamese forces fought a savage war of attrition for control of the whole of the area.

Background to war

French rule in Vietnam was the result of an intense imperial rivalry that began with the other great European powers in the mid-seventeenth century. Actual French colonization of Indo-China began in 1859 with the conquest and seizure of Saigon. It resulted in the conquest of all of southern Vietnam in 1867. By 1883, French troops had occupied all of northern Vietnam around Hanoi; and, by 1884, Tongkin (hereafter Tonkin). Afterwards, French businessmen and civil administrators arrived and absorbed the colony into the French Empire. Indo-China refers to the three states of Vietnam, Laos and Cambodia. After 1893 the French established the first Indo-Chinese Union to govern the area.

For the Vietnamese, French rule was both authoritarian and arbitrary. Several underground resistance movements took shape between 1890 and 1940, challenging French rule. The most strident were the Viet Nam Quoc Dan Dang (VNQDD), primarily a nationalist-based organization founded in 1927; and the Indo-Chinese Communist Party (ICP), led by Ho Chi Minh.

In 1930, the first of a series of local rebellions broke out in Tonkin, fuelling a peasant revolt under communist leadership. Sponsored by the VNQDD and ICP, the rebellions sought to drive out the French and establish an independent Vietnam. However, French and colonial troops suppressed the rebellions, and imprisoned many of its leaders including future North Vietnamese figures Le Duc Tho and General Vo Nguyen Giap. During this period the seeds of the First Indo-Chinese War were sown.

As the clouds of war appeared in Europe and Asia in the late 1930s, the chance that many Vietnamese nationalist leaders had hoped for arrived. France's fall to Germany in June 1940 signalled the second phase of Vietnam's drive for independence. In Indo-China, the Japanese occupied the Tonkin area but allowed the Vichy government to administer the rest of the region. Only in March 1945 did the Japanese intern French personnel and proclaim the autonomous state of Vietnam.

In 1940, Ho organized the ICP and other Vietnamese nationalist organizations into a single group which, with Nationalist Chinese support, carried out a sustained guerrilla campaign against the Japanese. This was the Viet Minh (Viet Nam Doc Lap Minh Hoi). After the US and Great Britain entered World War II in the Pacific, the Viet Minh began to receive arms and advisors from the US Office of Strategic Services (OSS).

Organized and trained by members of the OSS, Ho's forces undertook a guerrilla campaign against the Japanese, hitting munitions dumps, rescuing downed American airmen, and supplying Major-General Claire L. Chennault's China-based 14th Air Force with valuable intelligence. Encouraged by US President Roosevelt's and British Prime Minister Churchill's declaration of the Atlantic Charter, which supported the idea of self-government for the former European colonies in Asia and Africa, Ho organized what became Vietnam's first provisional government. With the sudden collapse of Japanese rule in all of Southeast Asia in August 1945, and the occupation of northern Vietnam by Chiang Kai-shek's Nationalist Chinese troops, Ho proclaimed the Democratic Republic of Vietnam (DRV).

Vietnam was occupied in the north by the Chinese, and in the south by British and Indian troops. Admiral Lord Louis Mountbatten, heading the Southeast Asia Command (SEAC), permitted French troops to re-enter southern Vietnam. Ho's request to the new US President Truman that pressure be applied on Paris to grant Vietnam the same semi-independent status the US gave the Philippines prior to independence in 1946 proved futile.

The communist Viet Minh made excellent use of the local terrain in their war against the French. Their use of waterways to transport men and materials through the dense jungle was effective, but it meant equipment had to be carried on foot.

With the fall of Chiang's Kuomintang government in China to Mao Zedong's communist forces, the Truman Administration became more sympathetic to France's claim in Indo-China, seeing it as a general war against communism.

As the Cold War between the US and the Soviet Union intensified, the outbreak of a "shooting" war on the Korean peninsula in June 1950 signalled the start of US military and economic assistance to France in Vietnam. Unable to defeat the elusive Viet Minh, Navarre set out to force Giap's forces into a major set-piece battle in the Dien Bien Phu Valley starting in November 1953. However, on the morning of 1 May 1954, after 209 days of combat, Dien Bien Phu fell. The Viet Minh victory had set the stage for the second and last war of independence against the US-supported regime of South Vietnam. North of the 17th Parallel Ho led the Democratic Republic of Vietnam.

War between France and the Viet Minh broke out while diplomatic negotiations continued in Paris. In September 1945, after having been released from Japanese captivity, French paratroopers and Legionnaires went on a rampage, shooting and clubbing innocent Vietnamese civilians in Tonkin. Shortly afterwards, French and Viet Minh forces exchanged small-arms and mortar fire in Saigon. In response to the violence, France's leader General Charles de Gaulle appointed the nationalist Admiral Georges Thierry d'Argenlieu as the high commissioner for Indo-China; and General Jacques Leclerc, the decorated war hero, as his military commander. Leclerc saw a negotiated settlement as the only way to end the chaos in the French colony, but heeded the words of General Douglas MacArthur: "Bring troops, more troops, as many as you can."[2]

Leclerc initiated a series of military offensives aimed at driving the Viet Minh away from Saigon and out of the Mekong Delta area. In tactics used against French and, later, American forces, the Viet Minh ambushed columns and conducted a scorched-earth policy wherever possible. After a five-month campaign, the regions in which Leclerc had been operating appeared to be pacified. However, a French soldier, Philippe Devillers, wrote that "once we departed, believing a region pacified, the Viet Minh would arrive on our heel". Devillers offered his view of what could be done to neutralize the Viet Minh: "There was only one possible defence, to multiply our posts, fortify them, arm and train the villagers, coordinate intelligence and police. What was required was not Leclerc's 35,000 troops but 100,000 – and Cochin China was not the only problem".[3]

Ho attempted to find a compromise. In 1946, he signalled his willingness to accept some sort of dominion status for Vietnam for five years and allow 25,000 French troops back into northern Vietnam. However, the instability of post-war French governments, coupled with d'Argenlieu's hard-line stance, meant that the eight weeks Ho spent negotiating in Paris were in vain.

On the morning of 20 November 1946, soon after Ho returned to Hanoi, a French gunboat attempted to seize a boat carrying

Vo Nguyen Giap (left), the Viet Minh general, instructs a liberation unit at Kao-Bak-Lang. General Giap was the mastermind behind the defeat of the French at Dien Bien Phu. Learning his trade against the Japanese during World War II, Giap became an effective general. Able to relate to the common man whilst mastering the finer points of strategy, he was an inspirational figure and a thorn in the side of his enemies.

Ho Chi Minh, one of history's most enigmatic and influential communist revolutionaries. He formed the League for the Independence of Vietnam, the Viet Minh, in 1941 with only one goal in mind – independence for his country.

Chinese smugglers. A Viet Minh patrol arrested three crew members of the French boat. Colonel Debes, the French commander on the scene, ordered an all-out assault against the Vietnamese. Shortly afterwards, French tanks rumbled through the streets of Haiphong Harbour. Viet Minh mortars thumped away against French troop positions as fighting enveloped the harbour area around Haiphong.

D'Argenlieu flew home to France where he received a "green light" to punish the Viet Minh. In a meeting with his Prime Minister Georges Bidault, d'Argenlieu asked if "we could use artillery?", to which the answer was, "even that".[4] Believing that he now had permission to strike out against the Viet Minh, d'Argenlieu radioed his counterpart in Saigon, General Etienne Valluy, to issue an order for Ho to pull all his forces out of Hanoi. Valluy in turn cabled General Morliere, his counterpart in Hanoi, to order the Viet Minh's evacuation from that city. Despite Morliere's assurances to Valluy that the ultimatum to Ho was unnecessary, he cabled Colonel Debes that "the moment has come for you to teach a severe lesson to those who have treacherously attacked you. Employ all means at your disposal to master Haiphong completely, and thereby bring the Vietnamese military leaders to a better understanding of the situation."[5]

The shelling of Haiphong

Debes ordered all Viet Minh units out of Haiphong within two hours. Debes' forces then moved into the harbour area while the French cruiser *Suffren* opened fire on the Vietnamese neighbourhood nearby. Sources later indicated that the Vietnamese suffered around 6000 deaths. Upon hearing of the attack, d'Argenlieu cabled a congratulatory message to Valluy in which he reaffirmed France's determination to remain in Indo-China. Ho warned the French that the Vietnamese would endure an atrocious struggle rather than renounce their liberty.

Events were spiralling out of control as Viet Minh troops killed three French soldiers. Valluy told newspaper reporters that "if these gooks want a fight, they'll get it".[6] A few days later, Valluy handed Ho an ultimatum: disarm the Viet Minh forces in and around Hanoi or face destruction. In response Giap deployed 30,000 troops.

On the evening of 19 December 1946, Valluy's forces struck, turning Hanoi into a battleground as they rounded up or killed suspected Viet Minh soldiers and sympathizers. Later that evening Giap issued a virtual declaration of war. He ordered "all soldiers and militia in the centre, south and north to stand together, go into battle, destroy the invaders, and save the nation". In words that would be prophetic, Giap added that, "the resistance will be long and arduous, but our cause is just and we will surely triumph".[7]

Throughout the first two months of 1947, French and Viet Minh forces conducted a series of hit-and-run raids on each other's installations in and around Hanoi. Starting in December 1946 and lasting until March 1947, the Viet Minh laid siege to most of Vietnam's principal towns, cutting their communications, blowing up bridges and tearing up roads. In Hue, the old imperial capital, the Viet Minh besieged a

battalion of French troops for nearly 46 days. In an emotional appeal to his countrymen, Ho exhorted them to "exert all of your efforts to carry out destruction work. We must destroy roads widely and deeply so that the French cannot use them. For the sake of the Fatherland we must make sacrifices and endure hardships for a certain time. Long live our victorious Resistance War! Long live independent Vietnam."[8]

However, by March 1947 the French had reopened the majority of roads during daylight hours and established full control of Hanoi. French troops in Vietnam numbered 94,000 officers and men, with a further 11,000 men en route from France. Meanwhile, Giap's Viet Minh forces numbered approximately 60,000 men, with an additional force of 100,000 militia and part-time guerrillas.[9]

The French had been organized along conventional lines, armed with US-supplied infantry weapons, M4 Sherman and M26 Chaffee tanks, and Dodge and General Motors support vehicles. The Viet Minh were armed with a variety of Japanese, Chinese, US and French weapons, while ammunition was produced in mobile and field workshops.

When the Viet Minh turned to a guerrilla strategy in 1947, the regular units were organized into independent companies,

A dead Viet Minh sniper lies in a roadside ditch. The French soldiers discovered him hiding whilst on patrol. It is worth noting how young the French soldiers are. As the photographer on patrol with them noted: "They are mostly young and inexperienced soldiers ... they are, however, excellently armed."

dispersed throughout northern Vietnam. Each company numbered approximately 100 men, including a company commander, a political officer and some communications personnel. Each company was organized into three combat sections, each consisting of three combat groups. The combat group included a leader with the rank of sergeant, an assistant group leader, a machine gunner and two assistants, three riflemen and a grenadier. When reinforced by a local militia force normally of company size, Viet Minh commanders carried out extensive hit-and-run attacks on French outposts. As Giap later recounted: "The soil of the Fatherland was being freed inch by inch right in the enemy's rear lines. There was no clearly defined front. It was where the enemy was. The front was nowhere, it was everywhere."[10]

Although the Viet Minh retained control of over half of the countryside, French military commanders believed that their own aggressiveness and superior firepower had enabled them to control the roads and major towns (at least by day). They were eager to defeat the Viet Minh decisively and neutralize Ho's claim to Vietnam. Many in the US State Department saw this as a sign that France was seeking to restore colonial rule in Indo-China. When US Ambassador to France Jefferson Caffery inquired as to

French intentions for large-scale military operations in Indo-China, French officials "assured him that France was carrying out no major offensives but only small-scale raids" in order to seize Viet Minh weapon caches, posts and to seal the border between China and Vietnam to prevent arms smuggling.[11]

Operation Lea

In fact, the French were already conducting battalion-sized operations throughout northern Vietnam with a total of 60,000 troops. The strategy was to cut the flow of arms reaching the Viet Minh, to kill Ho and the other leaders, and to destroy the Viet Minh Army.[12]

In the first phase of Operation Lea, in early October 1947, French paratroops descended on the Viet Minh headquarters at Bac Kan and captured a large cache of weapons, though none of the Viet Minh leaders. A combined force of tanks, engineers and artillery support pushed north of the border fort at Lang Son towards Cao Bang. Meanwhile, a river flotilla transported two battalions to Chiem Hoa. The second stage of the operation witnessed a further push northwards by nine reinforced battalions from Hai Duong. These moved north to clear the Viet Minh out of the Red River Delta east and northeast of Hanoi, while

other French forces operated in a blocking action north of the capital.

Operation Lea was only a partial success. In the three months it lasted, the French suffered 1000 combat deaths and a further 3000 wounded.[13] An American military observer who accompanied the French stated that he doubted they could undertake further such actions for some time, "as their equipment was rapidly deteriorating, morale was ... low, and replacements for paratroops, who had incurred especially heavy losses on the campaign, were, for the present, almost impossible to find."[14]

By 1948, French military activity in Indo-China had been reduced to patrol-sized operations. While French forces still had control of a few key towns and the road system, the Viet Minh tightened its grip on the countryside. One of France's major problems revolved around finding sufficient military manpower. This shortage had a debilitating effect on combat operations as the Viet Minh attacks continued to harass key military installations. For a time during 1948 the Viet Minh forced the French to dispense with the convoy system, and all but concede territory to their control. France mounted a few minor military operations in 1949, but these lacked the intensity of Operation Lea.

By the second year of France's war of attrition in Indo-China, US policy in Southeast Asia was about to undergo a fundamental change. As Mao's forces inflicted further defeats upon Chiang's Nationalist troops in China, and the Soviet Union took a harder line over the Korean peninsula, it became apparent that US interests in maintaining Japan's (and later Chiang's position on Taiwan) security rested on firming up its anti-communist stance in the region. Despite its past aloofness from the conflict in Indo-China, and its disapproval of re-establishing French rule there, it became apparent that military assistance might, as US Secretary of State Dean Acheson told a National Press Club audience, be the missing component in a problem that might otherwise remain unsolved. Acheson and other Western leaders saw the war as a drain on France's ability to defend Western Europe against the real enemy: the Soviet Union. A French military commander in Indo-China explained to an American observer that the cream of the French Army was in Indo-China instead of on the Rhine. By the time Operation Lea concluded, "highly competent military authorities in Tokyo" (i.e. General Douglas MacArthur) believed that the French might be able to hold off a concerted communist thrust if properly equipped. Yet there were differences of opinion in US circles regarding supporting the French. W. Walton Butterworth, the new head of the US State Department's Far East Division, warned that US economic and military aid to France was not necessarily the key to solving the Indo-China problem.

By the time of the French campaign north and east of Hanoi in the Red River Delta region, the US Army's Plans and Policies Division had drawn up a paper outlining the importance of Indo-China to US security in the region. The paper, entitled *The Position of the United States With Respect to Indo-China*, recommended that the US provide limited military assistance to the French only if they agreed to the complete transfer of sovereignty to Emperor Bao Dai, relinquish their claim to Indo-China as a colony, and acknowledge that military means alone would not work.

However, French Ambassador Henri Bonnet attempted to force the US's hand when he met with Acheson on 16 February 1950. Formally requesting economic and military assistance, Bonnet urged that the US affirm publicly its solidarity with France in its crusade against the communist menace in Asia. On 22 February, French officials put it more bluntly when they declared that, without a long-term programme of US military and economic assistance, they might find it necessary to cut their losses and withdraw from Indo-China.

Giap's strategy

Meanwhile, Giap was pursuing a three-phased plan to defeat the French Army based on Mao's concept of protracted warfare. With the French in control of the major cities and highways, and with garrisons at strategic points throughout the country, the Viet Minh resorted to the age-old tactics of guerrilla warfare. Aided by a sympathetic populace, Giap was able to launch what he called "la guerre mobile": a war without fixed fronts and rear areas. In fact, Giap carried out both conventional and guerrilla operations against the French to provide a window for conventional forces to be trained and equipped for a counteroffensive.

Giap's three-phased strategy pursued from 1950 to France's defeat in 1954 included a period of retreat and defence, during which the Viet Minh forces were to be retrained and consolidated; a period of equilibrium during which they could re-equip themselves with communist China's aid and eliminate the French-held posts in Viet Minh areas; and a period of general counteroffensives which eventually brought

Four French sailors man an antiaircraft gun on board a ship during Operation Toulouse. This action took place in early 1953 in the Qui Nhon region of Vietnam.

the French to total defeat. Giap and Ho correctly ascertained that the French would grow tired of a stalemated colonial war if pacification and victory on French terms could not be reached. Also, the Viet Minh leadership believed that if a few decisive blows could be dealt against the French Army, public opinion in France would demand a withdrawal. Hence, in the autumn of 1950 Viet Minh forces began a series of attacks against isolated French border positions along the Chinese border. These outposts, 480km (300 miles) away from the major French line, were surrounded by jungle and a hostile Viet Minh Army. Once they fell, the Viet Minh could receive uninterrupted military assistance from the Chinese communist forces.

By mid-1950, the Viet Minh Army had reportedly grown to 250,000 officers and men. The primary mission of the regular Viet Minh forces was purely offensive. All defensive and security tasks were handled by the regional and popular forces. Approximately 15,000 Chinese advisors and technicians helped to train, organize and arm the Viet Minh.

Too conventional a strategy?

For the French, the situation was growing increasingly desperate. In order to assess the situation, the US sent a team of civilian and military representatives to Indo-China to see first hand the French efforts on the battlefield. Heading the civilian side for the State Department was John F. Melby, while the veteran Major-General Graves B. Erskine, US Marine Corps, represented the Defense Department. Both concluded that the French Army might be able to hold its own in the face of a large-scale Viet Minh attack, but not against an attack in force by the Chinese communists. However, neither suggested that the French efforts were hopeless. This encouraged Washington to consider not only military assistance but a military advisory group to be sent to Indo-China to train both the French and their South Vietnamese allies in the use of US military equipment.

Meanwhile, French military fortunes continued to decline. Supported by an army of 15,000 military advisors from the People's Republic of China (PRC), along with advanced weaponry, the Viet Minh grew stronger. In one month, French military intelligence estimated that the Viet Minh received more than 50,000 bolt-action rifles, 150 semi-automatic rifles, 95 machine guns, 30 mortars, 32 75mm field guns, 8 37mm antitank guns and 4 130mm field guns from the PRC.[15]

The French Chiefs of Staff Committee recommended a regrouping of French forces to avoid a catastrophe. However, on 18 September 1950, the Viet Minh overran the French fortress at Dong Khe on the Chinese frontier. A few days later a French force of 4000 men along the frontier at Cao Bang was destroyed. One by one, the other isolated French bases along the border were captured or abandoned. Intelligence estimated that as many as 6000 men were killed or captured, and more than 10,000 rifles, mortars and machine guns lost.[16]

The defeats baffled Western military experts. General Douglas MacArthur, Commander-in-Chief of United Nations forces then fighting in Korea, told President Truman that the French had 150,000 of their best troops there with an officer of the highest reputation in command. He could not understand why they had not achieved victory. Truman responded: "I cannot understand it either." General J. Lawton "Lightning Joe" Collins was more blunt when he asserted: "France will be driven out of Indo-China, at the very least out of Tonkin, and they are wasting men and equipment trying to remain there."[17]

The newly appointed US Military Assistance Advisory Group (MAAG), headed by Brigadier-General Francis G. Brink, US Army, believed that what hampered French military efforts were poor intelligence, improvement in the Viet Minh forces, a lack of overall coordination between French air and ground forces, and the failure to organize forces larger than battalions. Brink reported that the French Army would be able to hold the Hanoi-Haiphong Delta area "if adequate military aid arrives within [the next] two months and French forces in Tonkin receive nine battalions and are reorganized and properly trained as the French plan".[18]

This military aid arrived in the form of an armoured regiment, an antiaircraft artillery regiment, a parachute battalion, two artillery battalions and five battalions of colonial infantry from North Africa and Senegal; and the appointment of General Jean de Lattre de Tassigny not only as Commander-in-Chief of all French forces in Indo-China, but also as High Commissioner. Almost immediately, de Lattre set about restoring the morale and fighting spirit of his beleaguered forces, creating a Vietnamese National Army and using American assistance more wisely.

The results of these initiatives had a positive effect on the French Army, with the timely arrival of a massive amount of US military equipment. When the Viet Minh attacked Vinh Yen on 13 January 1951, the French forces beat them back. However, they suffered substantial casualties and could not finish off the enemy. Two months later, the Viet Minh attacked the coastal enclave of Mao Khe, 30km (18.75 miles) northeast of Haiphong, and were again repelled. In June, the Viet Minh attempted to overrun the Catholic-dominated districts in the southwest corner of the Red River Delta around the towns of Ninh Binh and Phat Diem. Fighting in the open, French artillery and air power battered the Viet Minh, leading de Lattre to conclude that the battles had seriously eroded the enemy's strength.

In order to bolster US support for the war, de Lattre travelled to New York and Washington for talks with the Joint Chiefs of

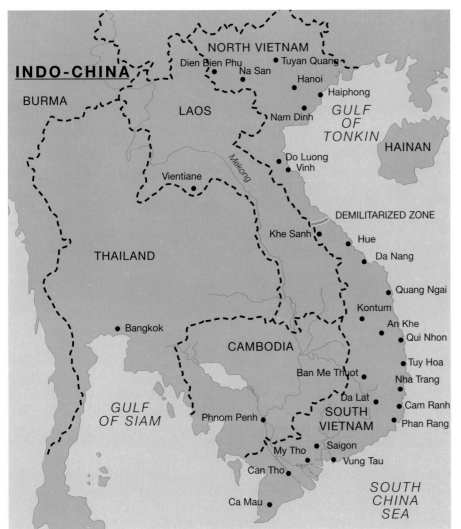

To American military officials, French military strategy appeared to be on the brink of collapse. While, with their superior firepower, French troops were able to force the Viet Minh to retreat, they remained wedded to their static defences. As one US military analysis concluded of the battles of Nghia Lo, Phu Doan and Na San, all part of Operation Lorraine, the French failed to take advantage of the defeats they inflicted on the Viet Minh. In fact, "a powerful French force, firmly established across the enemy's lines of communications" would have been in an excellent position "to fight a decisive battle under conditions of French choosing". French conduct of the entire campaign, the observers concluded, had been "timid, unimaginative and extremely defensive-minded".[20] Unwilling to use unconventional tactics, France saw the war drag on into 1953.

The Navarre Plan

Navarre assumed command of French forces in Indo-China that were in a poor condition. The failure to stage aggressive offensive operations, as well as field a sizeable Vietnamese National Army, suggested that France no longer had interests in Indo-China worth the cost of continuing the struggle.

With the assistance of US Army Lieutenant-General John W. O'Daniel, Navarre came up with a plan to take the initiative immediately using local attacks, with a full-scale offensive to follow in September 1953. In the interim, rear-area units in static defensive positions were to be consolidated into a mobile striking force. In addition, the Vietnamese National Army was to be trained at an accelerated pace and given greater responsibility in the conduct of military operations.

Staff, President Truman and the State Department. His objective was to convince US leaders that the Indo-China war and Korean conflict deserved equal priority. He told a crowd in New York City: "The war in Indo-China is not a colonial war. It is a war against Red colonialism. As in Korea, we are fighting on a Red battlefield for liberty and peace." At the Pentagon, de Lattre was even more blunt when he told the Joint Chiefs of Staff: "If Southeast Asia is lost, India will 'burn like a match' and there will be no barrier to the advance of communism before Suez and Africa."[19]

While de Lattre was able to secure more US assistance, the military chiefs and State Department remained sceptical of the French Army's ability to deal with the insurgency in Indo-China. This sentiment

gained support at the battle of Binh Hoa in November 1951, when the Viet Minh forced the French to retreat after the latter had briefly occupied the town. General de Lattre's death in January 1952 in Paris produced a renewed sense of pessimism that translated into a return to the poor battlefield performance exhibited before his command.

By autumn 1952, the Viet Minh had demonstrated a remarkable resilience in the face of superior French firepower, while France's efforts to train a force of native Vietnamese troops to legitimize their war effort met with limited success. A furious battle near the village of Na San, a strongpoint held by nine French infantry battalions, led to the slaughter of up to 7000 Viet Minh troops, but the clash left the French Army in a parlous state.

Viet Minh artillery on the hills surrounding Dien Bien Phu. The French severely underestimated Viet Minh ingenuity in getting guns into these positions. In fact, an army of porters manhandled the guns into place to give Giap an overwhelming firepower advantage.

The first phase of the Navarre Plan was to clear out the rear areas of Viet Minh forces. On 17 July 1953, two French airborne battalions were parachuted 240km (150 miles) behind Viet Minh lines at Lang Son, and destroyed a large depot of arms and ordnance. The paratroopers were withdrawn successfully to the coast where a French naval task force took them aboard. Operation Camargue followed, in which a number of Viet Minh-held fortified villages along Highway One were destroyed.

Giap continued to fight the French on his terms, though, using hit-and-run tactics, and in the process crushed a number of smaller French outposts. Another Viet Minh force attacked French outposts from the Annamese coast. Navarre remarked in his New Year (1954) message to his troops: "Having lost all hopes of winning a decisive battle in the Red River Delta, the Viet Minh disperses its forces. However, in that type of warfare, we have the advantage of being able to concentrate our forces rapidly ... a campaign begun under such conditions can but turn in our favour."[21]

As part of the Navarre Plan, on 20 November 1953, 3000 French paratroopers jumped close to the Laotian border near a Vietnamese village called Dien Bien Phu. O'Daniel felt that Navarre's decision to establish a base at Dien Bien Phu centred on the hope of luring the Viet Minh into a killing zone. However, he had serious misgivings about the decision, not least because the French base was completely surrounded by hills which, if reinforced by two or three battalions of medium artillery, could make the area untenable. Despite this pessimism, O'Daniel nonetheless conveyed in a report to Washington that the base could withstand any kind of attack the Viet Minh were capable of launching. He concluded that with the base at Dien Bien Phu, the French were in no danger of suffering a major military reverse but were gaining strength and confidence in their ability to fight the war to a successful conclusion. O'Daniel cabled Washington that the military situation at Dien Bien Phu was well in hand and would improve rapidly. The US Army attaché in Hanoi, however, reported that Navarre was, in reality, conducting a "holding action in Indo-China ... and that ... staff thinking and procedure is vintage 1935–1939".[22]

Navarre had at his disposal seven paratroop battalions, three North African battalions, one Vietnamese and two tribal Thai battalions, one combat engineer battalion, one truck company, 10 light tanks, two 75mm and 105mm artillery groups, and four 155mm howitzers, all located in a valley and in full view of the Viet Minh's reconnaissance parties. As for the Viet Minh, by late January 1954 Giap had concentrated no fewer than four infantry divisions around Dien Bien Phu. Giap's force in fact numbered some 35,000 men against about 5000 French troops inside the base.

By 18 February 1954, the Viet Minh had placed approximately 40,000 troops and numerous dug-in artillery positions in and around Dien Bien Phu, situated primarily along the high ground surrounding the French positions. The French base at Dien Bien Phu, broken into eight fire bases ("Anne Marie", "Huguette", "Claudine", "Eliane", "Dominique", "Béatrice", "Isabelle" and "Gabrielle"), had been surrounded.

Even as Navarre and other US military observers remained confident of the French Army's ability to blunt any Viet Minh offensive, Giap opened his assault on Dien Bien Phu. On the evening of 13 March 1954, Viet Minh infantry, with support from the artillery dug into the surrounding hills, launched a series of "human-wave" attacks and captured the French strongpoint "Béatrice". Four days later, similar assaults

The French camp at Dien Bien Phu. Between 13 March and 8 May 1954, the camp was captured piece by piece. Though the French fought hard, they lacked the resources to repel the Viet Minh.

resulted in the capture of "Gabrielle" and "Anne Marie". The French artillery commander, Colonel Charles Piroth, having made the boast that the Viet Minh could never emplace guns in the hills surrounding the French fire base, committed suicide.

Even as the US Joint Chiefs of Staff contemplated launching a series of air strikes and the possibility of dispatching troops to assist the beleaguered French paratroops in Operation Vulture, the situation in the Red River Valley Delta grew desperate. With his forces pinned down inside Dien Bien Phu, Navarre launched what appeared to be a meaningless combined land and sea attack against the Viet Minh forces in and around Tuy Hoa, along the central coastline of Vietnam. The amphibious attack readily achieved its initial objectives along the coast, but became bogged down in the surrounding mountains and valleys. Hoping to draw

Giap's forces away from Dien Bien Phu and relieve pressure on the base, the French were actually forced to withdraw by the Viet Minh.

The end at Dien Bien Phu came on 8 May 1954 as the final outpost, "Isabelle", fell to the Viet Minh in the last of a series of hard-fought battles by French Foreign Legionnaires and loyal Vietnamese troops. The defeat at Dien Bien Phu was not due to a lack of bravery on the part of the French or to over-optimistic strategic goals. Any analysis will clearly show that defeat came as a result of the French Government's refusal to reinforce Navarre's forces in Indo-China.

The decision not to reinforce Navarre or to commit troops from the Metropolitan Army forced French commanders in Indo-China to fight the war on the cheap. While Navarre can be blamed for his refusal to concentrate his forces to defeat the Viet Minh in a single, determined campaign while using firepower to his advantage, the general was a product of an army culture that forbade initiative and "unconventional" strategy.

In a post-battle analysis of the failure at Dien Bien Phu, General George Catroux asserted that: "Dien Bien Phu was incontestably the bitter fruit of a strategic error of General Navarre. But it also was a fulfilment. It was the harsh penalization of the defects of a military policy undertaken long before the advent of the Laniel Government and of methods ill-adapted to their purpose and furthermore imprecise. It was also the penalization of a defence organization of little coherence, which failed to define neatly the respective prerogatives of political power and military command."[23]

Ironically, Catroux's comments also apply to US efforts 11 years later, when US Marines landed at Da Nang to begin the Second Indo-China War.

The booty of war. Viet Minh troops stockpile French weaponry after the surrender of Dien Bien Phu. The Viet Minh also took over 10,500 prisoners, including one woman, a nurse.

A LACK OF IDEAS AND INITIATIVE

THE FRENCH ARMY WAS DEFEATED BECAUSE IT HAD TOTALLY FORGOTTEN MODERN WARFARE, RELATED ONE FRENCH ARMY OFFICER IN HIS PERSONAL JOURNAL:

This Indo-Chinese War might have been, should have been, even for those who hated it and wanted none of it, the crucible of a new army, modern in spirit and rejuvenated in its methods. Alas, the opposite occurred!

What had been weaknesses in metropolitan France here became monstrous vices. No imagination and no initiative were tolerated – or nothing, rather, that rose above the level of the "talent of the interpreter", the colonial cult of "residence" and a pious respect for the "period of command". There is bureaucracy, paper work, uselessness or paralysis of the "services" (determined to be of no service); pathetic technical resources (with one breakdown crane for the whole of Tonkin), with a handful of helicopters and mechanical equipment on the verge of collapse. The whole enormous machine is revolving to no end, or rather is not revolving at all.

Of course the individual combatant is often magnificent, and there are born leaders, but all is futile. We are fighting an outdated war ... against an adversary who until now had no artillery, no aviation and no tanks. We can no longer camouflage ourselves. We have fallen into the worst habits. We have forgotten modern warfare, tomorrow's form of land warfare. Defeat in the field is nothing, compared to the illusions, the sclerosis and the *non possumus* which have turned Indo-China into the grave of our army.[24]

French tanks take point as the army begins its daily ritual of clearing the road ahead of mines and snipers. It was a time-consuming task, requiring thousands of troops and vast quantities of weapons.

The French Army in Vietnam was a truly multinational force. Troops came from many of their colonial territories, including Vietnam itself.

COLONEL CHARLES LACHERORY STATED THAT IN VIETNAM:

It might have been thought that the military art would acquire a new form much less concerned, as in the past, with human values, and that we were heading for a "push button war". Yet … in the last 12 years not a day has gone by without French officers and men dying for their country in some corner of the globe, and they were not confronted by any "push button war" but by varied forms of conflict, insurrections, ideological wars, etc … or, in a word, revolutionary wars in which – more than at any other time and in any other form of conflict – human values revealed themselves preponderant.[25]

Near Ha Duong we came across a battalion of the newly formed Vietnamese National Army. The French did not rate these troops very highly and they let their Asian allies know it. This, in turn, meant that the Vietnamese soldiers lost confidence in themselves, and when the time came for them to go into action they had little heart for fighting. "Just look at that," the captain travelling with me said in disgust. "Instead of combing the ricefields and travelling light like the Viet Minh, those National Army soldiers always follow the roads and load themselves up with equipment and weapons so they're completely immobile. They should go barefoot instead of wearing marching boots."[26]

FRENCH JOURNALIST PETER SCHOLL-LATOUR RECALLED AN ENCOUNTER WITH *LES PETITS JAUNISSES* ("THE LITTLE YELLOW ONES"):

17

FIGHTING THE VIET MINH

The clouds were low in the leaden grey sky and a biting cold wind was blowing from the north. The legs of the little boys, sitting astride their buffaloes like Mowgli, were blue with cold. The soldiers who made up the army of the French Union were a motley bunch. The Moroccans wore thick *jellabas* with brown stripes. You could pick out the Algerians by their turbans. Who would have known at the time that the seeds of the Algerian

THE JOURNALIST SCHOLL-LATOUR TRAVELLED TO THE COASTAL ENCLAVE OF THAI BINH WHERE OPERATION MERCURY WAS IN PROGRESS. HERE, FRENCH AND VIETNAMESE NATIONAL FORCES REPORTEDLY ENCIRCLED TWO REGIMENTS OF THE VIET MINH'S 320TH DIVISION:

Revolution were being sown in those paddy fields? It was while they were in Indo-China that the *Maghrebis* became infected with the virus of nationalism. When we came across a lorry with the red and green insignia of the Foreign Legion on it, as often or not it would be snatches of German that carried over to us on the breeze. And by this time as much as a third of the strength of some French colonial infantry units was made up of Vietnamese. This growing predominance of native troops in the Expeditionary Force was known as *le jaunissement* ("the yellowing").

At the frontline command post of the 10th Mobile Group the road petered out. Nearby we could hear a battery firing at irregular intervals. The command post was located in an ancestral temple. Despite the thick clouds of cigarette smoke the scent of incense still hung in the air. Outside, two platoons of paratroopers were advancing on the last line of villages before the coast. They waded through the waters of the rice paddies, walking some distance apart, sometimes sinking up to their knees. Shots were fired at them from the outskirts of the village, but the firing was sporadic and it stopped altogether when they reached the first mud huts. The paratroopers showed us an underground fox-hole where the Viet Minh had dug in; a 13-year-old European would have been lucky to squeeze inside it. A soldier said: "When we comb the villages, they pull hunks of turf or brush-wood over their heads, and we can pass close to them for hours without spotting them."

A few soldiers with minor wounds came towards us along the narrow, slippery embankment. They were covered in mud from head to foot. At a crossroads, the paratroopers with machine guns at the ready were stopping and checking a stream of refugees who suddenly seemed to have appeared out of nowhere. The Viet Minh had herded them all together in the few remaining square miles of land on the edge of the

The Viet Minh used every asset available to them in their fight against the French. This included the use of bicycles for transportation. As the photo shows, the Viet Minh also recruited women into the army.

coast, the idea being that they could disappear among them and smuggle themselves through the French lines if necessary. The guerrillas of the Viet Minh 320th Division had, of course, donned the traditional black peasant costume before infiltrating the delta region. The French soldiers gave the young men among the refugees a thorough going-over. The tell-tale papers were easy to find – military documents, regimental orders, communist battle-songs tracts, photos of Ho Chi Minh. The weapons, however, lay buried somewhere in the rice fields.

It was not all success for the Viet Minh. At the Battle of Mao Khe in March 1951, the French gave the insurgent forces a sound beating. In the above photo, French troops stand over Viet Minh dead, savouring a rare victory against Ho Chi Minh's forces.

By sheer fluke the soldiers managed to track down the political commissar of a regiment. He was hiding in a fox-hole when the mine-detecting device in his wristwatch ... went off and gave him away. Now the man stared gloomily into the distance and refused to say anything. A thin drizzle was falling on the ... refugees. From a distance the black chain ... looked as if it was suspended between the sky and water like a mournful flight of migratory birds in an imaginary Chinese painting.[27]

> The Viet Minh guerrillas had donned peasant costume before infiltrating the delta region

VIET MINH STRATEGY

VO NGUYEN GIAP WAS THE VIET MINH COMMANDER WHOSE MASTERY OF GUERRILLA, AS WELL AS CONVENTIONAL, STRATEGY AND TACTICS LED TO THE VIET MINH VICTORY OVER THE FRENCH AT DIEN BIEN PHU:

We believed that in the French camp, the French General Staff and the military chiefs were well informed. They'd weighed up the pros and cons, and according to their forecasts Dien Bien Phu was impregnable. It has to be said that at the beginning of the autumn of 1953, for example, when our political headquarters were planning our autumn and winter campaigns, there was no mention of Dien Bien Phu. Why? Because, the Navarre Plan didn't mention it either. They had a whole series of manoeuvres planned.

For us, the problem was that Navarre wanted to retain the initiative whereas we wanted to seize it. There is a contradiction that exists in a war of aggression whereby you have to disperse your forces to occupy a territory but rally your mobile forces for offensive action. We took advantage of this contradiction and forced Navarre to disperse his forces. That's how it all started. We ordered our troops to advance in a number of directions, directions of key importance to the enemy although their presence wasn't significant. So the enemy had no choice but to disperse their troops. We sent divisions north, northwest, towards the centre, towards Laos; other divisions went in other directions. So to safeguard Laos and the northwest, Navarre had to parachute troops into Dien Bien Phu, and that's what happened at Dien Bien Phu. Before then, no one had heard of Dien Bien Phu. But afterwards, well that's history, isn't it? The French General Staff only planned to parachute in sufficient troops to stop us advancing on the northwest and Laos. Little by little, they planned to transform Dien Bien Phu into an enormous concentration camp, a fortified camp, the most powerful in Indo-China. They planned to draw our forces, break us, crush us, but the opposite took place. They wanted a decisive battle and that's exactly what they got at Dien Bien Phu – except that it was decisive for the Vietnamese and not for the French.

Dien Bien Phu was a victory in another era. What I mean is that in the latter half of the nineteenth century, when Western imperialism divided the world into colonies, a new problem emerged. How could a weak, economically backward people ever hope to regain its freedom? How could it hope to take on a modern Western army, backed by the resources of a modern capitalist state? And that's why it took us 100 years to fight off the French and French imperialism. Dien Bien Phu was the first great decisive victory after 100 years of war against French imperialism and US interventionism. That victory put an end to the war and marked the end of French aggression. From an international point of view, it was the first great victory for a weak, colonized people struggling against the full strength of modern Western forces. This is why it was the first great defeat for the West. It shook the foundations of colonialism and called on people to fight for their freedom – it was the beginning of international civilization.[28]

This map shows the French base at Dien Bien Phu. The Viet Minh assault began on 13 March 1954, and by 8 May, the last point of French resistance at fire base "Isabelle" had been overrun. The first attack, on "Béatrice", began as dusk fell over the valley. The massive Viet Minh force that had been surrounding the French descended en masse, and 24 hours later had taken the position. The insurgents then took the entire base piecemeal over the coming weeks.

FIGHTING AT DIEN BIEN PHU

DIEN BIEN PHU WAS THE DECISIVE ENGAGEMENT IN THE WAR, AND THE BATTLE WAS VICIOUS. MARCEL BIGEARD FOUGHT WITH THE 6TH COLONIAL PARACHUTE BATTALION:

"Bruno to everybody," Bigeard whispers into his radio. "In the following order, 6th, 8th, BEP [French Foreign Legion paratroopers], are you in position?" He reads off the list of units and waits for them to break radio silence twice, the conventional signal for "affirmative".

"What's the time, lieutenant?"

Berthumeyrie is breathing shallowly. This little Basque is one of the best men with a hand grenade in the 1st Company.

"Five to," replies Lieutenant Le Vigouroux.

Viet Minh shells explode near the airstrip at Dien Bien Phu. Few aircraft were able to make it in or out of the base, as artillery constantly pounded the runway.

It is six o'clock this 28th day of March, 1954. The artillery preparation has begun. The echo of the last shell burst has not died away before 300 paratroopers hurl themselves into the attack. The Viets recover and lay down a heavy fire on the assault troops. Facing them are the paratroopers, outnumbered four to one.

Air force fighters arrive with bullets and napalm. The earth trembles from the explosions, the rice paddies are smoking from tracer rounds. But the "paras" are not looking up: they are crawling, regrouping, dashing from rice paddy dike to ditch, now on their feet, now on the ground, pushing themselves forward through a dense curtain of bullets. Le Vigouroux's platoon is the point platoon. "Forward!" He moves his men, points out objectives, calls in artillery. "Berthu! On the left. A machine gun." The Basque rises on one elbow and lobs a grenade over a parapet. Two more grenades follow the same trajectory.

Le Vigouroux dashes ahead. At his side is Doan leading a squad of light infantry. He takes a few steps and falls. Dead. His men keep moving and fall in their turn.

Berthumeyrie jumps into the machine-gun nest. The machine gun is out of action, destroyed by shrapnel. Le Vigouroux jumps into the emplacement. Slaps Berthumeyrie on the back. "Well done!"

On the radio he contacts Bigeard directly.

"Bruno? It's going great. I've taken some losses but I've just gotten myself a machine gun."

Bruno is not surprised that a platoon leader reports to him personally. He likes the enthusiasm of his young officer graduates of Saint-Cyr [the French equivalent of West Point]. "Bravo, Vigouroux!"

The infantrymen distinctly heard Bigeard's "bravo". Then, stunned, they see the lieutenant fall, dropping the mike from his hand. A bullet has struck him in the middle of the forehead.[29]

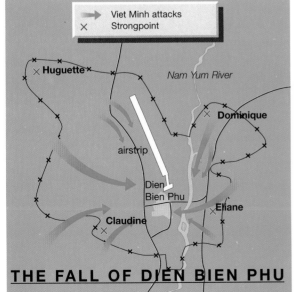

Viet Minh attacks
✕ Strongpoint

Huguette
Nam Yum River
Dominique
airstrip
Dien Bien Phu
Eliane
Claudine

THE FALL OF DIEN BIEN PHU

The assault into the main base came on 3 May against fire base "Huguette". By this point, however, the French were exhausted, and the Viet Minh completed their rout in days.

THE LONG MARCH

DEFEAT AT DIEN BIEN PHU MEANT IMPRISONMENT FOR THOUSANDS OF FRENCH SOLDIERS. THIS ACCOUNT OF THE MARCH INTO CAPTIVITY IS FROM A FRENCH MEDICAL OFFICER:

Then the exhausting 600km march began, towards the Chinese border, over the almost impassable mountains of the T'ai country, crossing rivers by boat or at fording sites, through thick forests, across rice fields.

French prisoners of war make their way into captivity under the watchful eyes of Viet Minh soldiers. Thousands of captured French soldiers were forced to march 600km (375 miles) to communist prison camps.

For the most part we were on poor trails cut into the mountain sides, strewn with rocks and made slippery by downpours. The sick and wounded who could no longer walk had to be carried by stretcher or on the backs of their comrades.

The march lasted one month, in stages of 20km per day on average and always at night in order to avoid airplanes.

During the day we were herded into the damp jungle. The only food we were given was a handful of cold rice, which often smelled of the oil from the containers in which it had been cooked. We chewed new leaves and drank from muddy, rain-swollen streams.

These mandatory halts allowed me to provide a little treatment for the wounded. I tried to comfort the most exhausted and to clean infected wounds with leaves, since we had neither bandages nor medicine. We all had dysentery and malaria which, of course, could not be treated. Our bare feet were covered with blood, but in time they hardened. We were also plagued by mosquitoes, flies, tics, lice and sometimes leeches. But those were only minor nuisances.

We were usually soaking wet and wading through mud since it was the rainy season. I don't think I have ever been so cold as on some of the nights in the mountains of the T'ai country.

> Comradeship allowed us to put one foot in front of the other and keep moving forward, for to fall out of the column meant death

One couldn't say morale was sunny, but then again the spirit of comradeship worked wonders. Even though we were exhausted, it allowed us to put one foot in front of the other and keep moving forward, for to fall out of the column meant death.

Noticing that the trucks returning from Dien Bien Phu were often empty, I would speak with the political commissar and insist that our wounded be loaded on to the trucks so that they could benefit more quickly from the Viet Minh hospitals. That request was always refused.

From time to time, we would pass through a village where the bell in the church steeple would ring out, giving us a vague but emotional reminder of the French countryside. These villages were apparently deserted; the rare inhabitants whom we met pretended not to see us.

At the end of the journey, our enlisted men and non-coms were sent to camps, which we learnt later were veritable death camps. Only the officers and warrant officers continued on to Camp No 1 near Tuyen Quang.[30]

PRISONER OF THE VIET MINH

For us it was almost like paradise: the end of the march, a roof over our head, the joy of finding comrades-in-arms who had been held prisoner for many years.

They at once showered us with their friendship and gave us the benefit of their experience of life in the prison camp. One of them, a medical lieutenant Andre, like St Martin, gave me a pair of shorts to replace my pants, which were in shreds. As for them, they were eager for news about France, the war, the movies in Paris … about life.

Every morning at formation "men" (rank did not exist) were chosen for the duties essential to our survival. The most important was the rice ration. About 30 men would go to get the rice about 20km away. A single *do-doi* [guard] would accompany them because any escape was impossible in a hostile country where even the water buffalo could pick us out by smell.

Political education was a daily event. We were to be made into "new men". There were news and training sessions where the same subjects were constantly rehashed: peace, the people's struggle, misdeeds of capitalist and imperialist policies, the "dirty" war in Indo-China, clemency of Ho Chi Minh (Uncle Ho), and the "valiant Vietnamese people" who not only spared our lives but allowed us to live and educate ourselves.

Finally, there were the self-criticism sessions where we were to confess our sins, mostly imaginary. They seemed to satisfy the camp authorities but caused us to laugh up our sleeve. The most unpleasant was the writing of manifestoes against the dirty war in Indo-China. These manifestoes posed serious problems for us. If we refused to participate, camp life gradually got worse: harder work details, fewer rations, disappearance of the little bit of medicine that we had and no distribution of the anxiously awaited mail. If we cooperated we knew that after interminable discussions the final text, which we couldn't agree with, would be written by the camp authorities.

Thanks to all the doctors in our camp and to the solidarity of all the prisoners, Camp No 1 did not experience the frightful death rates found in others.

On 20 July 1954 the Geneva Accords were signed. There was a festive atmosphere in the transition camp, organized and dictated by our captors. Early on, all of our possessions which had been confiscated were returned to us, at least those of us from Dien Bien Phu.

Then they issued us with two brand-new *do-doi* uniforms, a pith helmet and a pair of Ho Chi Minh sandals to replace the rags we had been wearing. As a fashionable accessory, we were entitled to a pin: a Picasso dove. And, lastly, they handed out to each one of us a tube of rice so we could survive in the corrupt capitalist world.

The next day, as we were boarding an LCT [Landing Craft, Tank] from the Navy base, the orchestra played, ironically, *"Ce n'est qu'un au revoir"* ("Till we meet again"). We didn't bother to listen, being too happy to be free.[31]

FOR FRENCH PRISONERS HELD IN VIETNAMESE CAMPS, LIFE ALTERNATED BETWEEN BOREDOM AND A FIGHT FOR SURVIVAL. THIS ACCOUNT IS FROM A PRISONER HELD AT CAMP NO 1:

The Viet Minh had little mercy for captured French soldiers. Many French were injured, exhausted and dying. Even when they got to the camps, death awaited many.

THE DIVISION OF VIETNAM

I still remember vividly the exodus from our village in the North to Saigon in 1955. I was six years old. My family were middle-level landlords – not rich, but with enough land to have hired hands. My father was killed in 1948, before I was born, in one of those periodic sweeps French troops made to villages in the Red River Delta. One of my maternal uncles, who worked for the Resistance, sent word that we should consider leaving because we owned too much land and would have problems in the coming land reform campaign. So my mother and her father's family, all supporters of the struggle against the French, fled to the South, together with about a million others, the majority of whom sided with the French.

THE AGREEMENTS CONCLUDED IN GENEVA BETWEEN APRIL AND JULY 1954 (COLLECTIVELY CALLED THE GENEVA ACCORDS), SIGNED BY FRENCH AND VIET MINH REPRESENTATIVES, DIVIDED THE COUNTRY AT THE 17TH PARALLEL. NGUYEN BA CHUNG'S FAMILY WAS ONE OF THOUSANDS TO FLEE SOUTH:

We settled in the suburbs of Saigon, then called Gia Dinh Province. I grew up in the South, graduated from high school, and went to college. In this milieu of schools, books, public discussion, I believed wholeheartedly in the causes of South Vietnam – the struggle for freedom and democracy against the "devilish" and "anti-nationalist" North Vietnamese. I was as gung-ho an anti-communist as any American conservative.

As I was an only child, I was exempt from the draft, but not from the turbulence of the war. The Buddhist uprising against Ngo Dinh Diem raised the first doubt in my mind about South Vietnam. It didn't make sense that a country of about 80 percent Buddhists, with a religious history stretching to the first century, had a Catholic president who had no faith in his Buddhist brethren. It perhaps made sense when the French created Ordinance No 10, which legally recognized Christianity, but not Buddhism. The French were, after all, well aware of the potential power of a Buddhist challenge. But it made absolutely no sense at all when Ngo Dinh Diem kept that ordinance in effect for the nine years he was in power.

There was something deeply wrong in the make-up of South Vietnam. I still remember the tremendous joy in Saigon when Diem was overthrown in 1963. I went into the streets, watching the city exploding into celebration.[32]

There was something deeply wrong in the make-up of South Vietnam

Desperate Vietnamese peasants from the North flood into the South to escape the ill-treatment dished out by communist forces. Most refugees were driven by fear and hunger as the Viet Minh took vast swathes of territory, and thus they rushed to the South to seek food and protection.

THE PEOPLE OF VIETNAM

VO NGUYEN GIAP PROVIDED CLUES AS TO WHY THE FRENCH FAILED IN VIETNAM, AND WHY THE AMERICANS WOULD FARE NO BETTER:

As a nation, Vietnam was formed very early on. It is said that, in theory, a nation can be formed only after the arrival of capitalism – according to Stalin's theory of the formation of nations, for instance. But our nation was formed very early, before the Christian era. Why? Because the risk of aggression from outside forces led all the various tribes to band together. And then there was the constant battle against the elements, against the harsh winter conditions that prevail here. In our legends, this struggle against the elements is seen as a unifying factor, a force for national cohesion. This, combined with the constant risk of invasion, made for greater cohesion and created a tradition – a tradition that gave us strength.

The Vietnamese people in general tend to be optimistic. Why? Because they've been facing up to vicissitudes for thousands of years, and for thousands of years they've been overcoming them.[33]

The High Command of the Viet Minh. General Vo Nguyen Giap (far right) and Ho Chi Minh (second from left) make plans for the attack on Dien Bien Phu. The siting of their artillery was crucial to the Viet Minh victory.

Victorious Viet Minh forces march back to base after an operation against the French. The soldier at the front carries the flag of the Viet Minh.

CHAPTER 2
THE AMERICANS TAKE CHARGE IN VIETNAM
1950-1964

Even as French paratroopers fought a losing battle at Dien Bien Phu, US military advisors – part of the newly created Military Advisory and Assistance Group, Vietnam (MAAG, Vietnam) – began to arrive in Saigon and Hanoi to train and assist French personnel. Little did they realize that they were the vanguard of what would become a very substantial commitment to the fledgling South Vietnamese state created in the aftermath of Dien Bien Phu.

"The beginning of a bad mess"
As early as 1948, the US State Department and Joint Chiefs of Staff began discussions on the type and extent of US economic and military assistance to the French. US officials hoped to use this aid as leverage to induce the French to grant the regime of Bao Dai real independence, as well as a sign of solidarity with the French war effort in order to counter the growing menace of communism throughout Southeast Asia.

On 1 March 1950, the Joint Chiefs of Staff and President Truman's National Security Council recommended an immediate military aid programme to Indo-China and Thailand. The president approved $15 million US of military assistance for the French war effort in Indo-China alone. Since 1948, the idea of a communist-dominated Vietnam had been unacceptable to Washington and, while the Joint Chiefs, the State Department and the president hoped to keep forces out, the commitment of military assistance and later advisors was seen as the least costly and the most acceptable option. In the short term, avoiding a French defeat became even more important to the US than to France. The

open-ended commitment was, as Charton Ogburn, a US State Department expert on the Far East, said, "the beginning of a very bad mess".[1]

In the wake of the French defeat at Dien Bien Phu, a MAAG team headed by Lieutenant-General John W. O'Daniel had been tasked to assess whether the French Army had a chance of succeeding in Vietnam. After meeting with his French counterpart, O'Daniel reported that the French Army in Indo-China (under Navarre) had become more aggressive in attitude. Admiral Arthur W. Radford, chairman of the US Joint Chiefs of Staff, therefore recommended that the US should give France its full support.

The first US military advisors
After Dien Bien Phu and France's subsequent decision to withdraw from Indo-China, the US assumed the role of training and equipping the South Vietnamese Army, or Army of the Republic of Vietnam (ARVN). After long resisting US suggestions to provide a training mission, French General Paul Ely eventually requested that O'Daniel and the US "join France in organizing and training the Army of Vietnam".[2] In fact, as early as 13 May 1953, long before the disaster at Dien Bien Phu, O'Daniel suggested an expansion of MAAG, Vietnam, and reorganizing the Vietnamese Army into nine divisions. Specifically, he wanted to train four light and five medium divisions, triangularly organized with each division consisting of three battalions and three regiments. After some hesitation, Secretary of State Dulles directed that O'Daniel might assist by advising on

the training activities of the ARVN. Dulles emphasized that the key word was advising, not training, since this might be construed as direct support of the French war effort.

While it now appeared that the US would engage in some kind of military assistance and advisory effort with the ARVN, there were those inside the Pentagon and State Department who placed conditions on such assistance. General Matthew B. Ridgway, the Army Chief of Staff, recommended that before the US assumed responsibility for training the forces of any of the Associated States, four essential conditions should be met. These were: (1) a reasonably strong, stable civil government in control; (2) a formal request from the government of the Associated States that the US assume responsibility for training its forces; (3) arrangements to be made with the French for the phased, orderly withdrawal of forces, officials and advisors; and (4) the size and composition of the forces of each of the Associated States to be dictated by the local military requirements and overall US interests.[3]

Ridgway's concerns aside, President Dwight D. Eisenhower approved National Security Council Memorandum 5429/2 which called upon the US to make every possible effort to defeat communist subversion and influence and to maintain and support friendly, non-communist governments in all of Southeast Asia with both military and economic assistance. The view held by the US Army leadership can be

South Vietnamese paratroopers, equipped with US helmets and semi-automatic weapons, search for communists in a coconut plantation southwest of Saigon.

summed up in the words of Lieutenant-General James M. Gavin: "We in the army were so relieved that we had blocked the decision to commit combat troops to Vietnam [prior to Dien Bien Phu] that we were in no mood to quibble". Little did they realize that the US Army would enter the Vietnam War through the "back door".

Throughout the remainder of 1954 and into 1955, French troops were replaced by US military and technical advisors under the auspices of MAAG, Vietnam, commander Lieutenant-General Samuel T. Williams. Williams' primary task was to build upon the Table of Organization established by his predecessor, O'Daniel, who had designed both a field and light division structure for the ARVN. O'Daniel's plans were built on the precept that the ARVN would be able to delay any invasion from the North while either Southeast Asian Treaty Organization forces or US forces could come to the assistance of South Vietnam.

Formally designated the Chief of the US Training Mission on 12 February 1955, O'Daniel assumed command of all American and French advisory and training personnel attached to the South Vietnamese units he was to train. By March 1955, the French contingent consisted of approximately 200 officers, all of whom had served in an advisory capacity to the ARVN, while the Americans initially numbered 68 from an approved number of 217 officers. By mid-July of the same year, however, the American figure had risen to 121.

Even as his advisors arrived in South Vietnam, O'Daniel organized the training mission into two parts: a staff echelon located at the level of a South Vietnamese armed forces headquarters; and a field and school echelon assigned to specific units and agencies of the ARVN.[4]

O'Daniel likewise drew up an offensive-minded plan that called for three ARVN divisions to act as a blocking force in front of the port of Da Nang, while three others

US President Harry S. Truman. He was keen to see the French remain in Vietnam, and was thus willing to send financial aid. However, he did not wish to commit US troops to the region.

would conduct an amphibious attack behind the communist lines at Vinh. At the same time, the US Joint Chiefs of Staff began to draw up preliminary plans to repulse overt Viet Minh aggression against South Vietnam, and to destroy the Viet Minh forces and take control of North Vietnam.

After dismissing the use of atomic weapons as prohibitive, "Campaign Plan - North Vietnam" concluded that the only effective response to an overt North Vietnamese attack would be the deployment of a large number of US ground combat troops in an effort comparable in size and scope to the Korean War.

Meanwhile, both O'Daniel and later Williams continued to train and organize the ARVN along conventional military lines as if to repel an overt North Korean-style invasion. Whereas O'Daniel believed that the territorial regiments could handle internal security, Williams maintained that specially trained paramilitary forces were required. He asserted that communist guerrillas had been destroyed in Greece, Korea, the Philippines and Iran, and they could be destroyed in Vietnam.

Having embarked upon a course that saw South Vietnam's problem as protecting itself from an invasion from North Vietnam, Williams' main task was to create an army in South Vietnam that resembled a minuscule version of the US armed forces. Therein lay the seeds of disaster in South Vietnam's

inability to deal with an internal insurgency even as the threat from the North continued to build from mid-1957 onwards.

Advising and supporting

During the first few years of MAAG, Vietnam, Williams and the US military advisors confronted many obstacles to their attempt to create a viable South Vietnamese Army. These included a language barrier, unfamiliarity with Vietnam's diverse ethnic culture, and the political instability (and illegitimacy) that surrounded the Saigon regime of Ngo Dinh Diem. Williams believed that exposure to US training schools and methods would solve many of the problems, and therefore wanted Vietnamese officers and enlisted men assigned to military schools in the US. This in itself created a severe language barrier as Vietnamese was not spoken in US schools, and many Vietnamese did not speak English.

The language barrier did much to derail the work of MAAG, Vietnam, during its first five years. Few Americans had knowledge of Vietnamese or even knew where the country was. Sergeant Leo Daugherty, Jr., a US Marine supply noncommissioned officer assigned to the US Marine Recruit Depot, Parris Island, South Carolina, recalled that in 1958 he checked out Master Sergeant Wiggins who had recently been assigned to MAAG, Vietnam. As he turned in his gear before his departure to Southeast Asia, Wiggins briefly chatted with Daugherty. Curious as to his next station of duty, Daugherty asked him: "Where are you going to?" Wiggins replied that he was "heading for some place called Vietnam to train South Vietnamese Marines". Daugherty, not knowing himself where

Vietnam was, recalled that he went home and looked it up on a map.[5]

Before his departure at the end of his tour of duty in Vietnam in 1956, O'Daniel recommended that officers being sent to Vietnam should learn some rudimentary Vietnamese. However, the US Army thought that setting up such a language programme would be extremely expensive.

For advisors sent to Vietnam, the conditions were as arduous as the mission. While some 40 US military personnel were authorized to have their families with them during their two-year tour of duty, the remaining 700 advisors normally served a one-year tour of duty that generally lasted only 11 months. This, in fact, was too short a tour to have any long-term benefits for either the advisors or their South Vietnamese counterparts. As one former US advisor noted, "one consequence of the short tour was that we had a number of people who merely wanted to get through. They'd spend three months getting oriented into their jobs and the last three months getting ready to leave".[6] Clearly this was a waste of both time and resources.

Another problem facing US advisors in South Vietnam was reporting and calculating battlefield effectiveness. Williams held a quarterly (later bi-monthly) meeting with all his senior advisors to discuss progress. As one officer from the Combat Arms Training Organization (the heart of the US advisory effort in Vietnam) recalled: "There was a tendency to report things optimistically. I believe that, in a number of cases, people held back a little bit in reporting anything wrong because they feared that it would reflect on them adversely."[7]

Brigadier-General Charles A. Symorski, another former advisor to the ARVN, reported that during one such Senior Advisors' Conference Colonel Russell M. Miner reported that while the South Vietnamese unit with which they were working was probably as good as, or better than, comparable units, "it couldn't really punch its way out of a paper bag". Williams was reportedly incensed at the negative overtones presented. Symorski added that after this incident people were afraid to speak or report on the true situation with respect to the ARVN's capabilities.[8]

There were few slots allotted to the US Air Force during the advisory years due to the fact that the French Air Force had been tasked to train and organize a Vietnamese air force. However, from August 1955 this changed as aircraft provided for the French under the Mutual Defense Assistance Program were given to the fledgling South Vietnamese Air Force (VNAF). In fact, by the time of the French withdrawal from the training mission under the terms of the Geneva Accords, the French transferred over to the VNAF 28 F-8F fighter-bombers, 35 C-47 Dakota transports, 60 L-19 liaison aircraft and a number of Sikorsky H-19 helicopters.[9] Because the French provided the VNAF with maintenance and logistical support, there was a shortage of spare parts and trained personnel to fix South Vietnamese aircraft. After the US took over the advisory effort, they replaced the ageing F-8F aircraft with the T-28 trainer.

The Vietnamese Air Force

While the VNAF had been configured primarily as a ground-support force for the ARVN, South Vietnamese soldiers received little if any training in spotting targets suitable for air strikes. What hampered the South Vietnamese military effort the most was the lack of proper coordination between the air force and the army. While observing the VNAF in action, a US Air Force liaison team visiting South Vietnam reported that "the high-level approval required for on-call fighter strikes, along with poor communications and/or procedures for requesting strikes, builds in excessive delays for efficient use of tactical air effort. This is particularly true in view of the hit-and-run guerrilla tactics of the Viet Cong."[10]

President Diem protested that other US allies in the region had received jet aircraft. After the crash of an F-8F, US Navy Admiral Harry D. Felt recommended to the Joint Chiefs of Staff that the VNAF be provided with the jet version of the T-33 trainer

Bao Dai, the last Emperor of Vietnam. After abdicating in 1945, he tried to assume power in the South after the division of the country following the French defeat. However, he was thwarted by the US-backed regime of Ngo Dinh Diem.

President Ngo Dinh Diem (right) of South Vietnam casting his vote in the second national legislative elections. The pro-Diem National Revolutionary Movement Party won majority control of the government in 1955.

aircraft and four RT-33 photo-reconnaissance aircraft. Still hampered by the terms of the 1954 Geneva Accords, which restricted the VNAF to propeller-driven aircraft, the US Navy refused and instead proposed that the South Vietnamese be provided with the AD-4 and later the AD-6.

After the decision by Ho Chi Minh and the Politburo to renew the war in order to unify all of Vietnam, the remnants of the Viet Minh, as well as those agents from North Vietnam who found their way back into South Vietnam amidst the political turmoil of the Diem years, formed in 1960 the National Liberation Front (whose military arm was the Viet Cong). With increased backing and support from both the Soviet Union and the People's Republic of China, Ho and his supporters brought renewed pressure to bear on Diem's government. The growing communist threat, not only in Southeast Asia but also in Europe, Africa and Cuba, prompted the Kennedy Administration to assist Laotian troops fighting the Pathet Lao communist guerrilla group, in addition to increasing its support for Diem. As President Kennedy struggled with the mounting communist challenge, the Joint Chiefs of Staff warned of another Korea-like situation unless the US was prepared to use all means at its disposal, including nuclear bombs.

General Emmett O'Donnell, commanding general of all US air forces in the Pacific, believed that the forces under his command could, if necessary, "prosecute a small war" in Laos with conventional weapons. However, he soberly asserted that such a conflict might bring in North Vietnam and China, and this would necessitate a massive increase in US ground and air forces. The Kennedy Administration, however, took the view of US Ambassador to India John Kenneth Galbraith, who believed that President Diem was "a wasting asset … who was losing, not gaining, popularity", and that the US should refrain from putting American ground troops into Vietnam and avoid over-committing to any war in Southeast Asia.

US Air Force personnel were nonetheless becoming increasingly involved as the US commitment grew during the early 1960s. *The New York Times* reported on 1 May 1962: "Sometimes an American instructor pilot has been at the controls in a strafing pass at jungle targets or on a bomb run. Americans are also flying on bombing and strafing missions. US Air Force pilots fly B-26 bombers and T-28 fighter-bombers in air strikes against the Viet Cong and in support of ground troops."[11]

By December 1962, the commitment to South Vietnam and the air war phase of the advisory effort was growing. The US Army had 199 aircraft in Vietnam, and the US Air Force 61; there were eight US Army generals, and three US Air Force generals. There was also a US Marine helicopter squadron, "Shu Fly", which transported both ARVN and South Vietnamese Marine units into battle led by Lieutenant-Colonel Archie L. Clapp.

One of the lingering criticisms of the Vietnam War has been that the US advisory effort failed to prepare the ARVN for the "other war" – the counter-insurgency effort in rural areas. Critics have argued that US Army advisors trained the ARVN according to conventional US Army doctrine to fight a Korea-like war. Nothing is further from the truth, as the comments of both Clapp and Williams illustrate. Clapp recorded in his *Shu-Fly Diary* that "while the government troops are heavier and pack more punch, there is no reason why they cannot be just as nimble as the VC, if the helicopters are employed to maximum advantage".[12]

The US Navy dispatched a small team of naval officers and enlisted men, as well as US Coast Guardsmen, to assist the newly established South Vietnamese Navy (VNN). Having already been established by the French as a coastal and riverine force, the primary task of the US naval advisors was to assist the South Vietnamese in preventing communist infiltration via the Gulf of Tonkin and South China Sea, as well as from the many rivers and inland waterways that traverse South Vietnam.

While the VNN struggled to patrol the extensive coastline and miles of inland rivers, the US Navy began an extensive training programme to make the VNN into an effective fighting force. American naval commanders "believed that the American training effort eventually would enable the South Vietnamese Sea Force to operate independently".[13]

Captain Joseph B. Drachnik, head of the US Navy's contingent assigned to MAAG in Saigon, proposed to establish a River Force that would consist of several river groups, each comprising a South Vietnamese rifle company, 15 river craft, 13 swimmer support boats, a UH-1B helicopter, a mother ship and a major support ship. Air support would be furnished by carrier and shore-based aircraft. As conceived by Drachnik, this River Warfare Force would be based at a river mouth or nearby port, and the mother ship 48–56km (30–35 miles) from the area of operations. The River Warfare Force would patrol the rivers in order to "locate, harass and destroy guerrilla-type insurgency units in order to assist a friendly government to resist covert aggression".[14]

Senior US naval leaders, however, resisted the creation of what they considered to be "special purpose units". Rear-Admiral Waldemar F.A. Wendt, the Navy's Director of Strategic Plans Division, considered it to be "uneconomical in manpower, equipment and money to develop specialized units and forces solely for counter-insurgency operations". Such activities, he said, "should be secondary to considerations of readiness for limited and general war". He added that while "the service could contribute significantly to meeting counter-insurgency requirements, these activities are primarily land-oriented and properly a primary responsibility of the Army".[15] In fact, the US Army's 9th Infantry Division assumed the mission as the US military's riverine force in 1967.

Individual junks came equipped with an array of small arms that consisted of M1 Garand Rifles, Browning Automatic Rifles (BARs), Thompson submachine guns and .45in pistols. In order to bolster the firepower of the junks, the US Navy had a contract with the Phan Thiet shipyards in Saigon that added mounts for both .30in and .50in machine guns.[16]

Marine security guards at war

Even as the US armed forces continued their advisory efforts, the Marines guarding the US Embassy in Saigon became eyewitnesses to the political turmoil that surrounded the Diem regime. Armed with little more than shotguns, carbines and pistols, US Marine embassy guards were in the first line of defence.

What the Marines could not know was that the Vietnam War was about to change dramatically. The US military would soon become an active participant in day-to-day combat operations. In fact, by 6 March 1965, the US Marines became the first troops ashore in "America's new war".

Instability in South Vietnam: loyalist troops patrol the streets of Saigon following the 30-hour armed revolt attempted by anti-Diem rebel paratroopers in November 1960.

STRATEGY FOR THE SOUTH

ASSESSING THE NEED FOR A VIETNAMESE ARMY, BRIGADIER-GENERAL T.J.H. TRAPNELL, CHIEF, US MILITARY ASSISTANCE ADVISORY GROUP, INDO-CHINA, ADVOCATED THE CREATION OF A LIGHTLY ARMED FORCE CAPABLE OF DEALING WITH THE GUERRILLA THREAT POSED BY THE VIET MINH:

It became increasingly evident after my arrival in Indo-China and seeing the terrain, visiting the troops and knowing the type of combat, that the most important and most immediate need to the successful conclusion of the war in Indo-China was more troops. During the past year, the Vietnamese Army has been organized as scheduled. However, most of these units have been activated by merely transferring and renaming units in the Vietnamese Army which were already in being in the French Colonial Army. I am convinced that additional Vietnamese battalions, over and above the units approved for support by the Joint Chiefs of Staff, should be activated.

In an informal conversation, the matter was discussed with General Salan, who agreed to the need but felt that the cost of many additional battalions and the cadre requirements were beyond the capacity of France to support, but that a realistic number should be set up to be supported and trained. In order to have a clear picture of the requirements, a study was made on the basis of an additional 40 battalions. In a short conference with General Alessandri, Military Advisor to his Majesty Bao Dai, he stated that he recognized the immediate need for additional Vietnamese troops, and he explained to me his concept for the organization of additional battalions. These troops would be armed only with shoulder weapons, light machine guns and 60mm mortars, and would be trained in manoeuvres over mountainous terrain, capable of finding and destroying the enemy in his own territory. Each battalion would be cadred with a minimum of seven French officers and 30 French noncommissioned officers. French cadres would be furnished as far as possible from the Vietnamese battalions already in being, but which are at present being employed on a static guard-duty basis. Military schools would be expanded in order to permit the battalions to be ready for a combat assignment in December 1953.[17]

US PRESIDENT EISENHOWER WAS EVEN MORE BLUNT IN HIS DETERMINATION TO PREVENT SOUTH VIETNAM FROM BEING OVERTHROWN BY HER COMMUNIST NORTHERN NEIGHBOUR WHEN HE TOLD HIS NATIONAL SECURITY COUNCIL:

What we want is a Vietnamese force which will support [Ngo Dinh] Diem … the obvious thing to do is simply to authorize O'Daniel to use up to X million dollars to produce the maximum number of Vietnamese units which Prime Minister Diem can depend on to sustain himself in power.[18]

US President Eisenhower in determined mood. He was adamant that South Vietnamese President Diem should be supported fully by the US.

GENERAL WILLIAMS SAW THE TRAINING OF THE SOUTH VIETNAMESE ARMY ALONG CONVENTIONAL, AS OPPOSED TO UNCONVENTIONAL, MEANS AS A NECESSITY. HE TOLD PRESIDENT DIEM:

Communist guerrilla strategy is simple. By using a small amount of arms and equipment and a few good military leaders, they force [their opponents] to utilize relatively large military forces in a campaign that is costly in money and men. In Korea in 1950, the South Koreans were using three divisions to fight less than 7000 guerrillas in the southeast. When the North Koreans attacked, the South Koreans suffered from this diversion as their army was not strategically or tactically deployed to meet the North Korean attack.[19]

Vietnamese villagers sit around the opening of the village storage pit. Though the villagers generally had honest uses for these holes in the ground, the Viet Cong would use them to conceal weapons and equipment.

By economizing on arms and men, communist guerrillas force their opponents into costly campaigns

THE FORCES OF THE SOUTH

THOSE SOUTH VIETNAMESE WHO ATTENDED ESTABLISHMENTS, SUCH AS THE US ARMY INFANTRY SCHOOL AT FORT BENNING, WERE OFTEN ASSIGNED TO SAIGON OR A LARGE HQ FAR AWAY FROM WHERE THEY WERE NEEDED MOST — IN THE FIELD. ONE FORMER US ADVISOR RECALLED:

One day during practice in firing the 60mm mortar, I was rather appalled at the complete lack of organization of the class. For example, there would be ladies, in their large straw conical hats, out selling bowls of soup and other things to nibble on right in among the class … that type of thing. The lieutenant in charge had a .45 automatic stuck in his back pocket, no belt, no holster or anything of that nature. And, finally, at the conclusion of the day, I went to this lieutenant and asked him: "You're just back from Fort Benning, aren't you?", and he said, "Yes, sir". "You had mortar instruction at Fort Benning?" "Yes, sir." And I said: "Well, what do you think? How do you compare the instruction you just finished giving with that which you received at Fort Benning?", and his answer was, "Oh, it was much better at Fort Benning". So I said, "Why?", and he said, "Well, sir, that was Fort Benning and this is Vietnam".[20]

Supported by two or three United States military advisors, South Vietnamese troops move towards their target. Note the tall radio antennae used for long-range communications being carried by the soldiers.

A US ADVISOR RECALLED
WITH AMUSEMENT
THE DIFFICULTIES
THE LANGUAGE
BARRIER CREATED:

He instructed the interpreter to tell their men, "About Face!". The interpreter looked at the major rather quizzically, then spoke rapidly to one of the trainees. The man broke from the ranks, went over to a pail of water, washed his face and then returned to the formation. Each time the advisor would attempt to teach this facing movement the same act would be repeated. Finally, after the third attempt, the trooper broke down. He told the major that there was nothing wrong with his face, that it was clean because he had washed it three times.[21]

COMMENTING ON THE
GROWTH OF THE SOUTH
VIETNAMESE AIR FORCE,
ADMIRAL ROBERT B.
PIRIE, THE US NAVY'S
DEPUTY CHIEF OF NAVAL
OPERATIONS (AIR), SAID:

While the other services ... are busily developing a multitude of new requirements, and programmes ... the US Navy is quietly contributing both a large share of the aircraft currently involved, and of those planned for use in the immediate future in South Vietnam, with very little credit redounding to us but with no little effort on training and readiness.[22]

US helicopters ferry 300 Vietnamese Rangers into the Plain of Reeds in the Mekong Delta. In this mission they destroyed five communist guerrilla villages and a training centre; 90 suspects were also arrested.

COMBAT TRAINING HAD TO
TAKE PRECEDENCE OVER
COUNTER-GUERRILLA
TACTICS, ARGUED
LIEUTENANT-GENERAL
WILLIAMS, COMMANDING
GENERAL OF MAAG:

The South Vietnamese soldier had the same mobility as the Viet Cong guerrilla, and his equipment was lighter and better. Anti-guerrilla training ... was a supplement to, and not a substitute for, individual and small unit combat training. Only when soldiers mastered the latter fundamentals could they ... go on to learn the more open style of warfare characteristic of counter-guerrilla operations. As an example, if two fire teams of a squad have not learned to advance with each other using extremely well-coordinated fire and movement ... they cannot be expected to perform effectively in attempting the same task with the extremely limited observation, the obstacles and the far greater control problems that characterize jungle or swamp operations.[23]

MARINE HELICOPTERS IN THE NAM

LIEUTENANT-COLONEL ARCHIE L. CLAPP, COMMANDING OFFICER OF THE ONLY MAJOR US MARINE CORPS UNIT IN SOUTH VIETNAM, RECORDED IN HIS DIARY DURING THE SUMMER OF 1962 THE DANGERS FACING MARINE PILOTS AND CREW MEMBERS OF THE SIKORSKY UH-34S FLOWN BY THE LEATHERNECKS:

A Sikorsky UH-34 Choctaw helicopter. This aircraft is synonymous with the Vietnam War, and was a vital weapon in the US arsenal. It could sustain a substantial amount of damage and still make it home.

Wednesday, 18 April: Two helicopters were requested to haul priority supplies from Ca Mau to Binh Hung. Ca Mau is the southern-most town in Vietnam that is under the control of the Vietnamese government; Binh Hung is Father Ho's famed "village that refuses to die". No roads lead to Binh Hung. The tree-lined canals and streams, which are the only surface routes of transportation, are ideal for ambush, and the VC [Viet Cong] control the surrounding countryside. Therefore, helicopters are the safest means of transportation between Binh Hung and the "outside world"…

Tuesday, 24 April: Operation Nightingale entailed landing troops of the 21st Division in eight separate landing sites. Enemy small-arms fire was received upon landing … and one helicopter was hit in an oil line. The pilot was able to take off and fly about a mile before landing in a rice paddy near a Self Defense Corps outpost. We were then able to make use of the "downed bird" procedure we had formulated, but had not yet tried. A wing-man landed and retrieved the crew, while a division of four helicopters proceeded to the forward loading site where it picked up the repair crew and troops … to form perimeter security. The repair crew determined what was needed to fix our downed bird; the part was flown in from Soc Trang, immediately installed, and the helicopter was then flown out and returned to base. The reserve troops were then lifted out of the area. The ground action went quite well also. The Viet Cong lost 52 troops killed and two captured, against three Vietnamese troops killed and six wounded…

Thursday, 26 April: The squadron went on its first "short-order" mission today. The III Corps briefing officer arrived at Soc Trang shortly after 0700. The crews were briefed, helicopters proceeded to the troop pick-up point, and landing was executed at 0900. Very light opposition was encountered upon landing, and the Vietnamese troops rounded up over 100 Viet Cong suspects for questioning…

Thursday, 10 May: The squadron returned to the scene of its first combat lift today. This time, however, there was a welcoming committee. As the flight approached the village, armed men could be seen scurrying out into the fields where they literally disappeared. A few of them, who happened to land in a sparse spot, could be seen lying on their backs firing upwards at the helicopters as they passed. The rest of them were presumably doing the same thing. One helicopter was hit, but was able to make it back to the forward loading site. This mission pointed up a cardinal principle of counter-guerrilla work: never repeat a previous manoeuvre. It is a tremendous temptation to repeat something that works well the first time, but there are few tactics more dangerous ... when operating helicopters against irregulars...

Monday, 7 June: The day started as a routine lift of 7th Division troops in the Plain of Reeds area. But it turned out to be our "Longest Day". When the troops landed on their first objective, a village situated at a stream junction, many armed and uniformed Viet Cong soldiers were flushed [out]. They headed north in the direction of the Cambodian border. The Division Commander decided to carry through with the second scheduled landing in approximately the same place as the first. He indicated that this was to give him a substantial holding force and he would start hitting [the enemy] from the other direction (i.e. this was to be his "anvil" and he intended to make other "hammer" landings and catch the VC in between)...

Thursday, 10 June: On a landing with 21st Division troops today, many people were flushed from the objective village while the helicopters were on the final approach. This was by no means the only time we were faced with this situation – the VC intermingling with the local population while they fired at us. If there is an answer to this problem, we didn't find it...

Saturday, 12 June: The VC ambushed a convoy to the north of Saigon, killed two American officers and several Vietnamese soldiers, and captured a quantity of weapons. The squadron was diverted from another mission to land troops in an attempt to head them off. The helicopters received small-arms fire. As soon as they had discharged their troops ... a radio call was received that requested them to land again and move some troops that had been placed in the wrong spot by another outfit. The request was denied...

Wednesday, 15 June: The largest helicopter lift in Vietnam to date took place today in a landing with 5th Division troops north of Saigon. The Marines led with 18 helicopters, the US Army came next with 12, and the Vietnamese Air Force followed with 11...[24]

Wednesday, 15 June: The largest helicopter lift in Vietnam to date took place today...

US Marine Corps UH-34s take off from an aircraft carrier. Helicopters were the mainstay of the airlift network in much of Vietnam.

37

A CREEPING COMMITMENT

GENERAL DECKER, US ARMY CHIEF OF STAFF, WARNED THE KENNEDY ADMINISTRATION THAT:

This is the last place in the world I would like to see … [US forces] committed unless absolutely necessary. If it were only the Pathet Lao that was involved, there would be no problem. But undoubtedly North Vietnamese would come in and probably the Chinese Communists, and when they do it is hard to predict where our commitment would stop.[25]

LIEUTENANT-COMMANDER BRUCE A. BRYER, US NAVY COASTAL FORCE ADVISOR, RATED THE NEW COASTAL "JUNK FORCE" HIGHLY:

The Junk Force [River Warfare Force] is a new and vital addition to the VNN. It will soon be the largest force afloat – both in personnel and number of craft. It has already demonstrated its potential in unconventional warfare. Due to recent publicity, the eyes of the free world are upon it. It will be spread over the entire 1500-mile coastline, making support problems acute. We must not allow this great new force to sink before it swims due to a lack of support from its Mother Navy.[26]

USAF AC-47 Dragon Ships at Pleiku Air Base. Each aircraft, nicknamed "Spooky", could deliver heavy firepower with its three Gatling guns.

US President John F. Kennedy. Taking up Eisenhower's mantle, he was keen to continue supporting the South.

IN NOVEMBER 1963, PRESIDENT JOHN F. KENNEDY WROTE TO ADMIRAL DAVID L. MCDONALD, CHIEF OF NAVAL OPERATIONS, AND MR PAUL NITZE, SECRETARY OF THE NAVY, EMPHASIZING THE US NAVY'S ROLE IN COUNTER-INSURGENCY OPERATIONS:

When I was in Norfolk in 1962 I noted particularly the members of the SEAL [Sea, Air and Land] Teams. I was impressed by them as individuals and with the capability they possess as a group. As missiles assume more and more of the nuclear deterrent role, and as your limited war mission grows, the need for special forces in the Navy and Marine Corps will increase.[27]

MASTER SERGEANT W.V. "BILL" EAST, US MARINE CORPS, WAS IN SAIGON IN THE LEAD-UP TO THE OVERTHROW OF DIEM IN NOVEMBER 1963:

We encountered several anti-American demonstrations. During one riot, I was on duty by myself in the embassy annexe. This riot/demonstration lasted three days and nights. There was a locker with several weapons stored there. I ... loaded all of them. I took a position on a balcony inside the front iron gate, and stayed there each night ... as that was when the crowds were the heaviest and rowdiest. During the day I would get some sleep, or rummage the annexe rooms for something to eat. All I could find was some candy bars and cookies in the secretaries' desks. There were several incidents of this sort during the rest of my tour.[28]

A light armoured car burns in the street in Saigon in 1963. It was hit by a rocket launched from the Independence Palace during the coup to oust President Diem.

CHAPTER 3
AMERICA GOES TO WAR
1964-1966

Even as the US advisory effort continued, political instability in Saigon threatened to undermine efforts to prevent a North Vietnamese invasion. The overall situation was made worse on the afternoon of 3 August 1964 when North Vietnamese patrol boats opened fire on the destroyer USS *Maddox*, 45km (28 miles) off the coast of North Vietnam. Terrorist bombs also exploded at various US installations in South Vietnam. These actions forced President Johnson to land the Marines.

"We're being fired upon"

In an effort to prevent North Vietnam from infiltrating men and material into South Vietnam, both the US and South Vietnamese Navies patrolled the Vietnam coast. The South Vietnamese Navy (VNN), with the assistance of the US, "conducted a series of minor, ineffectual raids against North Vietnamese coastal installations".[1] The US Navy sent its own ships in a programme called Operation De Soto, designed to detect North Vietnamese vessels.

On the evening of 30/31 July 1964, a South Vietnamese commando team had raided several installations off the port of Vinh. The USS *Maddox* was on a routine patrol 192km (120 miles) away. Thinking that the *Maddox* had been involved in the raid, North Vietnamese patrol boats fired upon the destroyer, now 45km (28 miles) off the coast and in international waters. The attackers fired torpedoes and machine guns at the *Maddox*. The *Maddox* returned fire with her 5in batteries and scored a hit. At 17:30 hours, F-8E Crusader jets flying off the aircraft carrier USS *Ticonderoga* fired rockets and strafed enemy vessels. When the aircraft broke contact, one ship lay dead in the water with two others limping away.[2]

Joined the next day by the USS *Turner Joy*, the *Maddox* continued its patrol. While US Navy fighter-bombers had been placed on alert, the National Security Council hesitated to take action, fearing it could have domestic political ramifications for President Johnson's re-election campaign. Then, sonar on board the *Turner Joy*, as well as communication intercepts by the National Security Agency, pointed to an impending attack by North Vietnamese vessels. Sailors aboard the *Turner Joy* reportedly heard the motors of enemy boats. Captain John Herrick, a veteran naval officer and the on-scene task force commander, raised some doubts as to whether a second attack occurred. Captain Herrick commented that the "entire action leaves many doubts except for an apparent attempt to ambush at the beginning".[3]

While critics were quick to accuse the Johnson Administration of making up the incident, North Vietnam indirectly confirmed it when it later admitted its torpedo squadrons chased the *Maddox* from its coastal waters, representing the first North Vietnamese victory over the US Navy. Furthermore, this claim only served to prove that the North Vietnamese purposely attacked the *Maddox* and *Turner Joy*. It therefore justified the retaliatory strikes ordered by President Johnson on 5 August 1964 against storage tanks located at Vinh. In the raid, US F-8 Crusaders and A-4 Skyhawks sank eight North Vietnamese patrol boats and damaged a further 24.

In a similar attack later in September 1964, the USS *Richard S. Edwards* and USS *Morton*, part of the Navy's De Soto patrols, came under attack by North Vietnamese vessels. Admiral Sharp recommended that the US hit Northern bases and other military targets. Sharp specifically wanted attacks against North Vietnam's supply depot at Vinh and the patrol boat base at Ben Thuy. The US Air Force wanted to hit enemy barracks Viet Thu Lu and Chap Le, as well as the ammunition depot at Xom Bang.

After an investigation of the reported clash between the USS *Morton* and USS *Richard S. Edwards* failed to turn up any evidence suggesting an attack, the Joint Chiefs of Staff once again backed away from any type of major retaliation. The Joint Chiefs now insisted that naval officers patrolling North Vietnamese waters send "flash" precedence messages alerting the authorities of any attack, real or unsubstantiated.

Admiral Thomas Moorer, the Commander-in-Chief, Pacific Fleet, had already anticipated some increased measure of involvement by US forces in Vietnam. He recommended the construction of piers, magazines for ammunition storage and fuel dump facilities, as well as the widening of existing airfields, particularly at Da Nang. He also called for a jet-capable airfield to be built at nearby Chu Lai. Moorer likewise proposed the deployment to these newly constructed sites of air defences and ground combat units to provide security.

Moorer stressed the fact that the US needed to expand the role of military

The A-4 Skyhawk as flown by the US Navy and Marines. This single-seat aircraft was designed for ground-attack missions, and was renowned for its bomb-load capacity.

personnel in the advisory effort and, in particular, the pacification campaign.

After attacks on US personnel at the Brinks Hotel and Bien Hoa airfield, the US Ambassador to South Vietnam, retired Army General Maxwell Taylor, dismissed the notion that what the war in Vietnam needed was US ground forces. However, he supported what General Westmoreland called a "tit-for-tat retaliation" through the use of sustained aerial bombing of the North to deter any future attacks.

"An entirely new war"

As the Viet Cong (VC) stepped up attacks on the Army of the Republic of Vietnam (ARVN) and US military installations, communist forces switched their guerrilla tactics to that of a fully fledged conventional war. Near the village of Binh Gia, two regiments of the 9th Viet Cong Division "ambushed and virtually destroyed two battalions of South Vietnamese troops, including the 4th Battalion, Vietnamese Marine Corps [VNMC], and inflicted heavy casualties on relieving armoured and mechanized forces".[4]

Westmoreland believed that Binh Gia signalled the start of the final communist offensive to absorb the South into North Vietnam. He was firmly convinced that the battle and other overt moves by the Viet Cong meant the beginning of an intensive military challenge which the South Vietnamese Government could not meet with its own resources.

After a visit to South Vietnam, the situation had deteriorated, according to President Johnson's Special Assistant McGeorge Bundy: "Without new US action, defeat appears inevitable – probably not in a matter of weeks or perhaps even months, but in the next year or so. There is time to turn it around, but not much."[5]

Following an attack by VC sappers on the US military compound at Pleiku in the Central Highlands, the war had come closer to involving US ground troops. Even

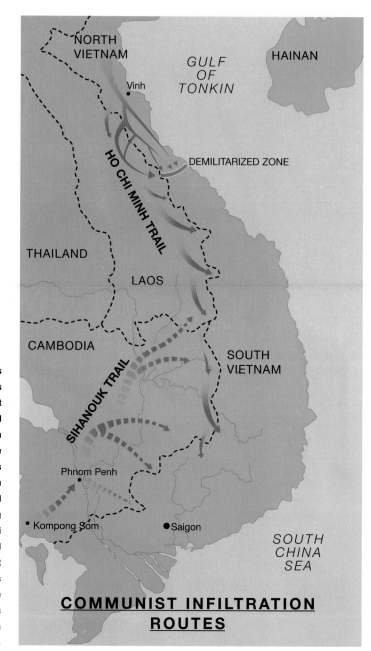

This map illustrates the infiltration routes taken by communist forces as they moved in and out of Vietnam in 1964. Utilizing the porous border regions that South Vietnam shared with Laos and Cambodia, including the infamous Ho Chi Minh Trail and Sihanouk Trail, Viet Cong and NVA troops were able to move men and materials into position with relative ease.

COMMUNIST INFILTRATION ROUTES

as US jet aircraft streaked towards North Vietnam on retaliatory raids, the US military build-up began with the deployment of a US Marine Hawk antiaircraft battalion to the base at Da Nang.

Several days later, on 10 February 1965, another VC unit attacked and destroyed a US Air Force enlisted men's barracks in the coastal city of Qui Nhon. There was the same response of air strikes, this time carried out by more than 100 US Navy fighter-bombers as a part of Operation Flaming Dart against military targets in North Vietnam.[6]

On 13 February, President Johnson approved the limited and measured bombing campaign codenamed Rolling Thunder. After another political coup in Saigon, Westmoreland, fearing that US troops were more vulnerable now than before, instructed his deputy commander, Lieutenant-General John L. Throckmorton, to determine what American ground troops were needed for base security. Throckmorton recommended the deployment of a three-battalion US Marine expeditionary brigade to Da Nang in order to guard the vital air base located there. Westmoreland later recalled that, "while sharing Throckmorton's sense of urgency, I nevertheless hoped to keep the number of US ground forces to a minimum and recommended instead landing only two battalions and holding a third aboard ship".[7]

On 22 February 1965, Westmoreland forwarded this request for the Marines to Admiral Sharp, who in turn informed the Joint Chiefs that, while he had some reservations about sending ground combat troops into Vietnam, he concurred with Westmoreland's assessment of the need for the Marines. Ambassador Taylor endorsed Westmoreland's request for a battalion of Marines to guard Da Nang.

The Marines land at Da Nang

By the end of February, President Johnson made the decision to commit a two-battalion Marine expeditionary force to Da Nang. On 25 February 1965, Brigadier-General Frederick J. Karch, the commanding general of the 9th Marine Expeditionary Brigade, had been alerted that a landing was soon to take place.

At 05:45 hours the next morning, Admiral Wulzen gave the order to land the troops. By 09:18 hours, the fourth and final assault wave went ashore. As the leathernecks scrambled from their landing craft, South Vietnamese troops secured the beachhead as young Vietnamese girls greeted the Marines with flowers and signs with the words, "Welcome, US Marines". By that evening, one-third of the Marine ground forces and two-thirds of the Marine helicopter squadrons in the Western Pacific had been committed to South Vietnam.[8]

Shortly after the Marines settled down into a routine of guarding and fortifying the area surrounding the airfield, the mission changed from a defensive to an offensive one. By the end of April 1965, US Marine

strength stood at 8878 officers and men. Karch was "confident that he could handle anything that the enemy could throw at him".[9] In order to expand the defensive perimeter surrounding Da Nang, Westmoreland sought and received permission from President Johnson to lift the restrictions placed on the Marines that prevented them from engaging in offensive combat operations. The new order authorized the Marines to engage in clearing operations within an 80km (50-mile) radius of their enclave at Da Nang.

Karch and South Vietnamese Major-General Nguyen Chanh Thi, I Corps Commander, met shortly thereafter to discuss the new tactical areas of responsibility (TAORs) for the Marines. After two days it was agreed that the Marine enclave in Da Nang would expand 6.4km (4 miles) beyond the perimeter, with the number of hamlets under Marine control expanding from 1 to 15, with a total population of 11,441 South Vietnamese villagers.[10]

When questioned at a US State Department press conference, Secretary of State Dean Rusk pointedly told the reporters that "we don't expect these men [the Marines] to sit there like hypnotized rabbits waiting for the Viet Cong to strike".[11] The Marines were given permission to expand their TAOR, Rusk maintained, in order to keep the enemy off balance and prevent major attacks against installations. Bill Moyers, President Johnson's press secretary, supported Rusk's comments and re-emphasized the defensive nature of the expanded TAOR. Moyers added that "there has been no change in the mission of the US ground combat units in Vietnam in recent days or weeks. The President has issued no order of any kind in this regard to General Westmoreland recently or at any other time." President Johnson's press secretary stressed the fact that "General Westmoreland also has authority within the assigned mission to employ these troops in support of

Vietnamese forces faced with aggressive attack when in his judgement the general military situation requires it".[12]

General Wallace M. Greene Jr., the US Marine Corps Commandant then on an inspection visit to Da Nang, summed it up when he told newsmen: "You don't defend a place by sitting on your ditty box."[13]

As the Marines stationed in and around Da Nang began active patrolling outside of their enclave, a high-level conference was convened at the headquarters of the Commander-in-Chief Pacific in Honolulu on 20 April 1965. It was attended by Secretary of Defense McNamara, General Earle Wheeler, the Chairman of the Joint Chiefs of Staff, General Westmoreland and Admiral Sharp.

After reviewing the situation in Vietnam, the attendees were in full agreement that, despite the presence of the Marines and the light VC activity in and around Da Nang, this represented nothing more than the calm before the storm. Additional US combat and logistical forces would be required. The delegates recommended the dispatch of 42,000 additional combat and support troops, including 5000 more Marines in order to establish another enclave at Chu Lai, 91km (57 miles) southeast of Da Nang.

Americanization of the war

While calling upon the services of the 173rd Airborne Brigade, Westmoreland concluded that without further reinforcements the ARVN would eventually crumble under the weight of the massive infusion of North Vietnamese troops that had begun by the spring of 1965. In addition to the deployment of the remainder of the 3rd Marine Division, as well as two US Army brigades and an airmobile division, Westmoreland requested a Republic of Korea division and other allied forces.[14]

Along with the troop requests, Westmoreland asked for authority to employ US forces in offensive operations against the

Soldiers of the ARVN traverse a river. The nature of the terrain in Vietnam made movement extremely difficult. Dense jungle and a multitude of waterways made even the simplest patrol arduous.

enemy. This was the birth of the so-called search-and-destroy operations. On 26 June 1965, President Johnson gave the Military Assistance Command, Vietnam (MACV) commander permission to commit US forces to battle in any situation.

When it had been reported that the 1st Viet Cong Regiment had been moving towards the Marine enclave at Chu Lai, both III Marine Expeditionary Force commander Lieutenant-General Lewis W. Walt and Westmoreland saw an opportunity to give the enemy a bloody nose. The Marines in I Corps Tactical Zone began preparations for a large-scale search-and-destroy mission they later named Operation Starlite.

Operation Starlite was a converging manoeuvre with the use of Marines assaulting from amphibious vehicles, a heliborne operation using troop-carrying helicopters, and employment of a classic amphibious assault with the use of naval gunfire as supporting artillery. A six-day battle killed at least 964 VC, and not only prevented an attack by the 1st Viet Cong Regiment but also made this same force combat-ineffective.[15]

In the follow-on operation known as Piranha, US Marines, South Vietnamese troops and elements of the 2nd ARVN Division attacked the VC enclave on the Batangan Peninsula. After three days of fighting, the Marines and ARVN killed a further 183 VC. Heavy losses were suffered by both sides during the battle in the Ia Drang Valley in October 1965, while in 1966 Operations Hastings (July–August) and Attleboro (October–November) witnessed the deployment of thousands of US troops.

While Westmoreland focused on the big unit war, Walt saw the key to winning in Vietnam as the struggle for the hearts and minds of the Vietnamese villagers. Long exploited by both the VC and the government of South Vietnam, the villagers living in the remote hamlets were fertile ground for VC propaganda and its campaign against the Saigon government.

Retired Marine General Edward H. Forney saw the idea of "pacification" as the way to make a significant contribution to beating the VC. He told General Greene that the Marine Corps should make pacification the cornerstone of its strategy.

In keeping with Walt's and Forney's emphasis on pacification, the Marines in I Corps Tactical Zone formed the combined action company (CAC), which was a Marine rifle squad assigned to a Popular Forces (South Vietnamese paramilitary units) platoon. Leadership roles were filled by both Marine noncommissioned officers and their Vietnamese counterparts.

The main objective was, according to Marine First Lieutenant Paul R. Ek, to "secure the people's loyalties, the security, counter-intelligence, obtaining the goodwill of the people. These formed the spokes of the wheel while training was the hub of the entire programme."[16]

Lieutenant-General Victor H. Krulak, Commanding General, Fleet Marine Force

The battle for the hearts and minds of the local population in South Vietnam was as important as the military effort. If the US could win the support of the local populace, then hunting down the VC would be easier.

Pacific (FMFPac), felt that victory could be achieved only if the Marines won this "other war". Westmoreland disagreed. Viewing 1966 as a transition year from defensive- to offensive-based strategy, the MACV commander wanted to husband his resources for a larger, more mobile phase in 1967. He believed that: "The Marines should have been trying to find the enemy's main forces and bring them to battle, thereby reducing the threat they posed to the population."[17]

Walt disagreed, and based his opposition on the fact that villagers were a good source of intelligence. The operational guidelines given to Walt by Westmoreland permitted the Marines to apply pacification tactics while conducting mobile operations against the enemy. Some Marine officers, Krulak among them, saw this dual operational and tactical approach as a formula for over-extending themselves. Walt's Marines would conduct a three-pronged effort in fighting the VC and North Vietnamese Army (NVA) that included search-and-destroy operations, counter-guerrilla operations and pacification.

Westmoreland fully understood the value of pacification, yet took the view that, by adopting a small-unit approach to fighting the Viet Cong and NVA, allied forces risked piecemeal annihilation. He recalled that pacification had been tried (and had failed) in

1964 by the ARVN's 22d Division in the coastal Binh Dinh Province. As the ARVN appeared to make some progress, "two main-force enemy regiments debouched from the hills and virtually destroyed the spread-out South Vietnamese units, making a shambles of the pacification programme".[18]

By the end of 1966, enemy units were employing superior Soviet-supplied weapons. VC and NVA sappers launched heavy mortar attacks against the Special Forces camp at Khe Sanh and the Da Nang airfield. The Soviet 120mm heavy mortars allowed the enemy to launch attacks against other major US military installations

and thereby increase the problems of base security. Westmoreland added that "Viet Cong local and guerrilla forces began to appear with AK-47 assault rifles".[19]

As 1966 ended, the US found itself fully engaged in the fighting in Vietnam. Where the French had hesitated, however, the US did not. Westmoreland acknowledged that "President Johnson never tried to tell me how to run the war. He deferred to my judgement, and he let me run the war ... as I saw fit. He backed me and supported me without exception."[20]

While General Westmoreland disagreed with the approach taken by Krulak and Walt regarding pacification measures in I Corps Tactical Zone, he accepted that "a long-term grinding machine would work in Vietnam".[21] It could be argued that he was indeed correct in this assessment in purely military terms.

Judged in terms of military effectiveness alone, the United States and its Free World allies set the stage for a number of victories in the South in 1967.

US and Vietnamese troops inspect the remains of a charred M113 armoured personnel carrier (APC) which had been ambushed by VC troops.

SUPPORTING A CRUMBLING ALLY

More faith must be put in the on-scene commander to do his job fully and make reports on his actions as quickly as is humanly possible. But the accomplishment of his mission must come first. This cannot be done when he is pummelled by flash precedence questions from all levels of superior echelons.[22]

Commencing with the 2 August [1964] attack on the *Maddox*, the Navy for the first time in warfare found itself required to feed near real-time details of the action into the complex international politico-military play in Washington. In order for the US to play the game to national advantage, our Navy had to feed accurate, detailed information to Washington at flash precedence.[23]

CAPTAIN HOLLYFIELD, US NAVY TASK FORCE COMMANDER OFF VIETNAM, WROTE TO THE CHIEF OF NAVAL OPERATIONS OVER PROCEDURES CONCERNING ENGAGEMENTS WITH THE NORTH VIETNAMESE:

ADMIRAL THOMAS MOORER, COMMANDING THE PACIFIC FLEET, WARNED OF THE NEED FOR A STABLE GOVERNMENT IN SAIGON:

Without a solid government, based on popular support, the military effort against the VC has little chance of success , as is rather conclusively borne out by the events and deteriorating situation which have been evidenced over the past year. The strategic concept required for success calls for a careful coordination of military operations with the governmental development of a national improvement programme aimed at urban and rural development to influence and benefit the masses. While it seems we have given this considerable lip service, this concept has never really been meaningfully applied.[24]

If we are really serious about Vietnam we should stop treading water in midstream and take positive action against NVN [North Vietnam]. Time is running out on us, and unless some drastic action is taken now, the US will be left with but little choice in the implementation of a full range of military measures against North Vietnam that include an all-out bombing campaign, aerial mining of ports, and a maritime blockade.[25]

Members of the US Joint Chiefs of Staff pose for a photograph in 1964. They are, from left to right, Admiral Zumvalt, General Westmoreland, Admiral Moorer, General Ryan and General Chapman.

We are faced here with a seriously deteriorating situation characterized by continued political turmoil, irresponsibility and division within the [South Viet-namese] Armed Forces, lethargy in the pacification programme, growing anti-US feelings, signs of mounting terrorism by the VC directed at US personnel, and deepening discouragement and loss of morale throughout SVN [South Vietnam].[26]

THE US AMBASSADOR TO SOUTH VIETNAM, RETIRED US ARMY GENERAL MAXWELL TAYLOR, WROTE TO PRESIDENT JOHNSON:

General Maxwell Taylor, US Ambassador to South Vietnam from July 1964 until July 1965. A former Chairman of the Joint Chiefs of Staff, he had enjoyed a long and successful career.

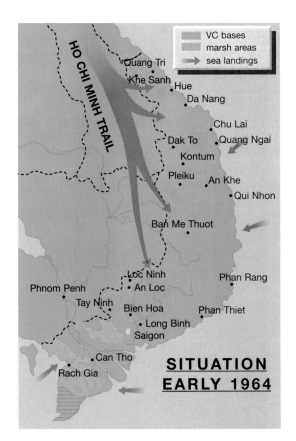

HO CHI MINH TRAIL

Quang Tri
Khe Sanh
Hue
Da Nang
Chu Lai
Dak To
Quang Ngai
Kontum
Pleiku
An Khe
Qui Nhon
Ban Me Thuot
Loc Ninh
Phan Rang
Phnom Penh
An Loc
Tay Ninh
Bien Hoa
Phan Thiet
Long Binh
Saigon
Can Tho
Rach Gia

VC bases
marsh areas
sea landings

SITUATION EARLY 1964

The situation in South Vietnam in early 1964. Communist supplies were pouring into the South by land and sea.

Over the next two days [of the Battle of Binh Gia], a Vietnamese Ranger battalion fought its way into the fringes of the hamlet. When a US Marine battalion arrived, the enemy retired to entrenchments in the rubber plantation. There the Marines came under a sharp attack that lasted until the VC broke off the engagement on New Year's Day. In the course of the fighting the Ranger battalions were virtually destroyed. However serious that result, the fact was that the enemy appeared to be moving from guerrilla and small-unit warfare into a new, and presumably final, phase – attacks by big units that would stand their ground.[27]

That was disturbing enough in itself. We would have been even more concerned had we known at the time that as early as September 1964 the North Vietnamese decided to commit North Vietnamese regiments and divisions in the south, a decision that went beyond mere support of the insurgency to direct intervention by regular units of the North Vietnamese Army.[28]

GENERAL WESTMORELAND RECALLED THAT THE BATTLE OF BINH GIA WAS THE FIRST TIME IN THE WAR THAT THE ENEMY HAD FORMED A DIVISION-SIZED UNIT:

CONTRARY TO WESTMORELAND'S BELIEF THAT BINH GIA REPRESENTED A SIGNIFICANT SHIFT IN NORTH VIETNAM'S TACTICAL APPROACH, TRUONG NHU TANG, A FORMER VIET CONG OFFICIAL, NOTED THAT:

This involved no change in strategy. Instead, we would intensify the political struggle on the rural and urban fronts. In the countryside, we moved to consolidate control in liberated areas and establish NLF government entities in disputed regions. The object was not to take land, but to create a strong NLF presence which villagers would accept as government. In the cities we took steps to accelerate pressure for negotiations. If we could weaken the regime's control of the rural population and galvanize pressure in the cities for talks, we might precipitate a political crisis. Depending on our success, we might now bring about a general uprising, which was our strategic objective, or catapult the unstable [General Nguyen] Khan (or his successor) into negotiations. Either development would distance, perhaps nullify, the spectre of American military intervention.[29]

Four Viet Cong (VC) soldiers take refuge in a cramped underground hideaway. As can be seen, women were also drafted into the VC to train as soldiers.

47

THE MARINES GO IN

BRIGADIER-GENERAL
FREDERICK J. KARCH,
THE COMMANDING GENERAL
OF THE 9TH MARINE
EXPEDITIONARY BRIGADE,
RECALLED THAT:

On 7 March [1965], I was sitting in my state room when Rear-Admiral [Don W.] Wulzen, US Navy, comes in and says, "Here is a dispatch", which said, "Close Da Nang, land the landing force". I looked at the dispatch. I looked at Admiral Wulzen, and I said: "Don, do you think in Washington they know what time it is in Da Nang? This means a night landing if we close Da Nang at this point."[30]

Charlie Company had been assigned the southern sector of the perimeter, its lines anchored on the left of the asphalt road that led into Da Nang city, and tied it in on the right with A Company. The MLR, or main line of resistance, was opposite the dirt road to our front. It consisted of a chain-link fence, a zigzag trench line connecting a series of stone watchtowers – relics from French colonial times – a double-apron barbed-wire fence, a minefield and a triple row of concertina wire. The MLR was manned by an ARVN regional force (militia) battalion, which we would formally relieve in two or three days.

LIEUTENANT CAPUTO
REMEMBERED THE OUTLAY
OF CHARLIE COMPANY,
1ST BATTALION, 3RD
MARINES' POSITION AT
DA NANG:

Until then, One-Three [1st Battalion, 3rd Marines] would serve as a secondary line of defence. [Captain] Peterson told us that the swathe of rice paddies and villages stretching southwards had been a communist stronghold for years and was considered the most likely avenue of approach for a Viet Cong attack. In simplest terms, if they hit [i.e. the Viet Cong], they would hit C Company first.[31]

DESPITE THE SLIGHTLY EXPANDED MARINE TAOR, CONTACT WITH THE ELUSIVE VIET CONG REMAINED RELATIVELY MINOR, CONFINED LARGELY TO HARASSMENT FROM SNIPERS AND BOOBY TRAPS AS THE MARINES CONDUCTED ROUTINE PATROLS. GENERAL KARCH NOTED THAT:

When we had reached the limit of our Phase II TAOR we still had encountered no VC in strength other than undersized platoons. After a few sniper shots were fired at the patrol and … [the Marines] moved out to attack, the VC disappeared. Also, the only attack … at Phu Bai could well have been a mistake … or a chance encounter … it was broken off immediately after the first exchange of fire.[32]

US bombers drop napalm on VC positions around Da Nang. The use of napalm was one of the most controversial aspects of the entire war, but it was effective when deployed accurately.

A group of young US Marines enjoy some of the local delicacies. The pineapples would have undoubtedly come as a welcome break from the day-to-day routine of C rations.

The patrol that morning had the nightmare quality which characterized most small-unit operations in the war. The trail looped and twisted. The company seemed to be marching into a vacuum, haunted by a sense of being surrounded by something we could not see. It was the inability to see that vexed us most. In that lies the jungle's power to cause fear. It arouses the instinct that makes us apprehensive of attics and dark alleys. Men with active imaginations were most prey to these fears. In Vietnam, the best soldiers were usually unimaginative men who did not feel afraid until there was obvious reason. The rest of us suffered from a constant expectancy, feeling that something was about to happen, waiting for it to happen, wishing it would happen just so the tension would be relieved.

Something finally did happen that morning, and when it did I damned near jumped out of my skin. It wasn't much – a burst of heavy rifle fire from the head of the column, the noise magnified by the dense woods. The shooting lasted no more than a few seconds, and then I heard my heart drumming against my chest. Widener took a call on the radio, a summons from [Captain] Peterson. I ran forward at a crouch, weaving around prone Marines. It felt good to be moving. I found Peterson standing in, of all things, a cornfield. A line of riflemen was moving cautiously through the rows of dead stalks. The field ended in a swathe of elephant grass, the same colour as the corn stalks, and beyond the grass rose a low, wooded edge. Hill 107 stood about 1000 yards away, to our left rear. From the ridge, a sniper had opened up on the point. Although the sniper had broken contact with the first burst of return fire, Peterson suspected an ambush. An enemy mortar crew atop Hill 107, and a few automatic riflemen on the ridge, could damage the company badly as it moved through the broad cornfield. Therefore, we would cross it one platoon at a time, each covering the other, while the skipper called in air strikes on the hill.[33]

LIEUTENANT CAPUTO REMEMBERED ONE PATROL AS THE MARINES IN HIS COMPANY MOVED AWAY FROM THE AIRFIELD AT DA NANG INTO THE SURROUNDING COUNTRYSIDE:

AN ESCALATION IN AID

ALONG WITH HIS DECISION TO REINFORCE US COMBAT STRENGTH IN VIETNAM, PRESIDENT JOHNSON ISSUED THE FOLLOWING STATEMENT ON 8 JUNE 1965:

If help is requested by the appropriate Vietnamese commander, General Westmoreland also has authority within the assigned mission to employ these troops in support of Vietnamese forces faced with aggressive attack when other effective reserves are not available and when, in his judgement, the general military situation urgently requires it.[34]

WESTMORELAND THOUGHT THAT A 44-BATTALION FORCE WOULD FINALLY CONVINCE THE VIET CONG AND NORTH VIETNAMESE THAT THEY COULD NOT WIN:

I saw the 44 battalions as no force for victory, but as a stop-gap measure to save the ARVN from defeat. The premise must be that we are in for the long pull. It is time all concerned face up to the fact that we must be prepared for a long war which will probably involve increasing numbers of US troops ... the enemy's shift to big-unit war was drawing ARVN troops away from the heavily populated regions ... American and Allied troops ... would have to assume the role of fighting the big units, leaving the ... ARVN free to protect the people. No more niceties about defensive posture and reaction ... we had to forget about enclaves and take the war to the enemy. [35]

US President Lyndon B. Johnson authorized the deployment of additional US assets into South Vietnam, and the expansion of their original mission brief.

US Army General William Westmoreland, chief of the Military Assistance Command, Vietnam (MACV), inspects a contingent of ARVN troops.

A US soldier searches for intelligence on the dead body of a VC guerrilla. He is looking for any kind of intelligence that might be used to achieve further success, such as maps, orders and codebooks.

NORTH VIETNAMESE COMMANDER-IN-CHIEF GIAP ADAPTED HIS TACTICS ACCORDINGLY TO DEAL WITH THE INCREASE IN US AID:

In a time of war, you have to take your lead from the enemy. You have to know your enemy well. When your enemy changes his strategy or tactics, you have to do the same. In every war, a strategy is always made up of a number of tactics, so you have to try to smash those tactics. If we took on the cavalry, for example, we'd do everything we could to smash that particular tactic. It was the same when the enemy made use of strategic weapons. And, when the Americans tried to apply their "search-and-destroy" tactic, we had to make their objective unattainable and destroy them instead. We had to … force the enemy to fight the way we wanted them to fight. We had to force the enemy to fight on unfamiliar territory.[36]

We had to force the enemy to fight on unfamiliar territory

THE BATTLE OF IA DRANG

PRIVATE FIRST CLASS JACK P. SMITH, 1ST CAVALRY DIVISION, FOUGHT AT IA DRANG IN OCTOBER 1965, IN A BLOODY BATTLE AGAINST THE NORTH VIETNAMESE ARMY:

The 1st Battalion had been fighting continuously for three or four days. They said little, just looked around with darting, nervous eyes. Whenever I heard a shell coming close, I'd duck, but they'd keep standing. After three days of constant bombardment you can tell from the sound how close a shell is going to land to within 50 to 75 feet. There were some wounded lying around, patched up with filthy shirts and bandages, smoking cigarettes or lying in a coma with plasma bottles hanging above them.

Late that morning the Viet Cong made a charge. About 100 jumped up and made for our lines. Then a couple of our Skyraiders came in. One of them dropped a lot of stuff that shimmered in the sun like green confetti. It looked like a ticker-tape parade, but when the things hit the ground the little pieces exploded. They were antipersonnel charges. Every one of the gooks was killed. Another group on the other side almost made it to the lines. There weren't enough GIs there, and they couldn't shoot them down fast enough. A plane dropped some napalm just in front of the line. I couldn't see the gooks, but I could hear them scream as they burned.

My company, Charlie Company, took over its sector of the battalion perimeter and started to dig in. At 03:00 hours another attack came. I didn't get any sleep that night. There was continuous firing until 04:00 hours, and it was as bright as day with the flares lighting up the sky. The order came for us to move out. The three battalions of NVA were destroyed. There must have been about 1000 rotting bodies out there. As we left the perimeter we walked by them. Some of them had been lying out there for four days.

The Cong opened up on our mortar platoon. It returned fire, killing about half the Cong. All of a sudden a dozen loud "crumph" sounds went off all around me. Assuming that all the GIs in front of them were dead, our mortar platoon had opened up with M79 grenade launchers. The Cong jumped up, moaning with fear, and the other [NVA] began to move around. They apparently knew the M79. Then a second series of explosions went off, killing all the Cong. One grenade landed between Thompson's head and Sergeant Moore's chest. Moore took the shrapnel in his side. A piece got me in the head.

It felt as if a white-hot sledge hammer had hit the right side of my face. Then something hit my left leg. I lost consciousness. I came out of it feeling intense pain in my leg and a numbness in my head. Blood was pouring down my forehead and filling my eyeglasses. It was also pouring out of my mouth. I slapped a bandage on the side of my face and tied it around my head. I suddenly felt better.

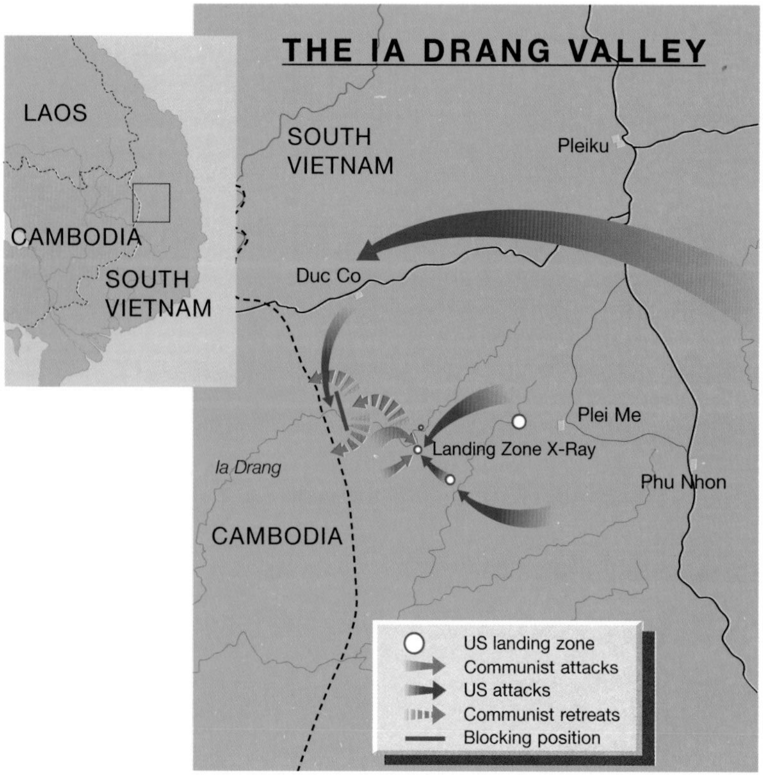

The Battle of the Ia Drang Valley. The US 7th Cavalry bravely and determinedly held off a numerically superior NVA force, but at a massive human cost.

THE IA DRANG VALLEY

LAOS

SOUTH VIETNAM

Pleiku

CAMBODIA

SOUTH VIETNAM

Duc Co

 la Drang

Plei Me

Landing Zone X-Ray

Phu Nhon

CAMBODIA

○ US landing zone
Communist attacks
US attacks
Communist retreats
Blocking position

The US air cavalry was one of the most effective units of the war. These heliborne troops could deploy deep into enemy territory, taking the fight to the VC and NVA.

I decided it was time to get out. None of my buddies appeared able to move.

I crawled over many bodies, all still. The 1st Platoon just didn't exist any more. The artillery was still keeping up a steady barrage, as were the planes. It was a miracle I didn't get shot by the snipers in the trees while I was moving.

At dusk the North Vietnamese started to mortar us. Suddenly the ground behind me lifted up, and there was a tremendous noise. At the same time I felt something white-hot go into my right thigh. I started screaming. The pain was terrible.

Still screaming, I ripped the bandage off my face and tied it around my thigh. It didn't fit, so I held it as tight as I could. I could feel the blood pouring out of the hole. It was hurting unbelievably. All night long the Cong had been killing the wounded. Every few minutes I heard some guy start screaming and then a burst of bullets.

When the light grew stronger, I could see dead men all around the tree. I found that the body I had been resting my head on was that of Burgess, one of my buddies. He was a professional saxophone player with only two weeks left in the army.

Half a dozen of the wounded were alive. Lord, who was full of shrapnel; Lieutenant Sheldon, with several bullet wounds; Sloan, with his fingers shot off; Olson, with his leg shot up and hands mutilated. The medics at the LZ [landing zone] cut off my boots and put bandages on me. My wounds were in pretty bad shape. We were out there for 24 hours.

I found that the body I had been resting my head on was one of my buddies

I heard the casualty figures later. The North Vietnamese unit had been wiped out. Out of some 500 men in our battalion, about 150 had been killed and only 84 returned to base camp. My company had 93 percent casualties – one half dead, one half wounded. Almost all the wounded were crippled for life.

Our unit is part of the 7th Cavalry, Custer's old unit. That day in the Ia Drang Valley history repeated itself. I ended up at Camp Zama in Japan. They tell me that I'll walk again, but no one can tell me when I will stop having nightmares.[37]

FRIENDLY FIRE AT IA DRANG

The 3rd platoon set off an ambush on approx. 30 NVA on the morning of the 8th near LZ X-Ray. Although blood trails were found, no bodies. The captain was, to say the least, "pissed". We started chasing them, doing butterfly sweeps, and had no further contact. I had just started carrying the radio that same morning. B Company hot-footed it towards LZ Juliet and caught a lift of Hueys. I ended up on one of the lead Hueys into the LZ, and that is when the kid jumped off and landed on an NVA soldier. I was handed the job of guarding the prisoner; he was the very last man in the company.

NOT ALL THE AMERICAN CASUALTIES AT IA DRANG WERE INFLICTED BY THE NVA. DENNIS BLESSING, WHO FOUGHT WITH THE 7TH CAVALRY REGIMENT, WROTE IN A LETTER:

We were on a well-worn trail going from the east towards the west. As we walked past some banana trees, the ground was still smoking from rockets. On the left of the trail were about 20 NVA, and 12–15 on the right. All seemed to be dead. Then one on the right sat up. The platoon sarg jumped off the trail and carefully approached the soldier with his rifle pointed at his head. He then turned and came back to the trail, and so I asked him why he hadn't shot the PAVN. The sarg said, pointing at his forehead: "Look there, he has a bullet hole in his forehead." And, sure enough, he did. When we got within your perimeter I can still remember some of the wounded yelling. That evening a soldier went outside the fox-hole line to take a crap. He told the fox-holes on his left and right he was out in front, but it was dusk and the fox-hole second away saw him coming in and shot him. I learnt a lesson from that.

The next week or so we corralled a lot of prisoners. You had taken the fight out of them. I remember guarding one, and as we walked through an old American position he stopped right in front of me and bent over and picked up a soggy old cracker a GI had thrown away and started eating it. I had to poke him with the business end of my M16 to get him to move along.[38]

A dead communist soldier after the vicious battle at Landing Zone X-Ray in the Ia Drang Valley.

THE VIEW OF THE BRASS

GENERAL WESTMORELAND WAS EXTREMELY SATISFIED WITH THE PERFORMANCE OF US TROOPS AT IA DRANG:

On 19 October [1965] the enemy opened his campaign with an attack on the Plei Mei Special Forces camp 25 miles southwest of Pleiku. He attacked the fortified camp with one regiment while holding the bulk of his division-size force in reserve. The Vietnamese Army counterattacked with the assistance of concentrated tactical air strikes. One brigade of the 1st Cavalry Division was moved into the area south and west of Pleiku to block any further enemy advance and to stand in readiness as a reaction force. On 27 October I directed the 1st Cavalry Division (Airmobile) to seek out and destroy the enemy force in western Pleiku Province. Thus began the month-long campaign known as the Battle of the Ia Drang Valley.

The principal engagements in the campaign were fought during the period 14–19 November around the base of the Chu Pong mountain. The performance of the 1st Cavalry Division was magnificent. In extended combat against a skilful and determined foe, it demonstrated the great effectiveness of the airmobile division concept and opened a new chapter in the history of land warfare. As the enemy withdrew his assault regiment from Plei Me, the regiment incurred several casualties from air strikes and pursuing air cavalry. However, when the cavalry division put a blocking force behind the withdrawing enemy and only a few miles from the Cambodian border, the North Vietnamese commander committed his remaining two regiments in an attempt to redeem his earlier failure at Plei Me and to destroy a major US unit. The 3rd Brigade, 1st Cavalry Division – barely 30 days in Vietnam – was the target. This gallant brigade decisively defeated each enemy regiment in turn. Altogether, the 1st Cavalry Division and ARVN troops killed an estimated 1800 North Vietnamese. Despite our troops' inexperience, the division's tactical leadership, training, tactical mobility, firepower and flexible doctrine enabled it to gain an impressive victory. This timely victory produced a sharp upturn in the morale of the South Vietnamese government and its armed forces.

The Plei Me/Ia Drang campaign also proved the worth of the lightweight, rapid-firing M16 rifle in battlefield competition with the communist AK-47 assault rifle. Up to this point, only a few US units had these weapons. At this time, I strongly recommended equipping all US Free World and Vietnamese forces with the M16 as soon as possible.[39]

Despite the heavy casualties, the US top brass, including General William Westmoreland (above), saw Ia Drang as a victory.

> In extended combat against a skilful and determined foe, it demonstrated the great effectiveness of the airmobile division concept

HEARTS AND MINDS

DURING MID-1965,
ACCORDING TO
GENERAL FORNEY,
A VETERAN
OF WORLD WAR II
AND KOREA:

The Marine Corps should get into the Vietnam job with both feet and it should be a real grassroots-level operation, not tied in with the MAAG, but rather an effort to be linked with the Civil Guard, the Self Defense Corps and the local militia in the village and boondock[40] level … around which the common people of South Vietnam would rally; this is the big deficiency in the present operation and one in which the USMC [US Marine Corps] could make a solid contribution.[41]

A 5th Special Forces sergeant treats a Montagnard woman in the village of Dak Sak. The methods of fighting the war for hearts and minds were many and varied. The provision of medical care to the local populace was but one method used to reach out to the Vietnamese villagers and bring them "on side", to use modern terminology.

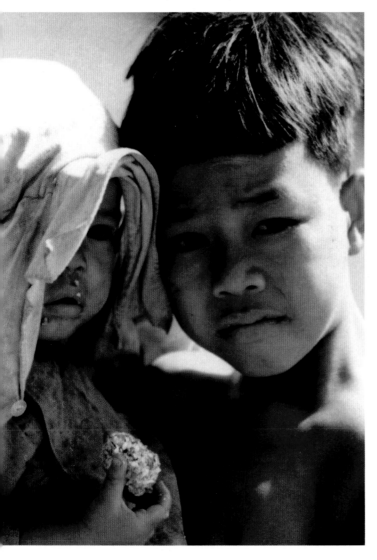

There was no virtue at all in seeking out the NVA in the mountains and jungle

THE MARINE CORPS' "BIBLE" ON SUCH PACIFICATION EFFORTS, CALLED *THE SMALL WARS MANUAL*, PUBLISHED IN 1940, STATED:

In small wars, tolerance, sympathy and kindness should be the keynote of our relationship with the mass of the population. The purpose should always be to restore normal government … and to establish peace, order, and security.[42]

A great many children were left without parents as a result of the war. Some parents had been killed accidentally in crossfire, whilst others had been dragged away by VC operatives on trumped-up charges of collaboration with the US. Children as young as 10, like this boy at Bien Hoa, were left looking after their orphaned younger siblings.

LIEUTENANT-GENERAL VICTOR H. KRULAK, WHO WAS COMMANDING GENERAL, FLEET MARINE FORCE PACIFIC (FMFPAC), AND ONE OF THE US MARINE CORPS' LEADING EXPERTS ON COUNTER-INSURGENCY, STATED:

There was no virtue at all in seeking out the NVA in the mountains and jungle; that so long as they stayed there they were a threat to nobody, that our efforts should be addressed to the rich, populous lowlands … [and that] … it is our conviction that if we can destroy the guerrilla fabric among the people, we will automatically deny the larger units the food and the intelligence and the other support they need. At the same time, if the big units want to sortie out of the mountains and come down where they can be cut up by our supporting arms, the Marines are glad to take them on, but the real war is among the people and not among these mountains.[43]

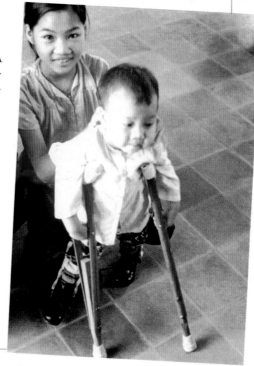

A young Vietnamese woman helps an injured child to walk with the aid of crutches. The US devoted millions of dollars towards helping injured civilians.

OPERATION HASTINGS

A US soldier trains his M60 machine gun. This awesome weapon can unleash an amazing amount of firepower – 550 rounds per minute – and was a firm favourite during the Vietnam War.

DURING OPERATION HASTINGS (7 JULY– 3 AUGUST 1966), THE MARINES FROM THE 3RD BATTALION, 4TH MARINES, KILLED A SUBSTANTIAL NUMBER OF NORTH VIETNAMESE IN A FIREFIGHT THAT BECAME A ROUT. STAFF SERGEANT JOHN J. MCGINTY, WHO COMMANDED THE 1ST PLATOON, K COMPANY, 3RD BATTALION, 4TH MARINES, TOOK PART IN THE BATTLE:

We started getting mortar fire, followed by automatic weapons fire from all sides … they were blowing bugles, and we could see them waving flags. "Charlie" moved in waves with small arms right behind the mortars, and we estimated we were being attacked by a thousand men. We just couldn't kill them fast enough. My squads were cut off from each other, and together we were cut off from the rest of the company. I had some of my men in the high grass, where our machine gunners had to get up on their knees to shoot, which exposed them. "Charlie" never overran us, but he got one or two of his squads between us.[44]

We were getting mortars right in the landing zone, and the bombs and napalm were dropping only 50 yards away from us. At one point, the NVA were trying to get the ammo out of those three wrecked helicopters that were still sitting there. Napalm got about 20 of them, and then another 40 in the middle of the landing zone. I remember one kid shouting: "Here come some more Marines!" But they weren't Marines at all – they were NVA. And when they saw us, they ducked into the river on our flank. All we could see were their heads and their rifles above water – it was like shooting pumpkins.[45]

CAPTAIN ROBERT J. MODREZEJEWSKI, COMPANY COMMANDER, 4TH MARINES, RECALLED THAT ONLY WHEN THE ENEMY WAS EXPOSED DURING AN ATTACK COULD US FORCES BRING THEIR FIREPOWER TO BEAR:

OPERATION ATTLEBORO

MARION L. ELLARD,
US 25TH INFANTRY
DIVISION, TOOK PART IN
OPERATION ATTLEBORO
IN LATE 1966:

US troops set fire to a wooden hut in a captured VC village. This seemingly unnecessary task was actually an effective method of preventing the VC from returning to the area too quickly.

On the morning of 1 November, Major Guy S. Meloy's battalion (500–1200 men) was alerted to enemy activity around Dau Tieng in War Zone C. Brigadier-General Edward H. De Saussure of the 25th Infantry Division was in command of the operation. Even then operations were under way to extract as much rice as possible from a newly discovered cache. The encounter began at approximately 11:00 hours when C Company (150 men), 1st Battalion, 27th Infantry (Wolfhounds) – 1/27 – was helilifted into a landing zone north-northwest of Tay Ninh.

A Company was to stay at Dau Tieng to secure the airstrip while B Company, under the command of Captain Robert P. Garrett, would approach an LZ just to the west of the Saigon River and at the northeastern extension of the forest, where the troops exited from hovering helicopters some 15 feet in the air into 12-foot-high elephant grass. At the time, what concerned me the most was the solidity of the ground. As it turned out, we landed into some two to three inches of water – much to our relief. Best of all, there was no mud present. An infantryman carries a lot of weight on his person, and to compound that by jumping from great heights into an unknown substance is enough to cause great concern.

We immediately lost coordination with units around us. Our unit's course was due west, so we set out in that direction hindered by the cutting edge of the tall grass. We soon came upon an abandoned VC village. One hour later, C Company, commanded by Frederick H. Henderson, was set down on another LZ on the far side of the forest. Plans were for A and C Companies to sweep north through the jungle growth, and B Company would set up a blocking action to prevent anyone from escaping.

At 15:30 hours, Major Meloy brought in A Company 1/27 to an LZ approximately 200 metres from the site of the engagement. Then Meloy had his helicopter, which was circling above the action, lead the airmobile assault at the LZ. Although not under direct attack, the LZ was swept by machine-gun and automatic weapons fire from the battle area. Once on the ground, A Company manoeuvred to the north, and then east to flank the VC force. Attacking across the flank of C Company, they routed the VC with the exception of stay-behind snipers. During the course of the battle, four air strikes were called in, one of which was within 100 metres of the forward positions. It consisted of jet-delivered 500lb bombs and napalm. As the afternoon progressed, additional reinforcements were sent in. The commanding general of the 196th Light Infantry Brigade, Brigadier-General De Saussure, sent in C Co. 3/21; and at dark, C and B Cos. 2/1 were airlifted in to help secure the LZ. This was deemed necessary because an earlier

ARVN soldiers on board an APC attack a Viet Cong stronghold following an air strike by Vietnamese Air Force A-4 Skyraiders during Attleboro.

Medium tanks of the US 1st Infantry Division are held up by a Vietnamese farmer and his oxen. The farmer is going to Trung Lap, near Saigon. The tanks are going to hunt down the Viet Cong.

dustoff [medical evacuation] helicopter had been shot down attempting to land, in spite of the intense artillery barrage called in for protection. It was eventually lifted out along with the casualties late in the afternoon. By dark, Meloy had five companies (750 men) on the ground under his command. B Company, 1/27, unable to reach its blocking position, returned to its original position where it was joined by 4th Bn., 31 Infantry, for night-time security. The plan for the next morning was to conduct a search-and-destroy operation through the jungle while manoeuvring to the northeast so the various companies could rejoin their parent battalions. However, the night was not quiet as the VC kept up almost constant probes – although refraining from mortar attacks. In response, Meloy called in artillery throughout the night. On the morning of 4 November, the major once ordered B Co. 1/27 to move west to meet the battalion. At 10.45 hours, B and C Cos. 2/1 headed due east to link up with their A Co., which was located with the 4/31. Forty-five minutes later, the remainder of the command moved out heading northeast. Leading was A Co. 1/27 with a rifle platoon two minutes ahead as point and point flank security. Following was C Co. 3/21 and the remainder of C Co. 1/27; Meloy positioned himself and a radio operator at the rear of A Co. 1/27 while this command group moved at the rear of C Co. 3/21.

The jungle was extremely dense, limiting visibility to approximately 10 metres or less. Fortunately, radio transmission was, and remained, good. Moving out in two columns, 40 metres apart, they were under way only a few minutes when the jungle erupted in fire. Major Meloy later recalled: "One moment it was quiet as can be, and the next instant it was like a Fort Benning Mad Minute." The contact we had

was greater than a battalion (500–1200 men), and it had the heaviest concentration of automatic weapons I have ever heard. We were immediately pinned down from three sides: north, northeast and east. For six hours the fire never diminished; we had to shout to be heard over the radio. The battalion fought off numerous suicide attacks by the enemy, who was equipped with automatic weapons, steel helmets, webbed gear and various uniforms. Even suicide assaults were launched against friendly forces.

Shortly thereafter, B Co. 1/27 reached the perimeter, having taken just two hours to make the trip through the jungle. With them were several AK-47 rifles taken from the VC attempting to escape. At that time, the observed enemy body count was well over 100 VC dead. At about 16:30 hours, Meloy sent word for the units to withdraw. C Co. 1/27 was first followed by headquarters. B Co. 1/27 set up a secondary blocking position, and the task force that had spent almost 30 hours under fire in a nose-to-nose battle began to pull back through their lines. My Bravo Company was left up front because it had sustained the fewest casualties during this operation. The

I was overjoyed to see the many Huey helicopters waiting in the clearing to helilift us back to base

troops started moving back 25 metres at a time. Every time we tried to lift the artillery, the enemy was right back with his full intensity of fire. It appeared the artillery bombardment had little effect because of the high canopy of trees he was using as cover. We later found out the artillery had indeed killed many of the enemy.

When I was ready to withdraw the last company, I didn't tell Bravo Co. to move until the artillery rounds had already been fired just on top of our position. Bravo Co. placed Claymore mines forward of their position in preparation of our retreat and waited for the VC to advance. After some movement to our front was spotted, word was given to detonate the mines and then pull out.

After the terrific explosion went off, we were engulfed in a massive dark cloud from the Claymore back blast, but before it could reach us we had pulled out. All of us were running as hard and fast as we could with all the gear we had to carry. I remember my legs felt like they were made of rubber, thus making it hard for me to keep my balance. However, the adrenalin was really flowing.

I didn't fall and soon ran into friendly troops who were to replace us and do some mopping-up action. These troops were the 1st Infantry Division (Big Red One), the 196th Brigade, and 5th Mechanized, making a total of somewhere around 14,000 combat troops to replace the departing combatants.

As we ran from the combat scene, I was overjoyed to see the many Huey helicopters waiting in the clearing to helilift our outfit back to base camp at Cu Chi. You cannot understand this euphoria unless you have been in combat, survived and then suddenly find yourself repatriated.[46]

WESTMORELAND'S WAR

GENERAL WILLIAM C. WESTMORELAND, COMMANDER USMACV, SUMMED UP US STRATEGY IN 1965 AND 1966, AND MADE CLEAR HIS INTENTIONS FOR 1967:

The military tasks that confronted us at the beginning of the year were many and varied. First, the protection of the government and the people; second, the protection and development of our installations and logistics bases to keep pace with the continuing deployment of major US troop units; third, the improvement of the South Vietnamese Armed Forces. We found it necessary to mount quick spoiling attacks against increasingly large enemy main force units building up in the border areas. We concentrated our efforts in the most vital areas. Elsewhere we applied the military principle of economy of force.

I judged that the critical regions requiring first attention were the populated areas around Saigon in III Corps, and the coastal lowlands in I and II Corps. The more important of these regions was that around the capital city. To the north, the central coastal provinces of Binh Dinh and Phu Yen were most critical. Not only were these provinces heavily populated and a prime source of VC support, but enemy forces there threatened to sever the country by linking up with North Vietnamese units operating in the Central Highlands. With these priorities and considerations in mind, I deployed the bulk of our reinforcements into these areas. For example, the remainder of the US 1st Infantry Division was deployed north of Saigon, and the US 25th Infantry Division was positioned just northwest of Saigon astride a major access route to the city. A new Vietnamese division, the 10th (later to be designated the 18th), was organized and positioned northeast of Saigon. The Republic of Korea 9th Infantry Division was deployed into the critical coastal areas of II Corps, and the US 1st Marine Division occupied the heavily populated southern provinces of I Corps. Although one brigade of the US 4th Infantry Division was initially positioned in the coastal area of Phu Yen Province, the entire division was eventually deployed to the Central Highlands to counter the steady build-up of North Vietnamese units in that region.

These deployments, which moved us beyond the "fire brigade" approach we had taken out of necessity in 1965, again affirmed my conviction that the combined US-South Vietnamese military effort must begin in the critical areas in which the population was concentrated. The enemy's view of the critical areas was much the same as ours. As a consequence, the major battles of the year developed in these areas. The largest battle, involving 22,000 American and South Vietnamese troops, took place northwest of Saigon in Operation Attleboro, where the Viet Cong 9th Division, reinforced by a North Vietnamese Regiment, was soundly defeated and driven back to the Cambodian border. In a series of savage battles, the 1st Cavalry Division, Korean units and ARVN forces cleared the northern half of Binh Dinh Province on the central coast, in Operation Masher/Whitewing/Thang Phong II. In the process they devastated [the NVA] Sao Vang Division, which was later to be designated the North Vietnamese 3rd Division. US Marines of the 3rd Division were progressively moved into the area of the two northern provinces and, in conjunction with South

US troops exchange fire with the enemy. The new M16 rifle being used was rushed into service with all US units after it proved its worth at the Battle of Ia Drang.

Troopers of the 101st Airborne Division fire from an old Viet Cong trench as they beat off an enemy attack during Operation Hawthorne in June 1966.

Vietnamese Army and other Marine Corps units, conducted a highly successful campaign (Operation Hastings) against enemy forces infiltrating across the DMZ.

This enemy build-up was met by the US 3rd Marine Division and by Vietnamese Army and Marine Corps units. I believe that the enemy opened this new front in order to divert our forces from the heavily populated region around Saigon. At the same time, we suspected that the enemy might try to seize this northern area and establish a liberation government. At this early date I was concerned that we would have to confront major North Vietnamese forces in the extreme northern area or abandon the region to the enemy. The threat in the north continued to mount during 1967 and 1968. The fact that we were able to meet this formidable threat of five to six enemy divisions without giving up any position of real value farther south is, to me, the major military feat of the war.

Pacification continued to be a disappointment. A Revolutionary Development Programme, introduced by the South Vietnamese Government in November, showed some progress. The most important development was the opening up of the Pacification Cadre School at Vung Tau and the deployment of 59-man Revolutionary Development teams into contested hamlets. The government's Chieu Hoi programme, which welcomed disillusioned Viet Cong back to government loyalty, made impressive gains – 20,242 returnees in 1966. Largely because of the presence of more US forces, the proportion of the population able to live in reasonable security increased to approx. 60 percent in 1966.

The coastal surveillance programme by the US and Vietnamese Navies began to reach a high stage of effectiveness in stopping enemy seaborne movements. Tactical air support procedures were refined; and US ground forces received superb support from the Seventh Air Force, the 1st Marine Air Wing and the Seventh Fleet. Additional Korean, Australian, New Zealand and Thai troops arrived and added a major and professional component to the growing allied force. By the year's end, our strength in Vietnam had

By the year's end, our strength in Vietnam had increased by over 200,000 men

increased by over 200,000 men. Understandably, this very rapid build-up placed heavy strains on the logistics system. The monthly tonnage of arriving supplies rose from 390,000 in December 1965 to over 600,000 a year later. By the end of 1966 sufficient forces had been deployed, together with their logistic support, so that the total allied military establishment was in a position for the first time to go over to the offensive on a broad and sustained basis in 1967.[47]

US Navy patrol boats off the South's coastline. The use of Mobile Riverine Forces was another vital component in taking the fight to the enemy.

CHAPTER 4
VOICES OF THE GI'S WAR
1965-1973

The Vietnam War was a conflict fought by both large and small detachments of troops in terrain that was often as much an enemy as the elusive Viet Cong (VC) and North Vietnamese Army (NVA) detachments. Unlike their South Vietnamese allies and NVA and VC foes, American soldiers remained on duty for 365 days from the time of arrival "in-country" until the time they boarded an awaiting "freedom bird" that took them back to the US. Indeed, the American serviceman, whose average age was 19 years, was much younger than his father who had served in World War II. Yet his performance on the battlefield was second to none. In fact, the American soldier who fought during 1965–75 was a member of the best field army ever sent into battle by the US.

This chapter is their story, as they fought and endured to survive amidst the whining of bullets, mortars and bombs in the jungles of Southeast Asia. Starting in 1965 and lasting until the final withdrawal from South Vietnam in April 1975, these are tales of bravery, told by young men who rose to the challenge and accredited themselves very well on the field of battle.

The GI's war: setting the stage

It is worth noting that the criticism the M16 rifle received as being inferior to the enemy's AK-47 Kalashnikov was largely unfounded. While teething problems did occur with this weapon, the M16 nonetheless proved itself more than a match for its Soviet-supplied counterpart.

In addition to their weapons and ordnance, each soldier and Marine wore the World War II-era steel helmet with a camouflaged cover. Reconnaissance troops wore either a floppy "boonie" hat or, as in the case of the US Army Special Forces, the famous "Green Beret". US Marines more often than not wore the heavy flak jacket in order to protect themselves against shrapnel wounds. Extra ammunition, canteen, bayonet and a combat knife or "K-bar" were attached to their webbing. Most Marines and soldiers wore the World War II-era marching pack that came with an entrenching tool. Total weight carried averaged 36–45kg (80–100lb). Both the Marines and US Army wore either the issued leather black boot or steel-tipped paratrooper jump boot. Later in the conflict, both services adopted the now-famous "jungle boot", which proved much more comfortable. Finally, both Marines and army personnel wore the World War II khaki-drab utility (fatigues) uniform. Special units (such as Long Range Reconnaissance Patrols), Marine Reconnaissance personnel and Navy SEALS wore specially made camouflaged uniforms that all American troops began to sport towards the end of the Vietnam War.

Training for the American soldiers and Marines was among the best (if not *the* best) in terms of preparing them for combat in Vietnam. US Army soldiers went through eight weeks of basic training and four weeks of advanced infantry training at one of many installations in the US. Marines spent approximately 12 weeks in recruit training at one of the two Marine Corps Recruit Depots: Parris Island, South Carolina, or San Diego, California. Marines received an additional four weeks of advanced infantry training called ITR (Infantry Training Regiment) at either Camp Lejeune, North Carolina, or Camp Pendleton, California.

US soldiers, Marines, air cavalrymen and Long Range Reconnaissance Patrol teams scoured the thick jungle looking for elusive VC and NVA detachments. The enemy was not just VC or NVA, however, but the occasional sniper and the mines and booby traps they planted in order to maim – two of the infantryman's most immediate fears.

Vietnam was the first major helicopter war in history. Helicopters were used as gunships, troop transports and in the medical evacuation role. Helicopters carried supplies to outlying fire bases such as Khe Sanh and Con Thien. Helicopters, such as the UH-1E "Huey" gunship, or its unarmed version called the "slick", became indispensable in a war marked by its battlefield mobility.

One little-known aspect of the war was the role played by US warships and aircraft carriers off the coast. "On Yankee Station" referred to the task force positioned north of the South Vietnamese coastline. Here, US Navy and Marine carrier-based aircraft launched bombing sorties against targets in North Vietnam.

The soldiers, Marines, airmen and sailors gave all they had during the Vietnam War. They were, like their fathers who served in World War II, among the "greatest generations" of young Americans sent into battle. The job they did was superlative in having never lost a battle to the veteran VC or NVA.

In the foreground a US soldier sits on lookout atop a defensive bunker position. He is holding an M79 grenade launcher, a weapon much used, and loved, during the Vietnam War.

THE AVERAGE GRUNT

STAFF SERGEANT JOHN NORWOOD JR., OF THE 11TH RRU, 1ST INFANTRY DIVISION, BEST SUMMED IT UP WHEN HE DESCRIBED THE AVERAGE GI OR MARINE OF THE VIETNAM WAR ERA:

The GI ... is the most complex person in this country ... the GI is many people, different in many ways, but with one single-minded purpose. He wants to be a good soldier (in the eyes of his fellow soldiers) and do the job he was sent here for. And get home safely to do the things he never appreciated before he was thrown into this thing called war. Invariably, they have impressed me as being very brave or having the guts to conceal fear and fight. I can recall cases in which companies of these kids stood and fought as long as there were Charlie left to fight. All the while their company was being wiped out. One company was C Company of the 2/16th, 1st Infantry Division, where there were 83 percent casualties, and the ones who were able to walk out weren't in real good shape themselves. I know a few of them who came back to Vietnam. I believe what we are doing over here is right and I'm glad to have had my chance to do my share.[1]

I've been going on the ground with the infantry whenever I can get out of flying. Some of the other pilots think I'm trying to get myself knocked off, but at least I have a chance to shoot back. It makes me realize what a hard job these infantry boys have. After tramping around the jungle for a couple of hours, carrying a rifle, canteen, ammo pouches, grenades, and such, you get pretty tired ... I was in the lead squad, about the third man back. The point man signalled for us to stop, and we crouched there looking up the trail. I guess this was too much for the Cong, because four or five of them broke and ran about 20 feet in front of us. We shot at them but didn't hit any. That jungle is so thick it makes it hard. I caught a glimpse of one running through the brush and fired a burst at him from my M16. Must have missed him by a mile. Sure feels funny to shoot at a human being. We followed them a short way, but figured they might be trying to lead us into an ambush, so we turned back.[2]

WO-1 ELLIOTT PRAISED THE WORK DONE BY THE US INFANTRY, WITH WHOM HE WORKED DURING SEVERAL OPERATIONS AS AN OBSERVER ON THE GROUND:

The average age of a US soldier in Vietnam was 19 years old. Despite their youth however, their senior NCOs heaped praise on the bravery and commitment many of them showed.

THE M16 RIFLE

He held up an M16 rifle … [and said] … "Brave soldiers and the M16 … brought this victory". [Lieutenant-Colonel] Moore and many of his soldiers told me that the M16 was the best individual infantry weapon ever made. Most American units at the time were equipped with the older M14 rifle, which was semi-automatic and too heavy for the jungle. Convinced that Moore and his men knew what they were talking about, I asked Secretary [of Defense Robert S.] McNamara as a matter of urgency to equip all American forces with the M16 and then also to equip the ARVN with it. Officials unfortunately disregarded the urgency of my request and failed to gear American industry to meet the need. Not until 1967 were there enough M16s for all American troops, and only then was I able to begin equipping the ARVN. The ARVN thus long fought at a serious disadvantage, armed as they were with WWII's [World War II's] semi-automatic M1. Armed with a light carbine, little more than a pea shooter when compared with the AK-47, the South Vietnamese militia were at an even worse disadvantage.

Just as the American press and some members of Congress during the early stages of WWII criticized the M1 Garand, which became the workhorse of American infantry during WWII and Korea, so critical attacks developed against the M16. It was admittedly a weapon that had to be cleaned meticulously, and ordnance experts were able to make some adjustments that improved performance; but from the first the M16 in the hands of troops experienced in its use and care was a superb weapon.[3]

The M16 assault rifle, seen here in the hands of a US Navy SEAL, had been barely introduced into the US Army when the war in Vietnam began. However, within a very short space of time it had established itself as one of the finest weapons in the world.

NAM — A UNIQUE WAR

A group of US troops relax in their hootch. Long periods of time were spent waiting for action, so solders used the opportunity to write home, play baseball and enjoy relative comforts.

THE FIRST US COMBAT TROOPS IN VIETNAM WERE THE MARINES. IN A DETAILED LETTER HOME, MAJOR-GENERAL LEWIS W. WALT DESCRIBED HIS MISSION AND THE PROBLEMS FACED BY THE MARINES:

I knew that before I came here and took over this assignment that I had a real challenge facing me, but I really had no idea how great this challenge was. My areas of responsibility include four enclaves, each of which has an airfield which must be defended. The northern enclave is Hue-Phu Bai, 40 miles south of it is the Da Nang Airbase, where my headquarters are located, 60 miles south of that is the Chu Lai Airbase, and 90 miles south is the Qui Nhon Airbase. To carry out the responsibilities I have to do a lot of air travel between these bases. In addition to the tactical responsibilities, I have all logistic supply and law and order responsibilities for US nationals in the area. You probably read about the attack on the Da Nang Airbase. I make no excuses for this having happened, but on the other hand it is not impossible for it to happen again. There are populated areas around all of the bases.

One of the biggest problems we have here … is to distinguish enemy from the friendlies. There is no question that we have constant surveillance by enemy agents. However, overall the picture is not as discouraging as you might think. Each day we free more people and have more South Vietnamese thankful for the protection we are giving them. It is heartwarming to see how grateful these poor people are to be free. I talked with an elderly lady through an interpreter. She and her family have been under VC domination for nearly 10 years. She lost both her husband and some of her children as a result of VC tactics. She told me that she had lived in terror during these years and she was so grateful that the Marines had liberated her village and had given her grandchildren and her daughter medical care. Children here are like children everywhere. They like to play and laugh and romp in the streets with the freedom that only a child can know. It seems so strange when we first take over a village to see how afraid the children are. They never laugh, nor do they even show a gesture of recognition. It takes about two weeks for them to get used to us and from then on they become real friends and the Marines, in true American fashion, adopt them all. If they were to be denied our protection by having us pull out, then all the people who have stepped forward as leaders to do things for the community would immediately become targets for brutal maltreatment and murder by the VC. You can win this war together with the Armed Forces of the South Vietnamese Government. It is going to take a long time. It is going to be difficult and costly. I believe that the US and the free world would make a great mistake if they don't carry this through.

Most of my officers and enlisted men are working an average of 16 hours a day, seven days a week. A few of us have old French barracks to live in, but 95 percent are living in tents or in fox-holes with a poncho over the top. At present, the weather is very hot and the dust is unbelievably fine and plentiful. It is a constant battle to keep the flies and mosquitoes under control. We have air conditioners only for our hospital tents and in food storage areas. The heat and dust really don't bother us as much as you'd think. After a week you become pretty used to it and the general health of the whole organization is excellent. Time passes rapidly because we are so busy. It is heartening to see how these young men, 18 and 19 years old, adapt themselves to the rigours of the situation. Those people who say our youth of today are soft and can't take it certainly are not referring to those we have in the Marine Corps. They not only can take it but they can dish it out in such a way that the enemy is beginning to have considerable respect for the US Marine. I am sure that this respect is going to grow over time.

The enemy is beginning to have considerable respect for the US Marine

This is a different kind of war than we have fought for a long time, and I think it is going to be longer than we have fought in my lifetime. I am sure that as time goes by and we develop more effective techniques, our efforts will improve and will show much more rapid progress. At present our efforts are confined to those objectives which will ensure the security of our bases. We have neither the forces nor the authority to do the entire job under the present policy guidance. I think the free world will soon have to decide whether or not we are going all the way in order to win this conflict.[4]

The "Zippo", a converted Monitor boat equipped with a flamethrower, was used to clear the banks of rivers. "Charlie" liked to ambush other boats and support ships from the lush undergrowth, and the "Zippo" was tasked with clearing the dense foliage. They were also used in a fire-support role.

FIRST COMBAT

US ARMY SPECIALIST
FOURTH-CLASS (SP-4)
KENNETH W. BAGBY
PROVIDED AN HONEST
AND GRUELLING
PERSONAL ACCOUNT OF
THE BATTLE OF THE
IA DRANG VALLEY:

We were crossing a field and were pinned down by automatic weapons fire from the enemy. We were pinned down for about 45 minutes before the rest of the platoon could get to us, and save the rest of us. So went the biggest and worst battle that any American force has had in Vietnam. We outdid the Marines and Airborne by a long shot. Estimated VC killed, 2000. Our casualties, I cannot give the information out. The battle took place on the Cambodian border. In another line of attack my platoon leader, Lieutenant Marm, was shot in the neck right beside me and Sp-4 Ahewan took him back through the lines to the aid station.

In another situation, me, Daily and Sergeant Riley captured two VC, and were bringing them back through the lines when we were pinned down again, as one of them spotted a buddy and tried to signal him. I was going to kill both of them but Sergeant Riley stopped me. Our battalion, the 1st B[attalio]n, 7th Cav[alry], is completely inactive due to the killed and wounded of its men. My squad consists of nine men, three came out: myself, Sergeant Scott and a boy named Stidell. The many men that died I will never forget. The odour of blood and decayed bodies, I will never forget. I am all right. I will never be the same, though, never, never, never. If I have to go into battle again, if I am not killed, I will come out insane. I cannot see and go through it again. I know I can't. The friends I lost and the many bodies I carried back to the helicopters to be lifted out, I will never forget. I met a boy on the ship coming over to Vietnam. He was my friend. We lived in the same tent together, went into An Khe together, and spent most of our free time together. I got to know this boy well, and he was my best friend, His name was Dan Davis. On Monday morning, the 15th November, he died in my arms of bullet wounds to the chest. He said, "Ken, I can't breathe". There was nothing I could do. To the right of me another friend, whose name was Balango, died of wounds in the throat. Up front, Sergeant Brown, my squad leader, was hit in the chest and leg. To my left Sp-4 A. Learn was hit in the ankle.

Folks, don't let these men die in vain. Appreciate what they are doing over here in Vietnam. They died protecting you all, and all the people in the US. We just cannot have the enemy get to the folks back home. [5]

Two soldiers from the reconnaissance element of the US 101st Airborne Division after clearing a hilltop LZ in Quang Tri Province.

PERSONAL COMBAT COULD BE CONFUSING
AND TERRIFYING AT THE SAME TIME.
JAMES F. MCCOLLOCH, US ARMY 9TH
INFANTRY, WAS AT LONG BINH IN 1967:

As we poked our way through the jungle, we did so in standard military patrol formation. Each man walked five metres (the maximum effective range of a grenade) behind the one in front, so if a grenade exploded the casualties would be minimal. We also used the standard five-man point, which means the primary point man travels in advance of

A section of US troops in a firefight with the VC. Most of the time shots were fired blind, since it was almost impossible to make out individual targets.

Large red ants trailed in and out of the wounds, carrying pieces of flesh

the main column and is flanked on the left and right by two men who maintain a certain lateral distance between themselves and the column. The point men are generally the ones who make first contact, so the newest members of the patrol or the guys who become known as "screw-ups" are generally given the point. I wasn't a "screw-up" but I was new, so I became a flanker in the point.

Travelling through the jungle at night is a frightening experience. I wasn't sure if my teeth were chattering because I was cold or afraid. I tried to ignore the knowledge that I might step on a booby trap or that "Charlie" might appear and run a bayonet through my chest. Although we were told they wouldn't stop a bullet, I decided to zip up my flak jacket as I walked and increased my grip on the rifle that had now become my best friend.

Suddenly, the silence of the night erupted with the sounds of an explosion and the cries of human anguish, followed by the unmistakable sound of an M16 on full automatic. The fear and apprehension I was experiencing only moments earlier suddenly disappeared and the instinct to survive overtook me. My partner and I both swung our rifles towards the noise of the explosion and screaming to lay down a base of fire in short, controlled bursts. I expended one magazine, reloaded, released my bolt and held ready to continue firing. The sound of rifle fire had ceased but the screams of human suffering continued.

The morning's first light found me anxiously awaiting its arrival. Even in the still dim light it was easy to see what had happened. A VC patrol detonated one of the Claymore mines our guys set up. Apparently, most of the patrol headed back the way they came, not even bothering to help their fallen comrades, the man and two women, dressed in black pajamas and armed with AK-47 rifles, who were caught in the initial blast.

My stomach was already queasy because of my nervousness when, as the day grew brighter, I noticed large red ants trailing in and out of the wounds on the bodies, carrying pieces of flesh. My mind raced to the events of the night before and I wondered if the ants were the cause of the screaming. The vomit was in my throat before I could stop it. I leaned against a tree and heaved.[6]

ARVN troops re-organize themselves after a firefight and treat their wounded.

CARVER'S WAR

US MARINE SERGEANT
GEORGE CARVER
RECALLED WHAT LIFE
WAS LIKE FOR THE
"GRUNT" IN THE FIELD
IN VIETNAM:

I've been so tired and tensed up that I hardly know what I am doing. It has gotten to the point where I'm still groggy an hour and a half after I've been up. I wish I knew when they were going to give us some time off. It had better be soon, as most of us have been working 18-20 hours a day, besides having 12 hours of guard duty every fourth night.

Was in VC territory this morning and had a couple of shots go whizzing past our vehicle. I wish these little SOBs [sons of bitches] would come out in the open so we could clean their clocks. We have a "code of ethics" over here. Don't shoot at them unless they shoot at you first … I have some good men, even though we do have some trying times. For the past three days, it was been 130–137 degrees. You'll never know how much we are wishing for rain. Monsoon season is way overdue. By then I'll be "bitching" about the rain and mud. Usually I carry an M14 rifle. It can fire semi- or full-automatic. At present I am armed with a .45-caliber pistol and a 12in throwing knife.[7]

We are dirty, muddy, wet and a bit discouraged. The rains have left us but the heat is overwhelming. After so many months of rain, we have forgotten the extreme change of climate. Very hectic night last night. We shot and wounded one Marine and captured two VC suspects. All three were about 600 yards in front of our perimeter. The Marine should have known better than to be out there after dark anyway. I feel very little remorse for him, as he was careless and stupid. He's lucky he only got hit in the upper leg. There was enough lead flying to kill 50 people.

Our little slant-eyed friends decided to play games this morning around 02:30 hours. They were firing mortar flares and cutting the fuses short so that they would land in our tent area and start a fire. They fired about 20 rounds before they got tired and found out they weren't doing any harm. VC activity has been quite in earnest the past three weeks. They've tried repeatedly to enter our base camp and cause havoc with our equipment.

Two weeks ago 100 to 150 hit an artillery camp a quarter of a mile from us. Six guns and 13 Marines were killed and wounded. One of these nights they're going to get "brave" and hit us like that. They keep their distance from us, though, as they have felt the "sting" of our machine guns and glare of our spotlights. Last night one of our trucks was grenaded and destroyed. The driver was only slightly wounded. Four nights ago we were roused out of a deep sleep because the VC had broken through an infantry company. We sat in our jeeps and trucks for three hours, waiting for the word to move out and engage. We have more days like this than I can remember. Sleep is a luxury to really enjoy! I've been getting an average of four hours a night. The circles under my eyes are almost as dark as my eyes are. There are some nights when I just lie awake all night.[8]

SERGEANT CARVER'S
COMMENTS RECALLED THE
CONDITIONS THAT US
SERVICEMEN FACED IN
VIETNAM. HE WROTE
TO HIS SISTER:

The "tail-end charlie" of a US patrol sweeps the jungle with his M16 rifle.

US soldiers on patrol keep a watchful eye for VC. The dense jungle vegetation made it very difficult to spot movement. The enemy was more likely to be heard first rather than seen.

Your impressions of a "firefight" are correct. The films that you see on TV have been cut. Filming of a firefight is usually covered by a "team" of reporters. Each team takes a separate assignment. In an engagement where you have ground troops, artillery and air support, you will have three or more teams covering this. The fact that the VC fired first is very common, as we can only return fire when fired upon. The Marines make an exception to this rule. When you read about the Marines in action, you should pay attention to the fact that we capture very few suspects or "POWs" [prisoners of war].

It is very hard to say how long an engagement will last. It may be a few minutes, a couple of hours, or many days. It depends on whether or not you are fighting VC or North Vietnamese regulars. If the odds are in their favour, they are like bulldogs, and will only retreat when they realize they have failed in their mission.

We are in an "operation" in the north of South Vietnam. I sit here and gaze across to the distant outline of trees where the VC wait. For days and days the infantry, artillery and air wing have been assaulting this tree line, and have driven the VC into their caves. Now the engineers must race against time across the long and lonely rice paddies to search out the tunnels and complexes of the VC.

It takes but a few minutes to cross the paddies, but they stretch into hours. Our rifles are grasped firmly and our demolition kits bounce wildly as we race toward our objective. TNT, fuse and igniter are ready. Toss! Hit the ground. One more hole is sealed. Just a few dozen to go. The dead and wounded are left where they have fallen to be given aid by the corpsmen and infantry that follow. Insanely, we race against the sun to close as many holes as possible to prevent the VC from regrouping. The night has descended, and we lie or sit in our ... fox-holes waiting for the sound or movement of "Charlie".

Our eyes are heavy and scratchy from lack of sleep. The false dawn of the Far East is here, and the endless heat of the day awaits us as we prepare for another day of battle.[9]

OPERATION STARLITE

Mom, I know I will never be the same Joe. Last night I lost one of my best buddies. It wasn't Bob, but he used to run around with us. Somehow the VC got through our lines and threw a grenade into where my buddy was sleeping. One of my buddies was wounded seriously and he's expected to die at any time. You know, Mom, things didn't really bother me until we got out here in the bad part of Da Nang. And now I lose two of my buddies. It's hard, Mom, to get over something like this, that's why I say it's gonna be different. I can't even smile any more, nothing seems funny to me, everything is so serious now. Once I get out of here I never want to hear another word about Vietnam or wars. You read in the papers about demonstrators and all this other bull … they ask why we are over here.

**IN A LETTER HOME,
US MARINE PRIVATE
FIRST CLASS JOE PAIS
DESCRIBED THE ACTION
AROUND DA NANG
IMMEDIATELY AFTER
OPERATION STARLITE:**

Well we're stopping communism over here instead of in the people's back yard back home in the US. We're doing a damn good job over here and we'll keep on doing a good job. Our Marine Corps saying is, "Death before Dishonour".

Well, the rainy season has finally moved in. It rains just about every day now. Sometimes all day and all night. I've moved to a new position now. I'm a squad leader. I'm in charge of six men. Of course, I'm still in heavy machine guns, our job is real dangerous, our life expectancy in combat is seven seconds. I'll be home, though, I won't let anything stop me.[10]

A soldier from the US 101st Airborne Division returns fire with an M-148 XM rifle. Nicknamed "Over and Under", the XM could fire a 40mm grenade from the underslung launcher, in addition to the standard 5.56mm ball round.

SPOOKING CHARLIE

ONE METHOD EMPLOYED
BY US TROOPS WAS TO
SPREAD FEAR AMONG
ENEMY SOLDIERS WHO
WERE SUPERSTITIOUS
ABOUT THE "ACE OF
SPADES" — SEEN AS
A DEADLY OMEN.
SECOND LIEUTENANT
CHARLES W. BROWN,
IN A LETTER TO
CONGRESSMAN CRAIG
HOSMER OF CALIFORNIA,
TOLD HOW HIS SOLDIERS
CARRIED A STACK OF
THE PLAYING CARD TO
LEAVE BEHIND FOR THE
VIET CONG:

The men and officers of Charlie Company are doing all we can to make as wide a distribution as possible of the "Ace". Our main area of operation is west of Pleiku in the Central Highlands region. At the present time I am on the battlefield but am happy to say that I'm not engaged in combat. I have been engaged lately and I am sure it won't be long until it starts again. Who knows what the next minute will bring. All of our men are carrying a basic load of "aces" as well as ammo. You might guess this causes us to receive harassment from sister units, but this helps our morale. "Charging Charlie" always has an ace up their sleeve. I cannot give an account of the effectiveness of our campaign. I will say that once we leave our cards, and then return some weeks later, there has been little or no VC activity there. You can arrive at your own conclusions.[11]

The helicopter was the weapon that the VC and NVA feared. However, they were more terrified of the "Ace of Spades" symbol. Here, a Huey has the "Ace of Spades" painted on its nose.

> "Charging Charlie"
> always has an ace up
> their sleeve

VC AMBUSH

US MARINE SERGEANTS AND STAFF NCOS OFTEN FOUND THEMSELVES LEADING PLATOONS INTO COMBAT, AS ON 8 JUNE 1966 AROUND HILL 55 AND THE LA THO RIVER BASIN. CAPTAIN WEST RECALLED:

Sergeant William Cunningham believed the 35-ton Amtracs would solve his problem. They would smash mined fences and tear up minefields. The platoon would walk in the tracks. A 60mm mortar would deal with the snipers. The platoon moved out in two columns in the wake of an Amtrac. They knew the area very well and hated it. The paddies and fields were separated by thick tree lines and many hamlets. The hamlets contained 1–10 houses.

Everywhere there were mines. They had been scattered at trail junctions, along fences, under gates. Having watched Marine patrols in this area, the VC buried their mines where they expected the Marines to walk. Sergeant Cunningham was aware of this. He was returning to the same hamlet complex so that the Amtracs could set off the mines. The enemy's supply wasn't inexhaustible, especially since most were M16 "Bouncing Betties" captured from the ARVN. The sergeant repeatedly warned his men to stay in the tracks of the Amtracs.

The column plodded south, strung out over a quarter of a mile. One Amtrac was in the lead; the second stayed back 200 yards in the middle of the column. After marching for 30 minutes, Sergeant Cunningham halted the column. In front of the lead Amtrac a thorn and bamboo fence ran at right angles to the line of march. Some 200 metres to the right front was a thick tree line in which the rooftops of four houses could be seen.

Sergeant Cunningham had seen his radioman and a squad leader trip a mine attached to that fence. Yesterday he had cautiously led his platoon across the fence and had been fired at. Today he told the lead tractor, "Rip that thing apart. Really tear it up". It crushed 30 feet of fence before its left track slipped into a ditch. The second Amtrac attached a rope and pulled the stranded vehicle out. Sergeant Cunningham decided to continue south to the minefields and wreck the fence on the return trip. "Move out," he shouted, "We'll come back to that bear later on." One Amtrac roared ahead while the second idled by the fence, waiting to turn into position. The point Marines, including Sergeant Cunningham, picked their way across the fence, stepping only in the tracks, and fell in behind the lead LVT [Landing Vehicle, Tracked]. The rest followed. Cunningham had walked 50 metres when he heard the explosion. Three Marines were sprawled on the ground. Corporal Raymond Lewis, leading the point squad, burst out: "Hey, why the hell don't they follow the goddamn tracks?" Sergeant Cunningham raced back, yelling in frustration and hurt, "I told you to follow me through here". A pause, then: "Okay, who got it?"

Feeling secure because there were many tracks near the fence and nine Marines had walked safely past, the 10th had wandered off the path. He had been following the dry trail of old tank treads. The VC had placed a mine on the old trail resting against the torn fence. The

A section of US soldiers lays down some smoke to obscure their movement across open ground during a VC ambush.

Following a VC ambush, US troops open fire on the enemy with an M60 machine gun.

Marine had tripped a mine, which flew knee-high, felling him and two Marines behind him. The column halted, well spread out but near no cover or concealment.

Then the sniping started. The first four to eight rounds were ignored. The sniping became steady fire and the targets were the wounded, the platoon leaders and the radioman. A light machine gun began firing short bursts. The VC had carefully planned the trap. No more than 20 seconds had passed since the VC had opened fire. They had better positions and had gained fire superiority from the start. The initial response was a matter of individual initiative as the Marines began returning fire.

Lewis's five men were heavily armed and he used all the weapons. The squad grenadier was pumping 40mm shells into the hamlet as fast as he could. Lewis turned his bazooka teams toward the hamlet. Corporal John Martin had his rocket launcher ready to fire. They agreed to target the houses. Martin fired from a kneeling position. A house shuddered and pitched at an angle. He fired again and a second house burst into flames. As he hit the third house, the machine gun stopped.

The 60mm mortar crew took up where the rocket launcher left off

The 60mm mortar crew took up where Martin left off. Less than 300 metres from the hamlet, the crew set up. Sergeant James Gibbs aimed while Lance Corporal Joe Dykes estimated the range. For two minutes, the crew walked rounds along the tree line. Under this cover, Sergeant Cunningham directed his 2nd Squad to secure a helicopter landing zone.

The Marines cleared the field by firepower and aggression. The mine severely wounded one Marine and put two out of action. During the rest of the day no sniper fired at the platoon. That was unusual. The following day, a Marine from the 3rd Platoon tripped a mine and five Marines were evacuated. The harassing fire that day was moderately heavy, inaccurate and delivered at long range. That was usual.[12]

HELICOPTERS AT WAR

US ARMY WARRANT OFFICER-1 RICHARD ELLIOTT OF THE 1ST CAVALRY DIVISION RECOUNTED THE DANGERS HELICOPTER PILOTS FACED DAY TO DAY ABOVE THE BATTLEFIELDS OF VIETNAM:

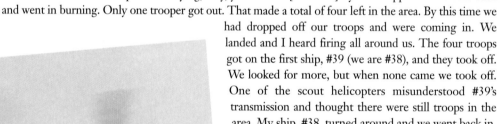

The gunner's view from a Huey. This US Navy airman fires his twin .30in machine guns at Viet Cong positions in the Mekong Delta.

Yesterday, the 30th, is a day that I will remember as long as I live. The scouts had spotted 30 or so PAVNs [People's Army of Vietnam] and a platoon went in to make contact. As they went in they captured a PAVN and he told them there were approximately 1000 others in that area. They tried to get out a bigger unit but the PAVNs jumped them and starting shooting them up. We, three ships, were being held in reserve in the rear area. We took off for that area, and they called the last ship (#37) back to drop off his troops and go out empty. I had come to know the pilot and co-pilot of this ship well.

Aside from close air support and casualty evacuation, the helicopter was vital in the resupply of troops in the field, since many places were inaccessible by road.

We got to the area, and were told to take our troops slightly west to secure a gunship that had been shot down. Then we were to return and get the troops, that were by now surrounded, out. Number 37, already empty, went in alone. He got in and loaded with troops. Total: nine infantry and four crew members. Before he even got off the ground they opened up almost at point blank. We were listening to him on the radio. The co-pilot was saying, "Fly, you mother [censored] fly". He flipped over on his back and went in burning. Only one trooper got out. That made a total of four left in the area. By this time we had dropped off our troops and were coming in. We landed and I heard firing all around us. The four troops got on the first ship, #39 (we are #38), and they took off. We looked for more, but when none came we took off. One of the scout helicopters misunderstood #39's transmission and thought there were still troops in the area. My ship, #38, turned around and we went back in. We found out later #39 had taken 31 hits.

In we came all alone, intending to land about 30 feet from the black, burning #37. At about four feet off the ground they hit us with everything. First our hydraulic system went out. Then our ship started to be rocked sidewards. At first I thought it was #37 exploding. Then, looking over, I realized it was their big guns hitting our ship. Dick, my pilot, and I both started pulling in power to get out of there. Just then, someone called over the radio and said, "38, you're on fire". Dick eyed the mike and said, "I know, we're all shot to hell". We cleared the trees and our engine finally quit. If it had done so three seconds sooner, I

would still be in that landing zone. Number 37 still is. I swear, there was only one area we could have landed in and it was full of stumps. We landed upright and piled out. All I grabbed was my pistol. Dick and I ran into the woods. I realized our gunner wasn't with us. "Where's Cliff?" I asked Dick. I went back to the ship to find him. He was ripping the machine gun off the side of the ship. We got it off, grabbed a belt of ammo, and cut out.

An armed US Navy Huey helicopter scans the terrain of the Mekong Delta.

We set up our defences, pointing towards where the PAVNs would come from, Dick with his grenade launcher, Cliff with his M16 and me with that machine gun. I kept my pistol in my lap. We sat there 40 minutes. The gunships were going over firing all the time. We lost two of them. Every time they went over they drew automatic gunfire. I was laying there, scared stiff, positive I was going to die, and wondering why our ships didn't pick us up. Later I found out they thought we were dead. We sat there waiting for Charlie to come when Cliff said, "PAVNs". We lay there watching the figures coming through the brush. It was our troops. We stayed hidden but held up our hand. Boy, I never thought a dirty, dog-faced soldier could look so good.

We picked up our weapons and fell in with them. We started moving again and the ship landed about 300 yards behind us. The three of us headed back towards it. It didn't see us, though, and took off.

Again, we headed after the troops. Bullets started sailing through the air around us so we hit the deck. The infantry fell back and their CO [commanding officer], a captain who I heard was killed, guided us back to where the mortar section was. We stayed there for a while, then started bringing in the wounded. We went back farther to another landing zone. Two ships came in and we loaded the wounded on, then got on ourselves. One of the door gunners (later) told me they got to #37. Both pilot and co-pilot were shot through the head by some large-calibre weapon. Two fine guys. Now more than ever I am determined to do everything possible to wipe these rotten bastards off the face of the earth.

Tomorrow we start trying to find Charlie again. Maybe I'll get to kill some

We found the Cong, now the division has to kill them off. Yesterday we caught 100 or so in the open. We bombed them, then our gunships went in and cut them down. We captured a 75mm recoilless rifle, though. We took a Special Forces team out the other day. They ran into some trouble, and we had to pick them up early. When we got them, one mountain tribesman came running up to the ship with a VC head in his hand. We are moving farther north tomorrow. Start trying to find Charlie again. Maybe I'll get to kill some. We moved, and now we are about 40 miles north of Pleiku. This place is crawling with VC. Right after we got here they jumped us while we were landing troops. One of our ships was shot down, pilot and co-pilot killed. This Bong Son area is loaded with Cong. Yesterday we found an estimated battalion. Of course we went in, we had to, but we knew we'd get shot to pieces. We picked up our troops after dark that night. While on a final approach, I could see the tracers that the VC were shooting coming at the ship. Kind of gives you a funny feeling.[13]

YANKEE STATION

METALSMITH SECOND CLASS EDDIE DORRIAN RECALLED FLIGHT OPERATIONS ABOARD THE AIRCRAFT CARRIER USS *KITTY HAWK*, THEN OFF "YANKEE STATION" IN THE SOUTH CHINA SEA:

Sailors stand by the planes and help to launch the planes. They have on headsets which we sailors call "Mickey Mouse" ears. The ears are worn to stop the sound of all jet engines. The goggles are to protect everyone's eyes from either jet blasts or something being blown into your face. Even though we wear those ears, we still hear the jets. Our catapults are almost the same thing as a slingshot. It doesn't look the same because it is operated by steam. They hook a plane up to the catapult by using a harness. A harness is a piece of steel cable about as thick as a baseball bat and as long as a couch. The plane has small hooks under the wings and each end of the harness is hooked up to each wing. The middle of the harness is then attached to the catapult. The catapult officer then gives the signal for the pilot to open up his engines. The pilot does this and salutes the catapult officer, which means he is ready.

The catapult officer gives the signal to the sailor, who presses a button and releases the catapult, sending the plane off the ship. The harness comes off the plane but stays on the ship because it is tied to the catapult track. When they test the catapult without a plane attached to it, the catapult goes 110 miles per hour.[14]

The aircraft carrier USS *Franklin D. Roosevelt* operating in the Gulf of Tonkin. On the deck it is possible to make out F-4 Phantoms and A-4 Skyhawks.

The US base at Khe Sanh comes under attack from VC mortars. US carrier aircraft provided valuable air support to bases under enemy attack during the war.

Two of my squadron's planes made everybody aboard ship sit up and take notice. They carried five tons of bombs apiece off the ship. Five bombs apiece at 2000 pounds apiece. We're still putting holes in Vietnam. Two days ago our planes really made some good score hits. They were aided by an army light plane, who knew the jungle area, and acted as a spotter by dropping smoke bombs on the area to be bombed. It was confirmed, we really did a lot of damage.

This morning at 03:00 hours, we're going after a pretty important target. I can't help saying a prayer to myself while the planes are being catapulted into the night, hoping they all return. It's a pretty good feeling, seeing the same number of planes return as you sent out. You can always tell by the pilot and the bombardier's faces how they made out on their mission. Last month, when we were out to get a railroad yard loaded with ammunition, our pilots returned and you should have heard them. WOW! They scored direct hits, and the explosion was said to throw debris 3000 feet into the air. Our "Skipper" gave us the ship's statistics of last month's period on North Vietnam, and it's unbelievable. We carried some 300,000 tons of bombs in three weeks. We sank 198 cargo junks and damaged 182 others; we destroyed 26 span bridges, a group of antiaircraft sites, Viet Cong headquarters, buildings, structures, radar sites, SAM [surface-to-air missile] sites, railroad yard, power factory and a lot of close air support for our troops there. As the Skipper puts it: "We're bringing the Viet Cong to the conference table."

METALSMITH DORRIAN SPECIFICALLY REMEMBERED SEVERAL COMBAT MISSIONS ABOARD THE USS *KITTY HAWK* THAT CAUSED SEVERE DAMAGE TO NORTH VIETNAM'S ARCHAIC MILITARY-INDUSTRIAL INFRASTRUCTURE:

The planes from my squadron carried so many bombs on the power plant strike (13 1000lb bombs per plane) that the Viet Cong said they were bombed by US Air Force B-52s. I hate to boast because it is all a result of team effort, but the majority of the statistics were made possible by the BLACK FALCONS of VA-85. They knew what they were doing when they called for an East Coast squadron. Of course, we had to pay a price also, but the job was done. Our planes made history by knocking out important sites even without seeing them. It's all done by systems incorporated into the aircraft.[15]

UNDER FIRE

RICHARD SHAND WAS IN CHARGE OF A "DUSTER" — TWIN 40MM GUNS MOUNTED ON A TANK CHASSIS — WHOSE MISSION WAS TO RESPOND TO ENEMY FIRE:

Two months as a "Duster" driver for headquarters battery left me little prepared for handling the guns. My total training consisted of firing four rounds in a gravel pit. Two days later I was put to the test and my inexperience showed. Our job was to respond immediately to any in-coming fire and, as happened in other actions, we had no time to put on helmets or flak jackets. Note: it was standard operating procedure to fire just one of the twin 40s and keep the other gun for back-up.

Now to the right, then to the left! I pump hard, stamping the pedal on the floor of the turret, gripping and turning the handles as I traverse and fire. BLAM! BLAM! BLAM! BLAM! The recoiling gun pounds and shakes the turret. Rounds explode in the wire and just beyond. Acrid smoke stings the nostrils.

We are under fire. Three 107mm rockets have just gone over our heads – SWOOSH – seemingly just above our radio antenna, and hit the guard tower at the opposite end of the compound. Now the radar dome beside us to our right is under attack.

RPG [rocket-propelled grenade] rounds fall short in bright popping explosions, like flash bulbs going off, right in front of our positions. This was not my first time in action, but it was the first time I ever had to aim and fire the guns. Old Mike behind me is loading away. I can hear him dropping the four-round clips into the loader as Fedor hands new clips to him. They work together like a well-greased piece of machinery.

In front of me is a tide of darkness. RPG launchers in the distance spark like matches being struck. My predecessor has neglected to put on the ring site necessary for aiming so our shooting is wild. The assistant gunner to the right of me calls off one target and I another. The guns traverse back and forth, spraying the countryside with flaring tracers and the percussive WUMPHS of explosions.

"Damn! Where's Fox?" Our section chief, Sgt. Fox, was unfortunately afflicted of loose bowels when under fire and is behind the bunker taking a crap into an ammo can. (These cans were shipped back to the States for reloading and I used to try to visualize the scenario when their contents were discovered.)

We fire perhaps five clips – 20 rounds, really far fewer than we should have, but we stop when the VC barrage in front of us halts abruptly. Echoes fade, the smoke clears and the ringing in my ears subsides. Purple after-images of the bright tracer flashes remain burnt into my retina.

The following morning the infantry swept the area in front of our position. They reported that the VC had run away so fast that they had left unfired weapons and sandals behind. If I had encountered the same situation a few months later I would have had the sight installed and probably would have placed at least another 50 rounds on target. But the past is past, and those who fought lived to fight another day. [16]

Communist in-coming fire outside the perimeter of a US base in South Vietnam. Being under artillery fire was a terrifying experience.

OURS OR THEIRS?

LZ [Landing Zone] Sally had our company of 40 men, a couple of infantry companies from the 101st, and an MP [military police] company. It was a very small compound, only the size of four or five city blocks square.

Day two at LZ Sally, and I pulled bunker guard. They wasted no time in getting me on the duty roster.

STEVE NIRK, 101ST AIRBORNE DIVISION, WAS AT LANDING ZONE SALLY WHEN HE CAME UNDER HEAVY ARTILLERY FIRE. HOWEVER, ALL WAS NOT WHAT IT SEEMED:

A US Navy warship shells an enemy position on the shore. Naval gun batteries could bring down a crippling amount of firepower onto a position with relative impunity.

At 02:00 hours, and well past my allotted time to sleep, I was still peering out into the darkness, scared to death and unable to even consider sleeping. That left three of us awake. Suddenly, my heart leaped out of my chest, and I gasped as I heard an unfamiliar, but very distinctive, sound of a large object flying through the air as it rapidly approached our position. It resembled the sound of a jet engine, but I realized it was an artillery round.

When the shell impacted the ground directly in front of the bunker but several hundred metres out, I shouted, "Oh shit, we're gittin' hit", as I dived for the bottom of the bunker and proceeded to attempt to crawl inside my helmet. As the echo of the explosion died out, I heard laughing and soon found out that it was directed at me.

"What the hell are you guys laughing at?" I asked from the floor of the bunker.

I looked up and noticed that they were still sitting up having quite a good time laughing at me.

"What the hell is going on?" I asked, just before I heard that same whooshing sound again, which by now was very familiar to me, even though I had only heard it once just a few seconds before.

KA-BOOOOOM!

The second round impacted even closer than the first, to which I responded with the same outcry of, "Holy shit, what the hell is going on, you guys?", as I cringed at the concussion that echoed in my ears again. They were laughing too hard to answer. By this time, I was not only pissed off at their taunting but confused about what was going on and their attitude toward the rounds.

"That was DTs," one of them finally told me, through his laughter.

"What the hell is a DT?" I asked, embarrassed at my ignorance and obvious over-reaction to a non-threatening situation.

"It's the Navy sitting off the coast and lobbing eight-inchers just outside our perimeter to keep Charlie off our butts. They're called defensive targets."

"Shit," I said. "Why didn't somebody tell me they were gonna do that, dammit. How in the hell do I tell DTs from in-coming?"

"You'll learn," he said. [17]

FIGHTING IN THE CLOUDS

Another day, another mission. This one must have been about November 1970 because bad weather had set in (monsoon) and Sgt. Fraizer was the Team Leader. We were inserted during a break in the clouds. We landed on a narrow ridgeline somewhere up in I Corps. I said "landed": I should have said jumped off, because the helicopter never stopped – it just slowed down as it passed over this very narrow ridgeline. Now that is also a thrill. To get out of the helicopter faster it was SOP [standard operating procedure] that as the helicopter made its final approach two men on each side would climb out on the skids. You would be holding your weapon out ready to fire if necessary and holding on to the helicopter with the other hand. On a mission like this in mountainous terrain, even though the helicopter was on final, you were climbing out on the skids while still 800 feet above the valley floor. As I said, it was a thrill.

The terrain in the Central Highlands differed greatly from the swamps and jungles of other parts of Vietnam. It made fighting on the ground and in the air decidedly more difficult.

VIETNAM ISN'T ALL SWAMPS AND JUNGLE. IN THE CENTRAL HIGHLANDS TROOPS HAD TO FIGHT AT HIGH ALTITUDE. RONNIE R. EDWARDS, US ARMY RANGERS, TOLD OF A MISSION IN 1970:

After landing we moved along a well-used trail towards the top of the hill. Walking a well-used trail is an invitation to trouble but I must say it was necessary in this case. This ridgeline was no more then 20–30 feet wide and dropped off at an 80-degree angle on each side. The sky we saw that day was the last we saw for five days. During the night the weather settled back in.

The next morning we were in the middle of a cloud. The Team Leader did not want to move because if we had contact we would not have any support. We were well outside artillery range – helicopters couldn't fly in that soup. Of course sitting on that trail on the ridgeline was no prize either.

We sat there for at least three days and never saw the sun. Couldn't see more than 10–15 feet in that soup. It is hard to sit in one place for four or five days and not make any noise. I had my guard lifesavers rationed out so I could have one every 20 minutes or so. During that three days or so I went through my memory and fantasized about making love to every single female I could remember. While we were there we heard wood chopping in a valley just beyond the next hilltop. I wanted to go check it out but the Team Leader did not want to lose our fragile communications. When we were finally extracted during another break in the clouds another team was inserted on the other hilltop to check out the wood chopping we had heard. This team ran into a pile of shit. When they went down to check out the wood chopping they ran into a whole regiment of NVA. The team moved back to the hilltop and were reinforced with more and more ground troops. It turned into a full-scale battle before it was over, and the whole reinforced mass ended up having to break out to another location to finally get out of there. Our dead on this mission were Drapp and Stoddard. It was just another lucky miss for me. [18]

THE NUI BA DEN

I have no pleasing memories of my war year, with one singular exception. The mountain. The Nui Ba Den.

I was drafted into the army in 1966 and served with the 25th Division in the middle of what the French called Cochin-China, assigned to a mechanized infantry battalion. We rode armoured personnel carriers (APCs): "tracks" we called them. We generally rode roughshod, armed to the teeth, through the countryside around Cu Chi and Dau Tieng, Trang Bang and Gau Da Ha and Tay Ninh, the Ho Bo and Bo Loi Woods. To make a long story short, we were not pleasant people and the war was not a pleasant business. I have no doubt we radicalized more southern Vietnamese to Ho Chi Minh's national revolution than we "saved".

The part of the world we fought in is as flat as the back of your hand. And above it stands the Nui Ba Den, 996 metres high, solid stone, and visible from almost any place, as if Mount McKinley were set in the middle of Kansas. On summer days, the very top of the mountain was wrapped with a bit of stone-white cloud, like a flat-brimmed, fraying hat.

VIETNAM'S GEOGRAPHY CAN BE BEAUTIFUL. MANY US TROOPS LEFT WITH VIVID MEMORIES. LARRY HEINEMANN SERVED IN THE US ARMY:

I always tried to take the last night guard, from three or four in the morning until breakfast. Night watches were mostly pathetically interminable reveries. And there in the moonlight the Nui Ba Den would be, like a fuzzy apparition. We watched in the darkness as processions of Viet Cong made their way up and around the mountain, each man carrying a tiny perfume bottle lamp, each light not much more than the flame of a birthday candle. The mountain seemed to shimmer at such times.

And then there were those few mad, murderous nights of fighting – "bitter fighting", as historians call it. My life's everlasting night horrors; the worst nights of my life. The killing would cease only when the sun rose, the smoke cleared, and the dew burned away. You looked up and there was nothing but meat and a wood line that looked like ruined drapes. And then you looked out across the way, and there, rising sharply above everything, was the Nui Ba Den.

Sitting guard in that last, long hour before dawn, the mountain would cut a clean silhouette from the scrub of dirty dark; soon a blunt, shadowy brunswick green; then a peculiar grey-green as the light gathered above us. The mountain was textured with the rubble of mould-stained boulders and thick stands of timber; then a transparent, seedling green; the sky all but blue. Then – boom – the sun rose, the world all colour, and there it would be, the Nui Ba Den, vivid and entire. The green of all green.

The Nui Ba Den has always loomed large in my memory of the war; in my 30 years of dreams and nightmares; in my imagination and my writing about that time of my life. Nowadays when I visit, I ride up highway 22 toward Tay Ninh, and just north of Gau Da Ha I see her. The Nui Ba Den, the widow who waits for her soldier's return, rises into view, and I feel I have come home.

How odd. [19]

A soldier's equipment rests on a sandbag wall. Vietnam had many glorious sunsets, but the outstanding natural beauty of the country was something most US troops never got to savour.

HIGHWAY TO HELL

GETTING SUPPLIES TO BASES WAS OFTEN HAZARDOUS. CHARLES ADAMS WAS A 5-TON TRUCK DRIVER TRANSPORTING 175MM AMMUNITION TO US FIRE BASES NEAR THE DEMILITARIZED ZONE:

While assigned to the first ammunition section of the Service Battery, 2nd Battalion, 94th Field Artillery, in the northern I Corps section of South Vietnam during the Vietnam War, we conducted many convoys of trucks delivering the tools of war to the guns on the fire bases on the DMZ.

The convoy started out from the huge American ammunition dump located at the Dong Ha Combat Base near the highway QL-1, near the coast in I Corps. Our destination was [the northernmost] American-occupied base at that time of the war called Fire Base Bastogne, located on a jungle mountain peak about 15 miles west of Dong Ha. The roads were very narrow in places so you could not turn around.

Our trucks consisted of 10 army 5-ton ammunition carriers, containing tons of 175mm high-explosive artillery rounds and very flammable crates of powder used to propel the artillery rounds, two fuel trucks containing mo-gas and diesel fuel, and some deuce 1/2s containing small-arms ammo and food. By this time all of the trusted and preferred convoy escorts, the "Duster" units of the 1/44th Arty with their twin-40s, had already stood down, turned their tracks over to the ARVN, and gone home. Instead of the "Dusters", our convoy escorts consisted of two old V-100s. The V-100s were left over from some long-gone MP unit. The Military Police vehicles were called all-terrain vehicles, but we called them worn-out pieces of junk because they kept breaking down.

We were only two hours into the all-day convoy when, as we were slowly moving up the winding jungle road about two miles out from Fire Base Bastogne, we heard on the radio, "CONTACT!". The word "contact" was the codeword for "convoy under attack".

I remember hearing firing up ahead of our truck. The firing was automatic small-arms up ahead, and I knew we had to move! Then we saw the mortar rounds start to impact near and above the road. The dinks were adjusting their fires as the telltale black smoke started to move up into the air from the rounds' impact.

The army 5-ton ammo carrier truck had 10 38-inch wheels on the ground, and all wheels were in drive because the 5-ton was an all-wheel-drive vehicle. I remember as I was downshifting to negotiate a hairpin ... I lost traction in the soft dirt and I bogged down to an almost stopped position. Well, the guy behind me, I think his name was Neese, slammed into my rear! It was a good hit, too, because I almost lost control. Finally, after my tires started to dig in my truck broke free and we were moving again!

We finally moved into the staging area just below Bastogne and parked. Everyone jumped out of their trucks and took cover. For about an hour we watched as the jets and the Cobra gunships bombed and machine-gunned the position from where the dinks were firing.

Luckily, all of our trucks arrived to Bastogne intact; however, a few of us had to change out of our pants!!

Our motto was, "We haul with style class 5". We were known on the DMZ as the "MOTHER TRUCKERS!". [20]

A pair of US truck-mounted antiaircraft guns wait to escort a convoy on its way from Ca Lu to the base at Khe Sanh.

WAR'S HARSH REALITIES

Our mission for the first day was to investigate an enemy base camp on a ridge a couple of klics [kilometres] to the west of the LZ [landing zone]. There were no villages in the vicinity; anybody we encountered was to be considered an enemy.

We reached the crest of the ridge and split up. The lead squad moved down the left side of the ridge towards a hooch and the crying baby. Part of my squad continued on the main trail which ran down the other side of the narrow ridge.

The crying baby was lying in a dead woman's lap at the bottom of a four-foot hole in one of the hooches. There was a dead man in the bottom of a similar hole in another hooch.

Fearing that the baby was booby trapped, they suspended the medic over the hole and he attached a web belt to the baby's ankle. Once attached they slowly pulled the baby out. They got the dead man and woman out using the same technique.

The baby was a girl, relatively healthy and very hungry. She couldn't have been more than a couple of days old. The man and woman were young, early 20s. They hadn't been dead long. They were still warm.

An American soldier carries a newly born Vietnamese baby to safety before an air strike is called in on the area.

They'd both been shot in the back of the head. There were no exit wounds. We originally assumed they were victims of the artillery prep; now it appeared that they had been executed by their compatriots.

I can only guess at what happened. The VC unit knew we were coming. They didn't have long to gather some necessities and get the hell out. They couldn't take the baby, it would make too much noise, or maybe the mother wasn't strong enough to travel. In either event the man wouldn't leave without them. So, some cold-blooded son of a bitch shot them and put them where it would delay us long enough for the rest of them to get away.

US TROOPS WERE OFTEN SURPRISED AT HOW HARSH THE VIET CONG COULD BE TO THEIR OWN PEOPLE. WES ZANONE WAS A GRUNT DURING AN OPERATION IN 1969:

It started to rain. We quickly destroyed everything we could. We pitched grenades into the tunnels and set fire to anything that would burn.

I saw the woman for the first time just before someone dumped a bag of rice on her. I looked into her face until it was covered. She had been somebody's daughter, and for a short while she had been somebody's mother. I wondered if her last thought was of her daughter and what would become of her.

I think half the guys in the platoon volunteered to carry the baby down the hill. Our medic was the logical choice; he was a conscientious objector and of course unarmed. I was jealous.

It was raining so hard that the choppers were grounded. That meant that the baby was spending the night with us. The medics came around and collected anything that would make the little girl more comfortable. I gave up a dry, almost clean, T-shirt that I had stashed in my fanny pack. We all gave up the sugar and powdered cream from what little rations there were.

The captain's radio operator sat up all night with her. The concoction he made with the sugar and powdered cream didn't work – she cried much of the night.

Having a baby in our midst gave new meaning to the war. We were protecting a totally innocent and helpless child. It was the first time that I felt like we were doing something worthwhile.

Early the next morning a Medivac came and took her away. I've often wondered what happened to her. If she survived, she'd be 27 years old around New Year's Day. [21]

NIGHT FIGHTING

Three Church is where we operated out of – many know that name rather than Three Tango. We worked directly with the Special Forces.

Captain said we were going on a mission to locate a battalion of NVA who had been wasting our base camps ... something does not look right since we have been given an azimuth to follow. Seems if they were looking for them, they would not tell us the direction to go.

Heard the point men on the radio say they saw boot prints with water still seeping in them, so they know we are here and going to be set up; better be taking up position, don't make any sense to keep going if we are where their outpost was at, means they are close.

Captain said to set up a perimeter, has that same gut feeling we are as close as we had better get. Not much daylight left.

Bringing the artillery in close, got a hot dog Forward Observer who says he can turn around and call it in backwards, no need for that. Dummy hit a fox-hole, don't need the NVA when we are doing a job on ourselves. Last night it was mistaken identity.

Here comes the mortars, amazing nobody got hit, really raked our perimeter good. Captain said to brace for an attack since that is how it goes, first the mortars, then it all cuts loose.

Heard the outpost say to get ready, they are coming, and there are thousands of them; lost radio contact. Hear our other outpost cut loose with the machine gun, Sgt. Reed went into shock, all he can say is, "Oh no, Oh no!".

A US soldier is silhouetted against the sunset. Visibility at night in Vietnam was barely a few feet, since little natural light pierced the dense jungle canopy.

FIGHTING IN DAYLIGHT WAS BAD ENOUGH, BUT BATTLING THE NORTH VIETNAMESE ARMY AT NIGHT WAS BOTH TERRIFYING AND CONFUSING. LOU TALLEY, US 4TH INFANTRY DIVISION, WAS IN JUST SUCH AN ACTION IN PLEIKU PROVINCE IN NOVEMBER 1966:

Got the artillery going, something wrong as it is going farther out instead of coming in closer. Captain has started calling it in himself.

Heard a pilot on the radio asking what was going on, says he is in the area (location being near a Special Forces camp in the area near Plei Djereng) and saw us in trouble, has a full load and can buy us some time, has an accent, Australian, not even our own air support. Had to call off the artillery since he is coming in low. The Aussie pilot (Powell) nailed them with rockets, 500 pound bomb, and several sweeps with his mounted machine gun. Not an exaggeration to say he came in so low they could have hit him with a rock and may well have had a few holes put in his aircraft since, in the clearing, he came in below treetop level and slow, just took a lot of balls to do that ... and in the dark of this evening attack!

Heard our air support, they need our location to get layout of battle area. Had somebody fire tracers from the centre of the perimeter to see where we are at. Never so glad to see those guys; almost all of us out of ammo and could not have held out two minutes longer.

Really did a job on those dudes, everything on fire from the napalm [powdered aluminium soap or a similar compound used to gelatinize oil or gasoline for use in bombs or flamethrowers], cooked many of them in front of us, no more enemy fire coming in.

Attack seems to be over. Said they will keep the perimeter lit up all night with illumination and want a body count at first light.

One man hit by our artillery is bleeding to death, captain trying to get him evacuated but no choppers will come in, action too hot and heavy. Captain said forget it since he just died.

Never prayed like that before in my life, plum scared to death, told God I was not going to promise anything since he knows what happened the last time. Please help us, please help us. Had to be honest, may not deserve anything good, just asking for help and can only promise I will try to play it straight.

Kind of strange that all that stuff reminded me of something in the Bible. Israel against the world and don't stand a chance, and that is when God steps in the scene so they know who delivered them and kept His Word to do that, kind of like when God used the enemy to punish His own house because of idolatry and stuff, and then He proceeded to restore.

NVA unit was said to be division size. Also found the body of a Chinese regular the next morning, who was not carried off, wearing black PJs [pajamas].

Lieutenant Paul Braim was shot by mistake at Regular Hill Base Camp by a private cleaning his rifle, replaced by Major Tom Rozelle.

Aussie Pilot: Wing Commander A.W. Powell, DASC Alpha

Type of aircraft: Canberra (not officially approved until April).

Bulldog Drummond was killed on 19 May 1967; and Powell was killed on 17 May 1968. Drummond was an FAC [forward air controller – a man on the ground who sees a target, identifies it, and calls in an aircraft to deliver air-to-surface weapons against it] pilot who Powell replaced; both were killed one year apart after they returned to Australia, both freak accidents. Drummond was well known in the 4th Division by ground troops, and always came in with his plane even if it was shot up.

Then there was the OP [observation post operator] who was caught in the crossfire, shot in both legs, climbed a tree, and survived all the napalm, rockets and bombs. The outpost gave us warning of the attack, but only one survived. [22]

Really did a job on those dudes ... cooked many of them in front of us

A US Special Forces trooper in full camouflage keeps a watchful eye out for Viet Cong activity during a night patrol.

MEDIC! MEDIC!

MEDICS WERE TO THE FORE IN MOST COMBATS, RETRIEVING THE WOUNDED AND EVACUATING THEM TO HOSPITAL. IN JUNE 1969 JOHN D. DENNISON WAS NEAR THE DONG NAI RIVER IN SOUTH VIETNAM:

In May 1969, I was transferred from the 229th Aviation Unit to HHC [Headquarters Company] 1st Bn., 8th Cav. Upon my arrival at the 8th Cav, I met a friend, named Preston Taylor. We had completed our Advanced Individual Training together at Fort Sam Houston to become Medics.

Preston was assigned to Alpha Company, commanded by Captain Marm, and I was assigned to Bravo Company, commanded by Captain Hottell. We flew out together in the same chopper since Alpha and Bravo Companies were on neighbouring islands, called Banana and Chicken Island, because of their shapes.

The companies were working a joint operation in the Long Khanh Province. Alpha Company was on one island while Bravo Company was on an adjacent island searching for a suspected enemy supply centre.

In the afternoon of 1 June 1969 Alpha Company discovered an enemy bunker complex with 13 bunkers (each measuring 15' x 10' x 6' with a 3' overhead) and also a hospital bunker (20' x 20'). One of the bunkers contained a cache of ammo consisting of 100 Chi Com grenades, 12 RPG [rocket-propelled grenade] rockets, 12 RPG boosters, 6 boxes of AK-47 ammo (3000 rounds) and 6 rounds of 75mm for a recoilless rifle.

Alpha Company had pulled back from the bunkers to a small clearing where an LZ could be set up to ship out the seized enemy weapons by chopper. Alpha Company would move back to the bunkers the following day and destroy them.

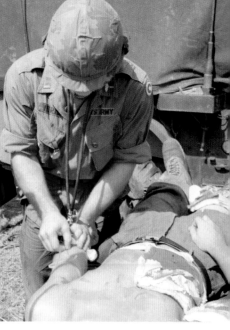

Medic! An injured US soldier receives treatment for his wounds from a US Army medic.

During the night the NVA moved back into the bunker complex unbeknownst to Alpha Company. It was estimated that the strength of the enemy was a company plus size. In the morning, Alpha Company began their approach on the bunker complex when they were met with heavy fire from machine guns and RPGs. Alpha Company took very heavy casualties from the enemy's intense fire and were forced to pull back, leaving five of their dead behind. Alpha Company then took up a defensive position while being supported by jets, gunships and artillery.

Upon my arrival into Alpha Company's LZ I met a fellow medic, David L. Adkins, and asked him how my friend Preston Taylor was doing. Adkins looked up and said that he had been killed. My stomach turned into a knot upon hearing of Preston's death.

There was no time to mourn my friend's death. There were still men who needed to be treated from Alpha Company and medevaced out. While I

Medical evacuation, or medevac, was one of the most crucial roles played by helicopters in Vietnam. Many lives were saved by choppers.

was at the LZ finishing medevacing Alpha Company's wounded and receiving additional supplies, Bravo Company's 1st, 2nd and 3rd Platoons attempted to recover our five dead troopers. They were again met with heavy fire from machine guns and RPGs. Snipers who had moved into the wood line near the LZ also opened up. I sought cover behind a fallen tree with three other men.

A call for stretchers came. I left the safety of the fallen tree, grabbed a stretcher and proceeded to the CP [command post]. I watched grunts seeking cover behind fallen trees and ground banks. I remembered my friends telling me how hard the grunts had it. I kept thinking to myself that, right now, grunts had it pretty nice, getting to stay behind cover. We all know the grunts took the brunt of the hardships in Vietnam, and it was only after the grunts spilled their blood that the medic's job became a little riskier. As I reached the CP I asked Captain Hottell for a guide to take me up to the wounded. We went about 100 yards when we started to receive fire from the opposite island. The guide said that I should go straight ahead and that he was going back to the CP. Straight ahead was a wood line with no one in sight. I laid on the ground with my back against a sand bank deciding if I should go forward or listen to my instincts and go to the left. I noticed a freedom bird coming in for a landing at Bien Hoa and my thoughts went to home. I wonder if I would ever get out of this living hell. As another burst of machine-gun fire came in my direction from the other island, I heard a voice call to me, "Doc ... Doc come over here". The voice was a sergeant calling for me to come to his location on my left. I later found out that there were enemy bunkers straight ahead.

After I finished treating the sergeant's wound, I got up and started to move forward. He grabbed my shoulder saying, "Stay here, Doc. We have all moved back now". We set up a medical treatment area where we finished treating the wounded and checked the men a second time for any missed wounds or injuries. The enemy fire finally let up enough so we could evacuate the wounded from our LZ.

While our artillery and gunships pounded the bunker complex, we dug our fox-holes extra deep for the long night ahead. As night fell, we could also hear the enemy digging.

In the morning, a mad minute of fire was ordered (when everyone fires their weapon at the enemy position). There was no return fire from the enemy. The enemy had moved out during the night and apparently crossed the

The digging we heard the night before was the enemy burying their dead

river. The order was given to put the men into body bags without identifying them. A small prayer service was said over all of the fallen men before they were sent out on a chopper. I still regret, after 30 years, not being able to say a separate prayer over my friend, Preston Taylor.

The digging, which we heard the night before, was the enemy burying their dead. [23]

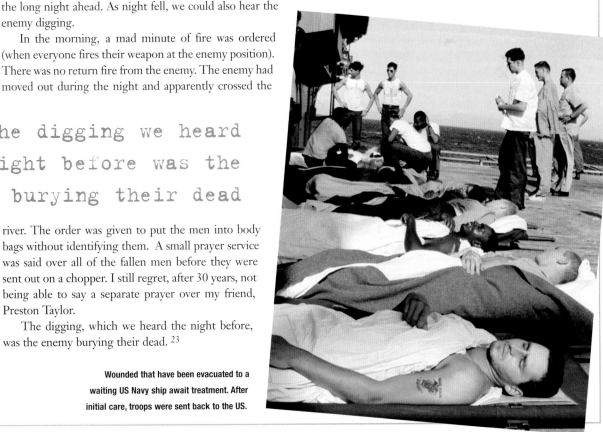

Wounded that have been evacuated to a waiting US Navy ship await treatment. After initial care, troops were sent back to the US.

EXPLOSIVES AND DEATH

BEING PUT DOWN ON A "HOT" LANDING ZONE WAS NOT A PLEASANT EXPERIENCE, AS TOM HAIN, 9TH INFANTRY MOBILE RIVERINE FORCE, RECOUNTED:

When we were on our way, one of the guys asked the door gunner what the LZ was like. He said it was HOT, and to get off quick and find cover as soon as we touched down. Our squad leader tried to give us instructions about sticking together, but the noise was too loud to hear him. I think we were all too scared to listen. Most of us had been in hot LZs before, but none of us had done it in the dark, and it was pitch black now.

As we approached the LZ, the door gunner told us to get ready. Damn, the LZ was hot! Even over the noise of the chopper we could hear the gunfire and sound of grenades. I looked down and saw the reflection of the stars and the tracers in the water in the rice paddies. It looked like we were about 50 feet in the air, so I stepped out on the skid. There were no lights on the chopper so I figured that the pilot was using night vision goggles. When he flared to land I would just step off and be running when I hit the ground. I had done it before and I was proficient at it. At least that was the plan.

We located the rest of my squad by radio and I was able to crawl to where they were, dragging my equipment behind me. They were positioned behind a dike and were busy laying down fire. I needed the time to clean my weapon. The firefight was still going strong. The red and green tracers were going in all directions. The artillery was pounding the treeline in front of us and it was clear that we were in deep shit. The guys around me were laying down grazing fire. The M60 gunner was yelling for more ammo, and everyone was yelling for air support.

I looked over to where the M60 was and the barrel was glowing a dull red. They had to let their weapons cool, and mine was stone cold. I put some rounds into half a dozen targets, and before I knew it I had fired five or six magazines and my barrel was hot, too. That's when Spooky showed up overhead.

The firepower from Spooky was a sight to behold. There were three multi-barrelled, electrically operated, high-speed guns sticking out the side of an old C47 airplane that the pilot could direct on to a target by flying a tight circle above it. The noise the guns made was like nothing else. Each gun could fire up to 6000 rounds of 7.62mm ammo per minute. Every fifth round was a tracer and they fired so fast that it looked like a single, bright red line. I loved Spooky. He worked out for a few minutes and then left. Afterwards, the intensity of the fighting was cut by 75 percent. Only sniper fire and an occasional mortar round were incoming. I loved Spooky!

Helicopters of 335 Assault Helicopter Company ferry troops from the 173rd Airborne Brigade to an LZ just north of Tuy Hoa during an operation.

UH-1 Hueys swoop in to pick up men of the US 12th Infantry, 199th Light Infantry Brigade, during Operation Toan Thang II in April 1968.

Three dead Viet Cong lay where they were shot. All their weapons and equipment have been stripped off them, so that comrades cannot return to salvage anything.

We were resupplied by chopper. We re-grouped, then started moving in the direction from where the fire had come. My squad was point. We moved into the treeline. There was no in-coming fire. We took a body count. There weren't many. We didn't expect a lot. The VC had time to drag their dead away. The smell was a mixture of mud, explosives and death. There was no noise except for the wet, muddy sound of our own footsteps. What was left of the treeline wasn't very deep, maybe 200 metres. Shell craters and trees cut down by artillery made it tough to walk. We were heading due east towards a town on a major river where we were supposed to be picked up by boat.

When we moved out after the dust-off left, I was out in front watching where I stepped and the open area ahead. One of the jobs of the pointman was to drop hand grenades into bunkers. As I came upon a trench that ran across my path I saw a bunker at the end. I stepped over the trench, walked up to the bunker, and dropped in a fragmentation grenade. BOOM! A few steps later one of the guys from behind yelled, "Hey Hain! You got one back here!"

My heart started doing double time and my stomach flipped over as I walked back. The poor SOB didn't move fast enough to get out of the bunker, and he paid for his lack of speed with his life. I felt good and bad about it, and I still do.

The SOP in our company said that since it was my KIA [killed in action], I had to go into the bunker and drag out any weapons or equipment. One of the other guys did it for me and came out with a brand-new SKS rifle. It was light and accurate and used by their snipers. It still had grease in the barrel. Because it was bolt-action, it was a trophy that he could take home. Only semi-auto and automatic weapons had to be turned in. It would have been mine if I had had the stomach to go into the bunker.

The fact that there was grease in the barrel didn't sink in until later. He had never fired the weapon! We found out later that we had walked into a VC training camp. The hot LZ the night before had killed most of the cadre. The VC that were left put the trainees up front to slow us down with sniper fire while they made their escape. This poor SOB was probably too scared to shoot and was hiding in that bunker hoping that we would just go away. If one of the guys behind the point would have found him, he probably would have surrendered to him. He didn't need to die. [24]

CHAPTER 5
"VICTOR CHARLIE" AND THE NVA
1965–1975

The soldiers who faced US troops on the battlefields of Vietnam were among the toughest opponents the US Army has faced. Beginning in 1965, and lasting until the final evacuation of US Marines from the US Embassy in Saigon in 1975, soldiers from the North Vietnamese Army (NVA) and South Vietnamese communists, known as Viet Cong (VC), demonstrated their fighting prowess in countless battles.

This chapter contains accounts from North Vietnamese soldiers and VC personnel, ranging from political officers to frontline soldiers, of the fighting that raged on their home soil for nearly a quarter of a century. For nearly 10 of those 25 bloody years, US troops, NVA and VC faced and fought each other on numerous battlefields in the South.

The central figure in all three of Vietnam's wars of liberation (1940–45 against the Japanese; 1946–54 against the French; and 1965–75 against the US) was North Vietnam's leader, Ho Chi Minh.

The Viet Minh (Viet Nam Doc Lap Dong Minh Hoi – League for the Independence of Vietnam) had been formed as early as 1941 as an indigenous anti-French resistance organization, fighting what was essentially a guerrilla war. Using a variety of weapons ranging from bamboo sticks to captured Japanese, Chinese and Soviet firearms, Viet Minh forces carried out a wide range of attacks on the French. By 1953 the ground rules had changed. Ho outlined the tactics his soldiers were to follow in a report to the Fourth Conference of the Party Central Committee which met early that year. He emphasized that the fighting would be both

long and arduous because the US and France would step up their efforts, hoping to "occupy our country and make it a military base from which to attack China".[1]

Ho's aim was to broaden the guerrilla war and conduct swift, mobile operations to annihilate the enemy's rear areas.

When the "Viet Minh War" ended in 1954, many young Vietnamese men left home and headed north to Hanoi to attend classes on "national language education". Here, the majority of them found their way into the ranks of the NVA. Le Ly Hayslip's brother Bon Nghe was one of them. She recalled how the South Vietnamese soldiers went into the jungle to look for the VC, and how "many Republican soldiers were killed on these sweeps because they carried so much equipment", making them clumsy and therefore noisy.[2]

The VC and ARVN

The fighting intensified between the VC and the Army of the Republic of Vietnam (ARVN) during the first three years of the 1960s. Often, after a target was attacked, the VC receded into their jungle camps to receive tuition in military operations and weapons, as well as political indoctrination. These "classes" often lasted four months at a time. "After the course," a VC soldier remembered, "we had a clearer idea of our mission. We saw it better against the background of the whole struggle; our men had a firmer political stand and their morale was heightened further."[3]

As victory in the Battle of Ap Bac in January 1963 demonstrated, the VC continued to improve. By the eve of the American intervention, in what became the

Second Indo-China, or Vietnam, War, both the VC and NVA had become formidable forces on the battlefield. As the next phase of this long struggle started with the arrival of US troops in March 1965, the VC and NVA reorganized and retrained to meet this even greater threat from a superbly trained, led and equipped US military force.

Fighting the Americans

The VC modified its tactics in order to counter the US advantage in firepower and mobility. They employed "hugging tactics" – remaining as close as possible to US troops, thereby negating the effects of air support. Well camouflaged and well armed, the VC often used hit-and-run techniques to inflict casualties. Nonetheless, in many engagements US forces, able to call upon accurate artillery support from fire bases, inflicted up to three times as many casualties on the VC and North Vietnamese troops.

The victory the NVA achieved over the army of South Vietnam came only after years of fighting and heavy losses. However, the NVA did not achieve this victory through its war with the US forces – it stood on the brink of defeat after the 1968 Tet Offensive, when US Marines and soldiers killed thousands of VC and NVA troops. In fact, it was North Vietnam that asked for peace talks. General Giap had not achieved against the Americans what he achieved against the French: a decisive military victory.

Three Viet Cong members stand triumphantly on top of a destroyed US M113 armoured personnel carrier. Note the typical black pajamas.

HO CHI MINH'S STRATEGY

IN DECEMBER 1946,
HAVING FAILED TO
NEGOTIATE VIETNAM'S
INDEPENDENCE, HO CHI
MINH URGED HIS
FOLLOWERS FORWARD:

As we desired peace, we made concessions. But the more we made concessions, the further the French colonialists went because they are resolved to invade our country again. No! We would rather sacrifice all than lose our country. We are determined not to be enslaved. Compatriots! Rise Up. Men and women, old and young, regardless of creeds, political parties or nationalities, all the Vietnamese must stand up to fight the French colonialists to save the Fatherland. Those who have rifles will use their rifles; those who have swords will use their swords; those who have no swords will use spades, hoes or sticks. Everyone must endeavour to oppose the colonialists and save his country. Army men, self-defence guards and militiamen! The hour for national salvation has struck. We must sacrifice even our last drop of blood to safeguard our country. Even if we have to endure hardship in the Resistance war ... victory will surely be ours.

Long live an independent and unified Vietnam! Long live the victorious Resistance! 4

The founding father of the communist movement in Vietnam, Ho Chi Minh. "Uncle Ho" was the main Viet Cong political strategist, and a talismanic figure.

1. Avoid strongpoints and attack weak points in order to disperse the enemy's forces and destroy the enemy's manpower and widen the free zone. That is our strategic line at present.

2. Main force troops on the North battlefield must use fluid, mobile warfare in order to annihilate the enemy's manpower bit by bit and weaken the enemy; and must coordinate it with attacks on fortified positions, one by one in order to take important points and small towns where the enemy has gaps or is weak. We do this in order to achieve the objective of fighting where we are sure of victory, and of broadening the free zone. At the same time, we may use positional warfare to draw the enemy's forces to us in order to attack them, disperse the enemy's forces, confuse the enemy's plans and create conditions for mobile warfare.

3. The battlefield in the enemy's rear must broaden guerrilla warfare in order to annihilate and wear down small parts of the enemy; in order to resist enemy sweeps, protect the lives and property of the people, harass, sabotage and dominate the enemy; propagandize and educate the masses in those zones, reduce the pool of recruitment of puppet troops, widen our guerrilla zones and guerrilla base areas, and establish and strengthen resistance bases in the enemy's rear.

4. Besides increasing main force troops, building up local troops, the free zone and rather large guerrilla bases, we must build guerrilla militia organizations not detached from production.

HO'S STRATEGY CONFORMED CLOSELY TO MAO ZEDONG'S PRINCIPLES ON HOW TO WAGE A SUCCESSFUL GUERRILLA WAR:

A VC instructor gives a lesson to Viet Cong troops. He is using the side of a burnt-out US M113 armoured personnel carrier as a teaching aid, which is a rather novel idea.

Those guerrilla militia organizations cannot only take responsibility for repression of counter-revolutionaries, security in the villages, protecting the interests of the masses and struggling with the enemy and coordinating combat with main force troops, but can also be used [as main force] replacements.

New recruits to the North Vietnamese Army, or NVA, are given lessons in firing a mortar. The NVA had over one million members by 1975.

5. Regarding the military guidance, we must combine the forms of struggle mentioned above in a flexible, shrewd manner. That would be profitable, on one hand, for the main force troops who can find many opportunities to annihilate the enemy; and, on the other hand, it can help guerrillas operate and help our guerrilla bases in the enemy's rear develop and be consolidated.

6. We must realize clearly the long-term character of resistance war. Therefore, we must pay much attention to maintaining the certain combat strength of the army, not causing it to be worn down or [be] too tired. At about the same time we must ask the troops to accept difficulty and hardship.

7. We must strengthen the political work, always raising the political level and class-consciousness of our troops; we must ensure the implementation of the policy of the Party and Government; we must thoroughly maintain self-conscious discipline regarding the military and political aspects.

8. We must strengthen military work, first of all always regarding training troops as important. We must strive to bring up cadres, force their thinking, and raise the level of political consciousness as well as the tactical and technical levels of the cadres.

9. We must have a common plan for the building and reinforcement of the army. Besides mobilizing youth in the free zone to join the army, we must pay much attention to winning over and reforming puppet troops who have surrendered to us. In organizing new troops, we must ... use the method of taking old troops and making them the foundation for broadening new troops.

10. We must ... improve gradually the equipment of our troops, especially the construction of artillery.[5]

MILITARY STRATEGY

GENERAL VO NGUYEN GIAP, THE CHIEF OF STAFF, OUTLINED THE MILITARY STRATEGY TO BE USED AGAINST THE FRENCH IN A DIRECTIVE TO HIS FORCES:

This directive by the general staff has the object of making clear for Resistance Committees at all levels, and for the entire army and military, the primary work which must be done to complete the task of activating guerrilla warfare. There must be one firm realization: guerrilla warfare is the base. Our resistance is an all-people resistance; that is the essential assurance for its final victory. Why do we call it an all-people resistance? All-people resistance means the entire people participate in the destruction of the invader.

Carrying it one step further, all-people resistance also means that on the battlefield of the entire nation there are not only regular troops but guerrillas ... and there are self-defence militia participating in the fighting. Therefore, to carry out all-people resistance, we must mobilize and arm the entire people.

In order to cope with the war generally, and to cope with the enemy's new tactics, activating guerrilla warfare is all the more urgent. With the enemy's fall-winter offensive, the war is expanding to our own rear area. Enemy troops will control the cities and main lines of communication; they will try to surround us from outside, forcing our troops into a position of encirclement. Thus the enemy army would have the initiative, and our army would be in a passive position. With the enemy's tactic of parachuting into many places, the rear could very swiftly become the frontline. Enemy troops may thoroughly exploit the gaps in our deployment in order to destroy our agencies and storehouses, and to murder and pillage our people. The only way to cope with that situation is quickly to develop guerrilla warfare. If we develop guerrilla warfare, it will follow that, even though the enemy comes to a place which has no troops, they will still meet resistance, will at least be harassed, gradually worn down and destroyed one small bit at a time, so that our troops will have time to deal with them. Our base of an entire people armed will submerge the cities and lines of communications controlled by the enemy in our own encirclement. From a position of being surrounded, we will shift to a position of surrounding the enemy. From a passive position, we will shift to the initiative. Therefore, if, generally speaking, activating guerrilla warfare is necessary, then, particularly at a time when a war is widening, activating guerrilla warfare is even more necessary.

What have we done to activate guerrilla warfare? We have put forward the slogan of guerrilla warfare for a long time. We have mobilized people to participate in it, organizing self-defence militia and guerrilla militia units. In Nambo, we have activated a fairly strong guerrilla movement. In many places, the regular troops have done their best to help the guerrillas to mature. However, because our realization has not yet been clear, because the tactics of application are not correct, because the idea of a people's war is not yet firm and arms are still lacking, guerrilla warfare at present has not yet developed strongly and widely:

The legendary North Vietnamese General, Vo Nguyen Giap. After defeating the French at Dien Bien Phu, he set about the US forces with vigour.

a) There are many localities where guerrillas are still weak and where neither the protection of localities, nor combat coordination with main forces, has yet been accomplished. In some places guerrilla warfare has developed but there are not yet units developed to the level of local troops.

b) There are places where guerrillas have not yet developed, so that the tendency to regularize has grown too soon, making it impossible for guerrilla warfare to develop. There are zones which have pushed guerrillas into the main force too hastily, to the point of weakening guerrilla bases. There are provinces in which the provincial unit has only been concerned with separate guerrillas, and not paid attention to bringing up guerrillas which are not separate. In wartime, there is also an inclination to attack according to regular methods, to join large battles, expending large amounts of ammunition, not regarding harassing attacks or scattered attacks, which have many results, as important.

c) Combat hamlets have not yet been actively constructed everywhere.

d) Main force troops do not yet have a concrete and active plan to develop guerrilla warfare.

How do we strengthen guerrilla warfare? In order to strengthen guerrilla warfare, we must immediately do the following things:

> In wartime, there is an inclination to attack via regular methods

1) Resistance committees must pay more attention to the problem of guerrilla militia. Each mountainous district, inter-district and district must have a factory manufacturing grenades, mines and ammunition. We must resolve correctly the problem of supplying arms to guerrillas. Guerrillas must ask the people to support and supply them and must capture arms from the enemy in order to increase equipment for themselves. Only in this way can guerrilla warfare develop to a high level.

2) Any detached guerrilla unit, when its activities and training have reached a certain level, can be recognized as local forces. Local forces ... can remain in combat in the locality, so that ... supply would be the responsibility of the local resistance and people's committees.

3) In the present situation, main forces have the task of activating guerrilla warfare in a direct and active manner. Help guerrillas with regard to cadres; of the cadres presently in the main forces, some must be moved back to the locality in order to command local guerrilla units. Help in regard to weapons: within the limits of capability, they must assist local guerrillas with arms; when they capture weapons from the enemy, they must divide them up with the guerrillas. But the most realistic and effective way of helping is to deploy main forces companies as independent companies in the localities in which guerrillas are still undeveloped. Besides the usual tasks, the independent company also has the task of helping the local guerrillas mature.

4) Regarding establishment of combat hamlets, they must be carried out more effectively.[6]

North Vietnamese recruits practise drill in a park in Hanoi. The North did not have many problems in finding willing new soldiers to replace those killed in action.

FIGHTING THE FRENCH AND AMERICANS

LE LY HAYSLIP, FROM KY LA IN CENTRAL VIETNAM, RECALLED HOW THE VILLAGERS HELPED THE VIET MINH:

Although I was too young to do anything against the French, I remember my sisters getting ready – cleaning up, brushing their hair and practising each night to sing and dance for the Viet Minh fighters who lived around our village. My sisters also prepared rice balls, bandages and other things the fighters would need in the field. Each evening, a Viet Minh representative came to the house of sympathetic villagers and took our gifts to the battle zones. We were never paid for these provisions, but then neither were the Viet Minh paid to fight on our behalf. Pay makes a soldier a mercenary, we thought, and money for supplies turns patriots into profiteers. The peasants of Ky La had not yet learnt to think of war as a business. My mother was more than patriotic. She had a secret tunnel dug under her bed, and once in a while I saw her or my father pass supplies into it. I never knew if the tunnel dead-ended below the house or if it led somewhere. I did not know that the Viet Minh spent most of their time underground, which made them difficult to find, even if you were a friend. The villagers kept them fed and clothed because if they appeared above ground during the day they would be shot like rats by the French. Unseen, they protected us like our ancestors.[7]

A Viet Cong Rural Development cadre receives a lesson in the city of Vung Tau in North Vietnam.

Our parents seemed relieved that he would not be involved in heavy fighting but would serve his country by spying on the enemy. Stealth and concealment would be his weapons. Still, he was a warrior ... and ... we had learnt that anything that had to do with the North had to do with ... suffering and dying. Everyone wanted peace, but Ho Chi Minh would settle for nothing short of victory.[8]

LE LY DISCOVERED THAT HER BROTHER HAD BECOME A LEADER OF A NORTH VIETNAMESE RECONNAISSANCE TEAM:

A French Sherman tank keeps watch for the Viet Minh as a truck convoy passes through.

The children were organized into committees to watch for informers and to run messages between the villagers and the Viet Cong in the field. The able-bodied men who were excused from duty with the guerrilla militia were organized into labour squads to dig tunnels that would allow the Viet Cong to pass into and out of the village without being seen. Families were ordered to build bunkers for their own protection and to have coffins ready, as if for the elderly, to be used for Viet Cong casualties after a fight. We received special training from the Viet Cong on what to do, and usually finished our work by oil lamps ... always listening for the sound of helicopters or the hollow "click" of rocket launchers.

The sand outside the village was easy to shovel, and we soon had a system of trenches along the roads both into and out of Ky La. On the paths used most frequently by the Republicans, the Viet Cong put cartridge traps (bullets held over a nail that discharged when you stepped on them), punji pits (spiked boards set knee-deep into the ground; when stepped on they ... sent poisoned barbs into the soldier's legs) and trip-wire grenade traps. Some fighters even filled coconuts with gunpowder and made pulling fuses for them, too. Although we knew how deadly these traps could be, we kids had no second thoughts about helping the Viet Cong make them or put them into place ... our enemy, we were assured, deserved everything bad that happened to them.[9]

LE LY RECALLED HOW THE VIET CONG ORGANIZED THE VILLAGERS TO RESIST THE SAIGON GOVERNMENT:

A deadly "punji pit" is displayed by an American GI. These nasty booby traps would be made by the VC along places where US troops patrolled.

FIGHTING THE ARVN

A VIET CONG GUERRILLA
LEADER RECALLED AN
UNSUCCESSFUL
ENGAGEMENT WITH
GOVERNMENT FORCES:

In February 1962 we attacked the Ba Tuc stronghold in Tay Ninh Province, near the Cambodian frontier. There was a complex of three posts: we destroyed 2, captured 25 guns and 20 prisoners. But we do not consider this action successful because we did not destroy the whole post and we had some casualties. But morale was high and we used this lesson to avoid future failures. Our preparations had not been as thorough as they should have been.[10]

Our men held their fire until the first line was only a few yards away and the last line was within range. Then they fired. Within seconds there were about 40 casualties, and they retreated. Between then and 07:30 hours there were three more assaults, each preceded by heavy air and artillery bombardment. In the fourth attack, the Diemists [ARVN] sent two platoons in an outflanking attack while the main force attacked in the centre again. They were all beaten back, and by that time they had taken about 100 casualties. That ended the first phase of the battle.

The second phase took place between 08:00 and 08:30 hours, and the enemy used two companies in three assaults. We used two platoons in counter-attacks, and the result was that the Diemists withdrew about half a mile behind the frontline. During this action the enemy used 15 helicopters and tried to land troops right in the centre of the battlefield. We had been expecting something like this from the beginning. Our 37mm heavy machine guns opened up, and three helicopters were shot down immediately. The rest tried

ON 1 JANUARY 1963, THE VIET CONG FORCES, LED BY "COMMANDER DUYEN", WERE DUG IN AROUND AP BAC:

to gain height and withdraw, but two more were downed as they flew over Van hamlet, just to the north. Within half an hour, assaults had been launched from the south, centre and north, and the Diemists had suffered 60 to 80 casualties. It was difficult for us to verify exactly, because they fell in the rice fields, and immediately after there was air and artillery bombardment which made our lads keep their heads down.

There was more shelling and bombing as the troops from the second attack withdrew, and then a third attack was launched with four fresh companies. One of their companies was completely wiped out. In that action we had our first casualties, one killed and two wounded. But the heavy air and artillery bombardments prevented us leaving our trenches to collect enemy weapons. After the third attack failed, Brigadier-General Van Cao, commander of the Third Army Corps, came over from Can Tho and personally took command.

There was a heavy artillery bombardment, over 200 shells fired in about 20 minutes, and then eight

Two young Viet Cong snipers search for a target in the Mekong Delta. An effective sniper could hold up a company of men for hours thanks to the terrain.

infantry companies were thrown into the central sector. The first wave advanced to within a hundred yards of our positions, fired and then withdrew. The second assault was spearheaded by the M113 tanks, the troops following on behind. We held our fire till they were about 30 or 40 yards distant, then opened up. Our special "steeled squad" moved out of the trenches with their antitank grenade launchers. Within seconds, four of the M113 tanks were ablaze and four others were damaged. All but two of our lads in the "steeled squad" sacrificed their lives in this heroic episode.

US infantry, supported by a number of M113s, advances towards the enemy. The ARVN was also equipped with American kit, including M113s.

The enemy was forced to withdraw one mile, the fourth phase ending at midday. Huynh Van Cao had done no better than Dam. Dam had lost five helicopters, and another eight had been damaged out of a total of 20, but Cao had succeeded in putting eight out of 13 amphibious tanks out of action. So the commander-in-chief of the Diemist army, Major-General Lee Van Ty, came from Saigon to assume personal command. He brought with him the 1st Airborne Battalion and reorganized all the forces that were left. At 15:00 hours, he launched the first of two major attacks from the centre and from the north, but both failed. At 17:00 hours, the battle was over.

Between the fourth and fifth phase, there was a curious incident. The Americans sent in technicians to salvage the damaged M113 tanks. We fired at them, but at the same moment their own artillery started pouring in shells. A lot of Americans were wounded, either by our fire or their own. US officer "advisors" ordered Vietnamese troops to go in and rescue them, but they refused. The Americans had to mobilize their cooks, technical personnel and others to go to the rescue of their tank repair teams. Some Diemist officers were court-martialled for this afterwards.[11]

DURING THE BATTLE FOR LOC NINH, A VIET CONG COMMANDER NOTED THAT: The Diemist troops simply refused to move forward: however, once we started firing they started getting casualties. The Americans exhorted them to advance but the troops refused to budge. Our forces slipped away during the night … leaving a few guerrillas behind as observers. The Americans did not know we had withdrawn, and early next morning opened up an artillery barrage against our positions. But they didn't try another attack; it was only a cover to pick up their wounded.[12]

VIET CONG TACTICS

LE LY HAYSLIP RECALLED THE HARSH CONDITIONS UNDER WHICH THE VIET CONG FOUGHT AND THEIR TENACITY IN BATTLE:

The VC were small, quick, and carried nothing but a weapon, some ammunition and a little dry rice. This kept them safe in battle, but it meant their day-to-day life was miserable. When they were hit, they had only herbal medicine to treat their wounds. When they were killed, their bodies were not removed, like the Republicans' were, for a decent burial at home. Usually, we peasants had to roll them up in mats and stick them in shallow graves before the authorities found them. When the Republicans caught us around a dead VC fighter, we had to act like we didn't know what was going on. We would tell the soldiers that nobody knew who the dead person was, even though his family might be standing right there, holding back their tears. We would claim the dead man was a vagabond or someone from another village. "Would you soldiers like to haul him away for us?" No, they would not. So we'd bury him, and the relatives would mourn in secret.

Unlike the Republicans, the Viet Cong fighters received no pay and their families seldom got pensions when they were killed. Wives lost husbands, parents lost sons, little kids lost fathers, and all had to pretend as if nothing had happened. The government came after the Viet Cong with boats, planes, tanks, trucks, artillery, flamethrowers and poisons, and still the Viet Cong fought back with what they had, which was mostly cleverness, courage, terror and the patience of the stones.[13]

Republican soldiers took out their frustrations on us: arresting nearby farmers and beating or shooting them on the spot, or carting anyone who looked suspicious off to jail. As these actions drove even more villagers to the Viet Cong cause, more and more of our houses were modified for Viet Cong use.

The cadremen told us that each family must have a place in which liberation troops could hide, so my father dug an underground tunnel beneath our heavy cookpot which could house half a dozen fighters … [while the children] were taught revolutionary songs … in praise of Uncle Ho – Ho Chi Minh – who, we were told, awaited news of our heroism like a kindly grandfather.[14]

LIEUTENANT LINH ANALYZED VIET CONG TACTICS IN A POST-WAR INTERVIEW:

We waited until they [the Americans] were very close. We were in our spider-hole firing positions – the Americans never saw us at all. I ordered my men to fire; one GI fell down, the others just stood around looking at him. They did not even know where the bullets had come from. We kept on shooting. Although their fellows kept falling down, they kept on advancing. Then, they called for artillery. When the first shells landed we simply went into the tunnels and went on to another place.[15]

This map shows the geography of the Mekong Delta region of Vietnam. The vast number of rivers and swamps made military operations very difficult. The delta was an area of high Viet Cong activity.

VC members under instruction. Just like the US Army, the VC also fought a battle for the hearts and minds of the South's rural population.

THIS COMMUNIQUE EXPLAINED THE TACTICS TO BE USED BY THE VIET CONG:

Male and female guerrillas and militia members! Cling to the enemy wherever he is ... using all weapons available, cut all communication lines, infiltrate deep into the enemy's rear and hit hard at his stores and airfields, tighten the noose on American posts, garrisons and military bases, snipe at him day and night. We will resolutely inflict upon the American expeditionary force – the most modern armed forces of the cruellest imperialist power – a bitter and ignominious defeat in the flaming sea of guerrilla warfare in South Vietnam.

Regional Army men! Make deep thrusts, hold on then fan out to fight and carry out other activities in enemy occupied areas, giving most effectual help to our compatriots ... in ... annihilating wicked thugs, in rising up to break the enemy's grip and win back the right to be masters of their land. Regular Army units! Deal deadly blows at American and puppet mobile troops; don't let them raise their heads![16]

THE NVA ON US TACTICS

NORTH VIETNAMESE GENERAL VAN TIEN DUNG, CHIEF OF THE NVA GENERAL STAFF, NOTED:

In operational conduct as well as in fighting, the Americans proceed from the point of view that everything is decided by firepower. They repose no confidence in the effectiveness of their infantry, which, in fact, is too faint-hearted and too weak to engage the NVA without firepower support, let alone annihilate them. They work out imposing plans but their possibilities to put them into effect are limited. Their firepower is strong when it is used from long distances, but the support which it actually gives to the infantry is also limited. Though commanding a great operational mobility in tactical and combat jobs, the US infantry usually huddles together in one place, not daring to fan out. As a result, this mobility only tires out their troops and makes their operations more costly. American planes, guns and tanks possess a big strike force, but they are greatly handicapped by the infantry (shock force), which is weak and, in some cases, even nil.

Clearly, the US ground forces cannot destroy the NVA, because their infantry has low morale, is weak and trained to fight on the battlefields with clear-cut frontlines, and their other services are incapable of great effectiveness. When fielded, American troops can form encirclement prongs rather quickly: however, as their infantry lacks combativeness, such a mobile deployment simply scatters their forces to be destroyed by chunks. In attacks, assaults and pursuits, they essentially count on the firepower of their air force and artillery, so that their "search-and-destroy" efforts prove futile. Instead, they are often intercepted and suffer heavy losses in men and material at the hands of the Liberation forces who turn up unexpectedly.

In the direction of their predatory war against a small country like Vietnam, the US imperialists are facing … insurmountable difficulties and deadlock in the political, strategic and tactical fields.[17]

New recruits to the Viet Cong photographed during a passing-out parade. The Viet Cong fought alongside the NVA during the battles in South Vietnam.

GIAP'S ASSESSMENT

With the strategic objective of completely liberating the South and completing the national-democratic revolution throughout the country, our army and people took a historic strategic decision: to launch a general offensive and uprising, a large-scale and decisive strategic battle to be waged throughout the South Vietnam battlefront aimed at wiping out and disbanding the entire puppet arm, smashing the entire puppet administration and regaining full power for the people.

THE BEST ASSESSMENT OF NORTH VIETNAM'S FINAL VICTORY CAME FROM GENERAL GIAP HIMSELF:

From our fighting experience ... we had clearly seen the limited capabilities of the US and its puppets, and these limitations were becoming more and more obvious. On the other hand, our ability to win great victories at a relatively fast tempo also became more and more evident. In view of our fundamental strong points and the enemy's fundamental weaknesses, and because the enemy could not avoid committing blunders due to their subjectivity and stubbornness, it was very likely that, in accordance with the law governing our step-by-step victory and the enemy's step-by-step defeat, a situation would arise in which the enemy would collapse very rapidly and we would win total victory in a relatively short period of time.

We made the maximum concentration of our forces with the highest determination to launch ever swifter battles, and started the historic Ho Chi Minh Campaign [on 26 April 1975] to deliver the decisive blow and conclude the war victoriously. Throughout the development of the Ho Chi Minh Campaign ... our Party closely followed the developments on the battlefield, as well as the new developments of the political situation in the country and the world. While leading the offensive and uprising we moved ahead with determination and daring, and won a complete and thorough victory.

Our strategic decision was very judicious, very revolutionary and scientific. It deeply reflected the thorough-going revolutionary spirit ... of our army and people in the protracted fight for the independence and freedom of our Fatherland.[18]

The communist forces of the North received large quantities of aid and equipment from other communist states around the world, most notably the USSR. The trucks in the photo are Russian-built and supplied.

CHAPTER 6
THE US AIR WAR IN VIETNAM 1956-1972

The Vietnam War witnessed one of the greatest uses of strategic and tactical air power in history. Air power was used both as an offensive and defensive weapon as the US attempted to halt the flow of men and material coming down the Ho Chi Minh Trail from North Vietnam. The arrival of a 68-man US Air Force (USAF) liaison team in 1956 to train and develop the fledgling South Vietnamese Air Force (VNAF) was the first element of what would be one of the largest air efforts by the US since World War II.

By early 1961, the VNAF numbered some 4000 personnel distributed among six squadrons that included: two transport squadrons flying C-47 Dakotas; two L-19 observation and liaison squadrons; one H-19 helicopter squadron; and an AD-6 (A-1H) Skyraider fighter-bomber squadron. Most of the VNAF's aircraft were obsolete, and it was short of trained pilots and technically proficient support staff.[1]

Despite this, the US Air Force advisors sent to South Vietnam in 1960–61 considered the VNAF capable of dealing with any situation it might be presented with in fighting the Viet Cong (VC). However, in an effort to illustrate the air force's commitment to the US military's new warfighting doctrine of counter-insurgency worldwide, General Curtis LeMay, the Air Force Chief of Staff, ordered the establishment of a unit within the Tactical Air Command, "to organize and equip a unit to train in WWII-type airplanes and prepare a limited number of these planes for transfer to friendly foreign governments".[2]

On 14 April, the US Air Force set up the 4400th Combat Crew Training Squadron (CCTS) at Hurlbert Field, Florida. It trained in both day and night operations; practised landings and take-offs from short, sodden airfields; low-level navigation; delivery of napalm; air-to-ground gunnery and rocketry. Initially, the 4400th CCTS squadron consisted of eight T-28Bs (trainers) acquired from the US Navy (armed with conventional bombs, rockets and, later, with AIM-9B Sidewinder heat-seeking missiles), and eight B-26 World War II light bombers from the air force reserve units, along with 16 Dakotas. By July 1961, the strength of the 4400th CCTS stood at 125 officers and 235 men.

In December 1961, the 4400th CCTS was posted to South Vietnam. From the Bien Hoa Air Base, the pilots and crews prepared to fly close air-support missions for the Army of the Republic of Vietnam (ARVN), as well as training VNAF personnel in combat flight operations to include closer air support and fighter tactics.

Meanwhile, the goal of US Air Force advisors in Vietnam was set at creating an independent air force capable of providing close air support to the ARVN, as well as dealing with any threat posed by North Vietnamese aircraft. Within a relatively short time after their arrival in South Vietnam, the advisors ascertained that they had "succeeded in converting the Vietnamese way of doing things from the French to the American".[3] Between 1962 and the beginning of 1965, the force grew from 4000 to more than 10,000 men. The six squadrons and 97 aircraft of 1962 had grown to 14 squadrons with 285 planes.[4]

Despite these Herculean efforts by the US to create virtually from scratch a modern air force, the VNAF still suffered from a lack of strong direction. At a top-level meeting at the Commander-in-Chief Pacific's headquarters in Honolulu on 1 June 1964, US State Department officials and military chiefs decided that the USAF would continue its efforts towards building the VNAF. It would provide combat support when the South Vietnamese were unable to handle the situation; and, if air attacks were necessary, would select targets near the Demilitarized Zone (DMZ) and, in concert with South Vietnamese aircraft, hit them.

Flaming Dart, Rolling Thunder

After the North Vietnamese fired on the USS *Maddox* and USS *Turner Joy* on 4 August 1964, the Joint Chiefs of Staff decided that a limited retaliation would be sufficient to demonstrate the serious consequences of continued aggressive acts by North Vietnam. On 5 August, carrier-based aircraft mounted attacks against North Vietnamese torpedo boat anchorages and oil dumps above the 17th Parallel, in a strike "that set the pattern for our future air strategy", according to General William W. Momyer, US Air Force. Momyer, who directed the air effort against Vietnam during much of the war, called this the "tit-for-tat strategy" that eventually hampered the US Air Force's ability to erode North Vietnam's will to fight.[5]

The level of attacks by the North Vietnamese increased as aircraft from the 1st Air Commando struck targets in Laos. The attacks by the 1st Air Commando,

A destroyed bridge in North Vietnam. The war in Vietnam saw one of the most determined uses of strategic air power by the USAF.

though, were "too few to significantly reduce the flow of material to the Viet Cong".[6] Major-General Joseph H. Moore, commanding officer of the 2nd Air Division (which controlled USAF operations in Vietnam between 1962 and 1966), requested the use of more force, but was turned down by the Johnson Administration.

However, after VC and North Vietnamese Army (NVA) troops attacked the US air base at Bien Hoa, destroying five bombers, the Joint Chiefs of Staff proposed a series of strikes against North Vietnam based on the "94-Target List".[7] President Johnson reluctantly decided to take action in order to convince the North Vietnamese that the US would not stand by and let South Vietnam fall to its communist northern neighbour. However, the President, Secretary of State Dean Rusk and Defense Secretary Robert S. McNamara were adamant that the primary role of air power in the Vietnam War was close air support and aerial interdiction of the lines of communication south of the 20th Parallel and in Laos. McNamara disagreed with LeMay and other senior airmen who argued for the destruction of North Vietnam's industrial base around Hanoi.

General John P. McConnell, LeMay's successor, agreed with McNamara that the primary mission of the USAF remained the support of the ARVN, but argued that a massive strategic air offensive was needed if the NVA and VC were to be defeated. The Joint Chiefs of Staff proposed a four-phased air campaign to: bomb targets on the 94-Target List; bomb below the 20th Parallel and thus interdict the flow of supplies flowing south from North Vietnam; bomb and mine the ports in the Haiphong-Hanoi area; and bomb the railroad lines between North Vietnam and China. President Johnson and Defense Secretary McNamara rejected the campaign on the grounds that it might bring the communist Chinese into the war, and that it would make little difference to US operations in South Vietnam. Attacks

were therefore limited to targets south of the 20th Parallel.

Operation Ranch Hand

Among the most controversial aspects of the air war in Vietnam was the use of chemical defoliants to strip away the jungle canopy that shielded the elusive VC and North Vietnamese. Operation Ranch Hand was the military term for spraying herbicides from modified US C-130 and C-123 aircraft. Between 1962 and 1971, 19 million gallons of herbicide were sprayed over six million acres in Southeast Asia, primarily in South Vietnam. Eleven million gallons of the total was the notorious Agent Orange, which poisoned crops and thus deprived the NVA and VC of sustenance.[8] In 1967 alone, more than 1.7 million acres were sprayed.

While there was very little foreign or domestic criticism at the time, doubts surrounding the effectiveness of the programme and the health hazards it posed to friend and foe alike began to surface in the autumn of 1969. Preliminary tests concluded that Agent Orange had caused birth defects in laboratory mice. After the release of a series of reports on Agent Orange and the birth defects it had "caused" in Southeast Asia, its use was banned. On 9 May 1970, the air force flew its last Ranch Hand operation.

Sergeant John J. Keating, who served in the US Marines during the late 1960s, was sprayed by a substance later identified as Agent Orange. He believes that it may "have led to a swollen gall bladder [later removed], a lapse in memory, diabetes and high blood pressure".[9]

Operation Ranch Hand remains one of the most controversial aspects of the Vietnam War.

One of the enduring questions of the Vietnam era was the effectiveness of the air campaign against North Vietnam. Operations Rolling Thunder (the bombing campaign that began in February 1965 and

lasted until October 1968) and Flaming Dart, as well as the naval air campaign, were limited in scope, due primarily to the Johnson Administration's desire to contain the war below the 20th Parallel. The fear of the Soviet Union or communist China intervening in the war ensured that the air campaign and its effects on North Vietnam remained limited.

This situation lasted until 1972, when a frustrated President Richard M. Nixon, in a final bid to end the war, launched a series of

A US Huey sprays chemical defoliant onto the jungle vegetation. The use of "Agent Orange" was one of the most controversial aspects of the entire war.

night. Tactical support forces such as the chaff flights [to block radar], fighter cover, 'Wild Weasel' [jamming missions] and Electronic-Counter-Measures [ECMs] comprised nearly 70 percent of the total sorties flown by tactical forces. Many of the support forces, however, delivered weapons against the enemy, and thus destroyed targets besides suppressing enemy defences for the B-52 and fighter strike forces. If the campaign had continued, more tactical forces would have returned to active strikes, for the enemy defences continued to deteriorate from the unrestricted attacks."[11]

The air war: a summary

In the final analysis, air power was decisive in ending the Vietnam War. As Linebacker II demonstrated, "the 11-day campaign came to a close on the 29th of December 1972 when the North Vietnamese responded to the potential threat of continued air attacks to the economic, political, social and military life of their country. It was apparent that air power was the decisive factor leading to the peace agreement of 15 January 1973. The concentrated application of air power produced the disruption, shock and disorganization that can be realized only by compressing the attack and striking at the heart with virtually no restraints on military targets which influence the enemy's will to fight."[12]

There is no doubt that the efforts and sacrifices of thousands of airmen, sailors, soldiers and Marine aviators during the Vietnam War contributed greatly to the lengthy US campaign. The maintenance crews and other support personnel also played an important part in mounting the US air war effort.

air offensives that eventually brought North Vietnam to the peace table (Operations Linebacker I and II). As Momyer recalled: "Linebacker I demonstrated that the US was ready to employ its air power decisively. The consequence of this employment would be the paralysis of North Vietnam's ability to feed and protect its citizens. Evidence of the strain the North Vietnamese nation was under came from a number of independent sources. Basically, the same situation had existed in the earlier campaign."[10]

Momyer asserted that, limited though Rolling Thunder was, there was evidence that the air campaign was on the verge of forcing the North Vietnamese to negotiate a settlement. The former commander of the 7th Air Force argued that had Haiphong and the other areas been bombed sooner than 1972, a peace settlement would have come more quickly. As Momyer remembered: "During the 11-day campaign, tactical forces flew 2123 sorties, of which 1082 were at night. B-52s flew 729 missions, all at

US AIR STRATEGY TAKES SHAPE

LIEUTENANT-GENERAL
LIONEL MCGARR TOLD US
DEPUTY SECRETARY OF
DEFENSE ROSWELL L.
GILPATRIC THAT:

The terrific firepower of the AD-6 [A-1H] mobile is not being capitalized upon. This stems from faulty organization, with consequently faulty decision-making of the RVNAF [Republic of Vietnam Armed Forces]. The VNAF has the capability of greatly assisting ground anti-guerrilla action by the ARVN. It can bomb, strafe, reconnoitre (both visual and photographic), carry troops, and effectively deliver CW [chemical warfare – i.e. gas] non-lethal munitions against any type of target in Vietnam. You must educate your advisors to the full and proper use of this asset.[13]

The first of these strikes, termed Flaming Dart, was conducted in February 1965 against targets above the DMZ in response to a series of attacks by the North Vietnamese and Viet Cong during that month. The enemy's February attacks on airfields, headquarters and advisory compounds throughout South Vietnam made it apparent that they were making an all-out effort to collapse the military and political structure, convinced that the US would not be able to halt their advance. Although the Flaming Dart strikes were essentially reprisals for attacks on American installations at Pleiku and Qui Nhon (and thus appeared to resemble our reprisals after the Tonkin Gulf attacks), these February raids were followed on 2 March by the first strikes of a continuing systematic air campaign termed Rolling Thunder.

Rolling Thunder was originally authorized to hit LOCs [lines of communication] in Laos and North Vietnam below the 19th Parallel, although it was understood that some targets in the Hanoi area would be released from time to time. General Curtis LeMay and his successor, General John P. McConnell (1 February 1965), and other senior airmen felt strongly that the initial conception of Rolling Thunder was too restrictive. They agreed that the LOCs below the 19th Parallel were important parts of the North Vietnamese logistical network, but the vital elements of the system were North Vietnam's

GENERAL MOMYER
RECALLED THE SEQUENCE
AND PURPOSE OF FLAMING
DART AND ROLLING
THUNDER IN THE
OVERALL AIR STRATEGY:

At Da Nang Air Base, a USAF F-100 Super Sabre returns from a successful bombing mission in the North.

ports, railroads, marshalling yards, bridges and supply centres; there were relatively few of these in the southern part of North Vietnam.

Three B-52 Stratofortresses deliver their devastating payload of 1000lb bombs onto a target 40km (25 miles) from the air base at Bien Hoa.

Furthermore, as supplies funnelled southwards, it became increasingly difficult to destroy them in large quantities because of the absence of open terrain and natural choke points. The dissemination of supplies among hundreds of jungle trails and thousands of porters guaranteed that air attacks in the south would be less efficient than attacks against the Kep Marshalling Yards, the Paul Doumer Bridge or the port of Haiphong. Thus senior airmen pressed for the expansion of Rolling Thunder into an air strategy focused upon the heart of North Vietnam.[14]

AMBASSADOR MAXWELL TAYLOR ARGUED THAT AIR POWER SHOULD BE: Designed to bolster the forces of South Vietnam and to cut the lines of communication in Laos. If attacks were to be made against North Vietnam, they should be in the DMZ [Demilitarized Zone], using US and South Vietnamese aircraft to demonstrate our joint resolve to expand the conflict if it continued in Laos and South Vietnam.[15]

HITTING THE NORTH

ADMIRAL ULYSSES SIMPSON GRANT SHARP, USN, COMMANDER-IN-CHIEF, PACIFIC, INFORMED THE JOINT CHIEFS OF STAFF ON 11 MAY 1965 THAT:

We must carefully weigh the capabilities and limitations of US air power operating within current political parameters and the vulnerabilities of [North Vietnam] within this framework. It is certain that we cannot expect interdiction, even when we attain a maximum feasible damage level, to stop completely supplies flowing to the VC through southern [North Vietnam] and Laos routes. Further, we cannot predict how successful the VC will be in procuring weapons and ammunition through other sources and channels. Although the immediate military objective is to reduce the movement of personnel and supplies to support the VC ... in our effort to accomplish this we must first develop and drive home to the [North's] leadership the idea that our staying power is greater than theirs. To do this we should raise their direct costs in terms of manpower and military, logistic and support facilities and in the indirect economic effects.

Secondly, and perhaps more importantly, the characteristics of the air campaign should be such as to generate pessimism and a feeling of helplessness among the military; and general frustration, anxiety and fear among the people. The total impact would be realized the in degradation of supervision, military training, cadre replacement and build-up for Laos and [South Vietnam], as well as in the reduction of supplies. The concept [should be to make] it as difficult and costly as possible for [the North] to support insurrection in Laos and [South Vietnam]. Its success will be realized when [North Vietnam] is convinced that the cost of aggression is too high. The concept we propose calls for a demonstration of US air power carrying out an around-the-clock programme of immobilization, attrition and harassment.[16]

Although still not satisfied with the changing strategy, other senior airmen and I believed that air power was beginning to affect the enemy's logistical system as it had in Korea. We did not believe, however, that our air power could be as effective as it had been in World War II unless we were authorized to strike the full range of interdiction targets.

The authorization to attack oil storage facilities in the closing days of June 1966 was the beginning of a new phase in the strategy of gradually increasing pressure on the North Vietnamese by attacking targets closer and closer to the vital power centre of their government. But this piecemeal application of air power was relatively ineffective because it still avoided many of the targets that were of most value to the North Vietnamese. Consequently, the message conveyed by these strikes on the oil facilities lacked the necessary ring of authority. Though harsh, the tone seemed also hesitant and uncertain to the North Vietnamese.

GENERAL MOMYER RECALLED THAT BY 1966 THE AIR CAMPAIGN WAS HAVING AN EFFECT:

Throughout the remainder of 1966, additional targets above the 20th Parallel were released one by one. Although the frequency of the strikes and the size of the striking forces were still very closely controlled in Washington, some change in strategy was becoming evident; and it was expected by most commanders from [Admiral] Sharp on down that it was only a matter of time until the most important targets would be released.[17]

Three young North Vietnamese women practise antiaircraft drills with their rifles. Such tactics were ineffective against high-altitude bombers.

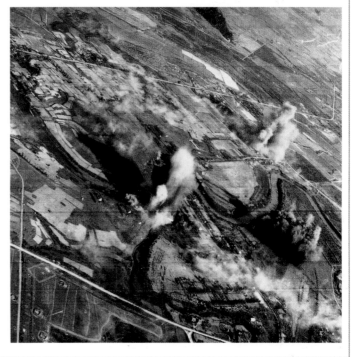

The B-52 Stratofortress is capable of carrying 31,500kg (70,000lb) of mixed ordnance, including "dumb" bombs, smart bombs, mines and missiles.

Insisted that air and naval power had to be employed more aggressively against North Vietnam if the war were to be ended soon. Since becoming CINCPAC [Commander-in-Chief, Pacific], Sharp had often advocated attacking targets near Hanoi and mining the Haiphong Harbour. Although Admiral Sharp believed vigorous action was needed ... to contain the North Vietnamese, he felt the full use of air power against all suitable military targets [in] North Vietnam, Laos and Cambodia should be the basis of our strategy. Lacking any evidence of North Vietnamese willingness to negotiate a settlement, the Joint Chiefs supported Sharp in his proposals for an expanded ground war.[18]

GENERAL MOMYER ADDED THAT ADMIRAL SHARP:

A USAF F-105 Thunderchief attacks the Xuan Mai Army barracks in North Vietnam. This is the view from the air as the F-105's 750lb bombs hit their targets.

SKYRAIDER PILOT

MAJOR THEODORE J. SHORACK, USAF, WROTE TO HIS FAMILY SHORTLY BEFORE BEING KILLED IN MID-1966:

Flew on first mission today – actually was riding right seat with one of the old-timers. There is a big rice bowl area about 40 miles northeast of Bien Hoa that extends for about 20 miles by 10 miles. It's getting close to harvest time and the ARVN and US Army are trying to protect the area so the farmers can harvest the rice and put it into normal market channels, instead of having 90 percent of it confiscated by the VC, as it has been in the past several years.

So far, it's been pretty quiet – little contact with the VC. We CAPed [Combat Air Patrol] for two-and-a-half hours, standing by in case the army should make contact and need help. Nothing developed so a spotter plane directed us in against an area in the jungle where he thought some VC might be hiding. We dive-bombed and napalmed along a strip. There seemed to be two small secondary (in addition to the bombs) explosions so we might have hit something. This operation could develop into something yet, since it will be a couple of weeks before the rice is harvested. If it does ... you'll read about it. The mission I mentioned in the other letter did not materialize. The NVA apparently did cross over but have been hiding.

Just a short note – I have to go on to night alert in about 45 min for a "Snipe Hunt". This is a special deal we run each night – have a couple A-1s standing by while the army runs around the delta with a Mohawk which carries side-looking radar.

> The VC are deathly afraid of aerial bombing: the big bombs really bother them

They check around the waterway with this gear. If they catch anything moving we scramble and go strike it with rockets. Haven't flown one yet but it sounds ... interesting. Will go out and set up one aircraft at 22:30 hours, then stand by until 00:30 hours, if nothing comes up by then we turn in. Beautiful moonlit night tonight – nice night for flying. Because it is so bright out, the VC will probably be very cautious.

Was on a mission this morning over the Michelin rubber plantation. No activity there today, though yesterday Ed King and another pilot killed a bunch of VC when the army flushed them. Ed said that he could see them running around in the brush, which is unusual. Our FAC spotted a bunch of people on a bicycle riding around the plantation. We made a couple of low passes to see if we could draw fire. They either rode nonchalantly along or stopped and waved at us. Maybe they were shaking their fists! We expended ordnance on some trails in the woods where the army would be travelling throughout the afternoon. Oh yes, the first couple of hours we patrolled the area where the army was extracting troops by helicopter. If there are VC in the area the aircraft overhead seem to discourage them from attacking unless they have a real good reason for it.

Interrogation of captured and defecting VC indicated that they are deathly afraid of aerial bombing – not so much strafing but the big bombs ... really bother them.[19]

A US ground crew attaches a fresh weapons package to an A-1 Skyraider. The A-1 was used in ground-attack and FAC (forward air controller) roles.

Despite its relative age and technological inferiority compared to the jets, the A-1 Skyraider was a remarkable success in Vietnam. Able to take a lot of punishment and carry a large payload, "Sandy" was a firm favourite.

MAJOR SHORACK DESCRIBED AN AIR OPERATION ON THE EDGE OF THE RICE BOWL NEAR THE MICHELIN PLANTATION:

There was an operation on the edge of the Rice Bowl last night and we flew two sorties up there in support of the 10th ARVN Division. We definitely got some VC last night. Hit 'em with about 10 airplanes under the cover of night, and then hit 'em again as they tried to evacuate their wounded. Ground troops reported that they could hear an awful lot of crying, groaning and calls for help out in front of them. Won't be a body count probably for a day or two yet. The fact ... that impresses me most is that I'd sure hate like hell to be a VC. The air control communication is now efficient enough that whenever they start something ... air power is on them.[20]

The only apprehension you feel is when you roll in on a target from which you know they are firing at you. Then you make yourself as small as possible and crouch in the cockpit behind the engine and the armour glass in the front panel of the windshield. Dive-bombing isn't bad – 'cause you stay high – napalming you come down low and feel rather exposed as you grind on by at about 100 feet altitude. Napalm is jellied gasoline that we drop on the VC to burn them. It's nasty stuff but they are nasty and this is war.

MAJOR SHORACK DESCRIBED WHAT IT WAS LIKE TO FLY AN A-1 SKYRAIDER:

Was on alert for 24 hours ending this AM at 07:00 hours. Tomorrow morning will be on a mission just this side of the Cambodian border, where it is suspected they store goodies that come down the Ho Chi Minh Trail. Should be an interesting target – one you can see, at least, but must be real careful not to get into Cambodian airspace. Too bad the rules of the game don't allow us to cut 'em off in Cambodia.

Had a real interesting mission this afternoon. Not because it was particularly good, but because it was rather hairy. We followed the FAC up a river valley where the clouds closed down on the tops of the mountains on both sides. The margin between the outcroppings and the cloud bases was pretty slim. You had to dodge around ridges and knobs and level bomb in a narrow pocket in the edge of the valley, about as much a hazard from your own bombs as from people on the ground. However, if they have a 50-calibre down there, with you trapped against a low ceiling and hampered in manoeuvrability by the "mountings", you can really get the devil shot out of you. We went in, circled in the tight little pocket, dropped our bombs, heaved a big sigh of relief, and got the hell out of there.[21]

117

RETRIEVING DOWNED AIRMEN

COLONEL DARRELL D. WHITCOMB, USAF, A CARGO PILOT, DESCRIBED THE RESCUE OF THE CREW FROM A STRICKEN EB-66 IN SPRING 1972:

At approximately 15:15 hours on 6 April, US Air Force Captain Fred Boli took off from the American air base at Da Nang in a prop-driven Douglas A-1 Skyraider fighter-bomber (known as a "Sandy"). With Boli, whose call sign was Sandy 01, were three other A-1s, Sandys 02, 05 and 06, and two Sikorsky HH-53 rescue helicopters (known as "Jolly Greens"), Jolly Greens 67 and 60. A few minutes later two more Jolly Greens, led by Captain Mark Schibler, took off as back-ups.

Colonel Hambleton and Lieutenant Clark, EB-66 survivors, had now been on the ground four days and needed to be resupplied. Therefore, one A-1 (Boli's) was rigged to drop him a Madden resupply kit with food, water, ammunition and extra radios. A rescue attempt could also be made if Boli, the Sandy leader, felt the situation warranted it. It would be Boli's last call.

Boli noticed a friendly tank position approximately six kilometres south of the survivors, and decided to make the final holding point for the helicopters right over them. At 16:15 hours, Boli directed the two FACs [on station] to terminate the air strikes so that he could overfly the survivor's immediate area. He ... tried to drop the Madden supply kit to Hambleton, but the arming wire on the device failed and the kit did not release from the aircraft. Boli did not know that, however, until he landed back at Da Nang. Boli also strafed a few suspected NVA locations with his 20mm cannons, and had Sandy 02 drop several cluster bombs on the other areas, widening his area of search as he did so. Boli directed the FACs to hit several areas with more air strikes. While all of that was going on, Boli ordered Jolly Green 60 to hold southeast of Quang Tri, and ordered Jolly Green 67 and Sandys 05 and 06 to proceed to the final holding point.

As the aircraft were repositioning, Captain Boli began his final briefing for all the participants in the rescue attempt. They would first try to extract Clark. The two would be picked up either by Jolly Green 67 or one of the other choppers. But the briefing was rudely interrupted by a SAM [surface-to-air missile] call, which forced all of the aircraft to dive for the deck to avoid the missiles.

Boli directed the task force to execute the pickup. Sandy 02 immediately laid down his marks for the helicopters to follow to Hambleton. Sandy 03 put down his smoke screen. Sandys 02, 05 and 06 began the "daisy chain" to protect the vulnerable helicopter and began dropping cluster bombs and strafing with their 20mm cannons. A slight wind shift caused some of the smoke screen partly to obscure Hambleton's position. But the confusion was quickly resolved, and the force pressed on.

As Jolly Green 67 crossed the river near Cam Lo, the helicopter began to take ground fire from all quarters. Seconds later, as it approached to within 100 metres of Hambleton, Boli called for the survivor to pop his red smoke so that the Jolly Green crew could locate him. Almost simultaneously, someone on Jolly Green 67 called, "I'm hit". Hambleton heard ... this on his survivor's radio and, realizing the gravity of the situation, did not pop his smoke and reveal his position. The crew of Jolly Green 67 fought to control their damaged aircraft. Boli had briefed the helicopter crew that if they began taking ground fire, they

A US Army OH-6 Cayuse helicopter takes off from Da Nang Air Base. These aircraft were often used in FAC roles during search and rescue (SAR) missions.

A US Army Huey is supported by an A-1 Skyraider. In a SAR mission, the A-1s would provide support for the vulnerable helicopters picking up downed pilots.

were immediately to exit the area on a southeast heading. Realizing their desperate situation, the crew began to turn their craft to escape the cauldron of withering fire ... Jolly Green lay on its side, a heap of burning, smoking wreckage. It would continue to burn and smoke for several days, with intermittent explosions of the ordnance on board. The fire would become so hot that some of the metal would melt into the ground. There were no survivors, and there would be no search-and-rescue attempt. Instead, the names of six more Americans – Chapman, Call, Prater, Pearson, Avery and Alley – were added to the mounting bill for Hambleton. Back at Da Nang, the men of the rescue forces were stunned by the tragic loss of Jolly Green 67 and its crew.

In their hiding places near Cam Lo, the two survivors had been witnesses to Jolly Green's downing. Lieutenant Clark later recalled that there had been so much firing going on that he could not distinguish who was firing at whom. But as the Jolly Green passed over him heading south, he could tell that it was not gaining altitude. When he heard it crash, Clark was devastated. His immediate thought was: "I really cocked this up. Six more guys dying because I f——d up." And then the realization set in that he was not going to be picked up that day. Clark felt desperately lonely. Colonel Hambleton ... cried for the six brave men who had lost their lives lost trying to save his own.

Although he was tired, hungry and demoralized, the 53-year-old navigator resolved then and there, "Hell, I'm going to get out of this regardless". Hambleton and Clark did get out. But not by helicopter. No more of the vulnerable choppers would be sent in. Instead, a small ground team was dispatched, commanded by US Marine Lt. Col. Andy Anderson and led by Navy SEAL Lieutenant Tom Norris. Within a week, the team would infiltrate behind enemy lines to rescue the downed flyers. It was a risky and dangerous mission, but it got done. The two lucky fliers returned home as heroes.

Nothing could be done, however, for the brave crew of Jolly Green 67. They were lost forever, part of the larger cost of the war. It would be 22 years before their remains would be found and returned to the United States.[22]

119

CARRIER AIRCRAFT

SEAMAN DENNIS BARR, USN, SERVED AS AN E-4 MECHANIC OR ASSISTANT PLANE CAPTAIN ABOARD THE AIRCRAFT CARRIER USS *AMERICA*:

I'm an E-4, an assistant plane captain on an A-7C Corsair attack aircraft of squadron VA-86, the "Sidewinders", one of six squadrons in the *America*'s embarked air wings. We're on a Westpac [West Pacific] cruise which will keep us away from our home base at Norfolk, Virginia, for five months. It is September 1972 and the *America* is involved in the Linebacker bombing campaign against North Vietnam. My job is straightforward. I'm to assist Petty Officer Engels, crew chief for A-7C Corsair number 156799, in getting the plane ready for launch and recovering it after the mission. The pilot of our plane is Lieutenant J.G. Murphy. He'll be number two in a two-plane diversion hurtling aloft after dark to search for "Wiblicks". That's a WBLC or Waterborne Logistics Craft. Much of the war is being fought by daylight against targets deep in the enemy's homeland, but the *America* is a round-the-clock operation and it's important to harry the boats infiltrating supplies into South Vietnam.

I feel a keen sense of personal responsibility, knowing that the pilot's life may depend on how well I keep the Corsair flying. We check everything – control surfaces, cockpit, instruments, air intake ... you name it. It's as if 799 is being scrutinized under a microscope. This plane's gripe sheet indicates a persistent problem with the electrical system, so I get an electrician who checks it over and pronounces it okay. At 03:00 hours, as Lieutenant Murphy is being briefed, we review the bomb load of six 600lb Mark 81 bombs hung under the wing. I perform a walk-around check of airplane 156799, looking for a sign that anything might be wrong.[23]

Unsung heroes. Leaving the glory to the pilots, the ground crews who kept US aircraft in the skies were a vital cog in the American war machine. Here, a crewman onboard an aircraft carrier refuels his plane.

ROUTINE MAINTENANCE

GARY DOSS WAS A HELICOPTER PILOT AT PHU BAI ON 14 SEPTEMBER 1967:

After breakfast, it was a trip to the armoury to check out the M60s and a couple of cans of belted 7.62 ammo. Then it was off to the flight line to prepare the old helicopter for another flight.

A US sailor enjoys the view as the sun sets in the Gulf of Tonkin. All ground crews felt a profound sense of personal responsibility to the pilots and aircraft in their charge, and worked hard to keep them both in the air.

The first light was just enough to see the old bird sitting chocked behind the double-stacked row of 55-gallon, sand-filled drums called the revetment. Her dark green skin had a low sheen, she was clean inside and out and ready to fly. The early light of dawn carried enough light to allow the pilots to do their visual walk-around. Sometimes it was a kick of the tyres and light the fire look. Sometimes it was a more detailed inspection. It didn't matter: the old bird was always in top shape. Fuel tanks were topped off, fluids serviced, rotor head and tail rotor full of grease and wiped down. This was all routine maintenance after each flight. If we were to go down, it would not be caused by a preventable mechanical problem.

The pilots climbed up to the cockpit, slid back the windows and crawled into their seats and buckled in. With a flip of the battery switch, the instrument panel came to life and the artificial horizon globe slowly rolled into the straight and level position. The checklist was read and the instruments were in order. On signal, the powerful starter was engaged and whined loudly as the massive pistons deep inside the engine began to rotate. The crew chief stood fire guard by the exhaust stack as the pilot turned the "Mag" switch, closed the auxiliary air door on the huge air intake on the carburettor and pushed the throttle to idle. The engine belched smoke, caught hold, seemingly only on five or six cylinders, then all were engaged and she quickly reached idle speed.[24]

COBRA GUNSHIP

MIKE AUSTIN (196TH LIB 1971-72) AND DON DUNNINGTON (101ST AIRBORNE 1969-70) BOTH FLEW THE FORMIDABLE AH-1G HUEY COBRA:

The AH-1G Huey Cobra was the world's first helicopter engineered to be a true gunship, and every effort had been made to create a fast and stable weapons platform. With a top speed of 190 knots (230mph) in a dive, it was nearly twice as fast as the Huey. Also, it possessed a system of electronic flight stabilizers, called SCAS for Stability Control Augmentation System, which dampened out wind gusts and turbulence much better than the Huey's mechanical stabilizers.

Considered in its design was the fact that a gunship had to dive directly towards its target, which was just as likely shooting back. Even though the aircraft was almost 45 feet long and over 13 feet tall, the fuselage was barely three feet wide, providing an extremely narrow profile when viewed straight on, thus making it a difficult target to hit. Its greatest vulnerability was immediately after breaking from the diving rocket run, when the unprotected sides and belly were exposed, a fact that Charlie-Model and Mike-Model Huey gunpilots, with their door gunners to cover the break, liked to point out. Regardless of its few shortcomings, the newer Cobra had almost universally replaced these famous gunships in Vietnam. For sheer firepower, no chopper could match the Snake.

The types of rockets were mixed as well between high-explosive, white phosphorus and flechettes, each having its own special purpose. High-explosive, HE, was the most commonly used, especially when shooting at a fixed target such as a hooch or bunker. White phosphorus, WP or "Willy Pete", was used to start fires with its white-hot chemical reaction, impervious even to water. Willy Pete was also handy to mark targets and landing zones with the prodigious white smoke its explosion produced.

The strangest, and probably most fearsome, was the flechette rocket or "nail". Strictly designed to be used against troops caught out in the open or when firing at a general position such as "the treeline at nine o'clock", each warhead contained 2200 steel nails with fins stamped on one end, resembling tiny darts. After the solid-fuel motor propelled the rocket to supersonic speed in less than two seconds, the warhead exploded a few hundred feet above the terrain, leaving a red dye cloud to mark the release point. From there, the nails would drop at a steeper angle because of their resistance to the wind. The shower then

struck the ground in an elliptical pattern ... the size of a football field. The pilot used the puffs of dye to adjust the firing angle indirectly since he rarely could see any signs of impact.

While conducting the mission, Cav[alry] gunships followed two basic rules: maintain constant visual contact with the scout loach and always be in position to cover him with fire. Compared to loaches, gunships had it easy. Protected to a certain extent by altitude, we enjoyed an even greater advantage in being easily recognized. The enemy knew us as an arsenal of death that required their respect. They had to be desperate to take us on in a direct confrontation, although they wouldn't hesitate if cornered. The low and slow scout, on the other hand, was a tempting target, even though they knew a diving Cobra would result from any threat to the loach.[25]

The Vietnam War witnessed the birth of a dedicated attack helicopter. The AH-1 Cobra, developed from the UH-1 Huey gunship, was a phenomenal success.

THE THUD

SURFACE-TO-AIR MISSILES (SAMS) WERE A CONSTANT THREAT TO US AIRCRAFT, AS F-105 PILOT G.I. BASEL RECOUNTED:

The Isle of Madeline was far behind. I was seeing North Vietnam from a lower altitude than ever before, and I didn't like it. Without a heavy bomb-load, carrying just Shrikes [antiradar missiles], we were able to get a lot more speed from the planes.

A formation of F-105 Thunderchiefs drop their bomb loads over a target in North Vietnam. The "Thud" was used for 75 percent of strike missions in Vietnam.

High above us and far to the rear, the force was turning inbound for Bak Giang. They were above the cloud layer and unable to see the ground.

"Roger, Bear Lead. Otter's got you covered."

On the instrument panel in front of me, a large red warning light suddenly flashed. At the same instant, a loud squeal filled my headset. I flinched. The word "Launch!" screamed in the middle of the light. A SAM was up!

"Valid Launch! Valid Launch, Bear! Take it down!"

Bob had already turned towards the missile site. We started down to build more speed while Bob sent the second element up to fire. "Otter Three, get him!"

"Rodge, three's up to fire!"

Down we went, turning left. I could hear Dale Leatham, "Bear! Hard left turn, take it down!"

The big armada of airplanes manoeuvred in controlled alarm, diving towards the clouds and turning hard left; knowing a blazing missile would soon burst from the clouds below and seek one of the struggling airplanes. It was escape time. Bob and I were swinging around to the right and down to the deck, then back left to head towards the active SAM. I was all hands and elbows trying to keep in formation. Vapour streamers poured from Bob's wing-tips as we pulled around to the left. No sooner had we lined up on the telltale strobe of hostile radar, than we began a hard pull straight up. Streamers again.

"Ready, Otter Two?"

"Ready!" My Shrike had been ready for many minutes, gibbering and squeaking in my headset at the random signals in the air. It now began to squall anxiously at me as it sensed the strong radar beam from the enemy site. "Set me free! Let me go! Want eat!" I was pulling hard on the stick, following Bob upwards in a steep climb. We punched through the layer of clouds together. The sense of speed was startling.

"Otter Two; Fire Now!" My thumb punched the button. The missile left the wing with a swoosh, freed at last to seek and gobble radar food.

"G.I., it's after you! Take it down, fast!" The second and third missiles had been launched on ... me! Bob's use of my name instead of the call-sign was really unnerving, implying total disaster.

I was still hanging there, rotating in slow motion ... when the missile exploded. Our Shrikes had ... knocked out the site ... saving my ass.[26]

An NVA SA-2 surface-to-air missile (SAM) is prepared by communist troops. SAMs accounted for the loss of 196 US aircraft during the war.

HITTING THE TRAIL

Slightly after midnight, I am sitting in the cockpit of my airplane. It is a jet fighter, a Phantom, and it's a good airplane. We don't actually get into the thing, we put it on. I am attached to my craft by two hoses, three wires, lap belt, shoulder harness and two calf garters to keep my legs from flailing about in a high-speed bailout. The gear I wear – gun, G-suit, survival vest, parachute harness, is bulky, uncomfortable – and means life or death.

I start the engines, check the myriad systems, electronic, radar, engine, fire control, navigation, all systems; receive certain information from the control tower, and am ready to taxi.

Throttles forward and outboard, gauges OK, afterburners ignite, nose wheel steering, rudder effective, line speed, rotation speed. We are off, leaving behind only a ripping, tearing, gut noise as we split into the low black overcast, afterburner glow not even visible any more.

Steadily we climb, turning a few degrees, easing stick forward some, trimming, climbing, climbing, then suddenly, on top! Soon I make radio contact with another craft, a big one, a gunship, painted black and flying very low. His guns flick and flash, scream and moan, long amber tongues lick the ground, the trail, the trucks. I am there to keep enemy guns off him and to help him kill trucks. Funny, he can see the trucks but not the guns 'til they're on him. I cannot see the trucks but pick the guns up as soon as the first rounds flash out on the muzzles.

MAJOR MARK E. BERENT FLEW WITH THE 8TH TFW "WOLF PACK", TARGETING THE HO CHI MINH TRAIL USED BY NORTH VIETNAM TO INFILTRATE TROOPS AND SUPPLIES:

Sometimes when I drop, pass after pass, great fire balls will roll and boil upwards; and a large, rather rectangular fire will let us know we've hit another supply truck. Then we will probe with firepower all around that truck to find if there are more. Often we will touch off several, their fires outlining the trail or truck park.

Many times garden-hose streams of cherry balls will arc and curve up, seeming to float so slowly towards me. Those are from the smaller-calibre, rapid-fire quads; and then the big stuff opens up, clip after clip of 37mm and 57mm follow the garden-hose, which is trying to pinpoint me like a search light. Good fire discipline – no one shoots except on command.

But my lights are out, and I'm moving, jinking. The master fire controller down there tries to find me by sound. His rising shells burst harmlessly around me. The heavier stuff in clips of five and seven rounds goes off way behind.

Soon I have no more ammunition. We, the gunship and I, gravely thank each other, and I pull up to thirty or so thousand feet, turn my navigation lights back on, and start across the Laos border to my home base. In spite of an air-conditioning system working hard enough to cool a five-room house, I'm sweating. I'm tired. My neck is sore.[27]

A USAF F-4 Phantom. This formidable aircraft was used extensively in Vietnam, in both fighter and ground-attack roles, including along the Ho Chi Minh Trail.

SPECTRE IN THE NIGHT SKY

Take a four-engine cargo plane off the shelf, bolt half-a-dozen cannons to the deck pointing ominously out the left side, put in some sensors to see in the dark, add a gunsight for the pilot and a computer to help him with the ballistics, and you have the ingredients of an airborne gunship.

The hunt was on. Charlie would be well advised to lay low and wait until this Spectre returned to its nest. But Charlie had other ideas.

"Charlie, Charlie, Charlie," drawled a sensor operator in a deep southern brogue! The first truck was sighted in the sophisticated cat eyes of the gunship.

"He's going down the road into some trees."

The other sensors slewed around to peer at the truck racing for cover.

The deadly C-130 "Spectre" gunship wrought havoc on the communist forces trying to smuggle supplies along the Ho Chi Minh Trail.

"Hell! He's stopped in the trees," the voice groaned. "I see him again. Okay, let's shoot him right there."

The forties [40mm] began their deadly work. Circling overhead, the gunship sought satisfaction. Crash after thunderous crash as the big shells were launched into the jungle.

"Triple A at 12 o'clock," announced the right scanner who was leaning out of the airplane into the slipstream looking at the first red balls of 37mm antiaircraft shells coming up.

LIEUTENANT-COLONEL JAMES F. HUMPHRIES FLEW AC-130 SPECTRE GUNSHIPS AGAINST THE HO CHI MINH TRAIL:

"Four o'clock underneath. No threat," called another scanner lying on his stomach leaning out over the edge of the cargo ramp looking straight down into the black void below. Charlie was going to fight back.

In this sector, the enemy gunners had earned the reputation of being "nine levels", the best in the game. The first rounds sped by harmlessly, lighting up the sky high above with quick, bright flashes as they were detonated by their fuses. Minutes raced by as the gunship orbited the abandoned truck, whose driver by now was probably on top of the nearest hill.

"Seven rounds underneath. Roll out, pilot!" the unseen voice warned excitedly. "Whew, that was a bit close!" Charlie was firing in anger.

Back into the orbit and more broadsides from the big guns. A burst of flame signalled a hit on the trapped supply truck.

"You got him! He's burning!" cheered the southern voice. "Big fire!"

"Let's safe the guns and go home," called the pilot. Hours in the target area had passed quickly. But suddenly everyone felt the weight of the heavy flak helmets and the dull pain of ears long pressed under sweaty earphones, the eye strain of trying to see electronic blobs as trucks, and the weariness of feeding heavy ammunition into the hungry guns.[28]

125

PURE TORTURE

CAPTURED IN NORTH VIETNAM IN JANUARY 1968, THOMAS MOE WAS RELEASED IN 1973. HE RETIRED FROM THE US AIR FORCE IN 1995:

I was hiding under a log. Doing my best to masquerade as North Vietnam terrain, I'd pulled branches on top of me, smeared mud on my face, and arranged leaves and other foliage to stick out of my clothes. I was 20 miles behind enemy lines, having parachuted out of my F-4C fighter aircraft when a weapon malfunction blew it, along with my wingman, to bits.

I was eventually betrayed by a small hole in my camouflage through which I poked my radio antenna. Within seconds a zillion rifles were pointed straight at my head. Thus began a month-long, 100-mile journey to the "Hanoi Hilton" to begin my five years as a prisoner of war [POW] – where I would get to know pain on a personal basis.

North Vietnamese policy was that POWs were war criminals, a policy that supposedly justified brutal treatment and total control. That control was reflected by a list of regulations posted in each cell. Rule number one was the catch-all: "Criminals will strictly follow all regulations or be severely punished". The scenario was quite simple. An interrogator would tell you to do something, like give out military information. When, predictably, you would refuse, you were told you had violated the regulations and had to be punished. The word "punish" still evokes in me a slight feeling of nausea

A ceremony held in a POW camp celebrating the release of SSG Gregory on 30 May 1969. Of the known 766 US POWs, 116 were killed while in communist captivity.

since it meant, at the very least, beatings that would last several days and nights. Punishment ultimately meant torture. Torture is methodically applied pain to produce a wearing effect – to make you submit. Usually the pain would reach a level just short of stopping vital functions, although it could continue even after one lost consciousness. Its preliminary stages could start with something as simple as being sat on a stool, dressed in long pajamas (in summer) or just shorts (in the winter). The summer jungle air was suffocating; the damp, cold winter air was penetrating. After a while, you became a lump of huddled misery, sitting in the heat or biting cold. During a single session I sat on a stool in the same position 24 hours a day for 10 straight days.

What I was not prepared for were the effects of solitary confinement. For the first nine months of my captivity, and sporadically later, I didn't see, hear or talk to another American. Although physical pain was inflicted on me deliberately and effectively, I would discover what an incredible burden mental pain would add to my suffering, how a dark fog slowly could creep over my consciousness, trying to rob me of my remaining power of reasoning. I saw that the mind could convince life itself to slip away through the beckoning black hole that pain created. I learnt how vital it was to keep the mind as sharp as possible.

This was necessary to get through interrogations and also for survival. If you didn't keep your mind clear, the "V", as we called the North Vietnamese, would crush you through a steady dose of pain that eroded mind and body like a vicious chemical.

The body is first to give up. You cannot keep yourself from passing out, throwing up, screaming. I discovered that the more the body convulsed involuntarily, the more I could observe it as though it belonged to someone else. I found I could intellectualize pain, which allowed me to take a quantum leap in my tolerance of it. Sometimes, though, the problem was staying in touch with reality enough to keep alive. Detaching oneself too much has an insidious narcotic effect that invades one's reason and dulls normal danger signals. This is probably the way nature helps us die without being all tensed up.

Things started with long sessions of standing immobile around the clock; next I was put on my knees for three, four, six hours at a time. This went on for days. It was the first phase, sort of a limbering-up session to wear me out and take the edge off my powers of reasoning. Then I was told to write a war-crimes confession, saying I was sorry I'd participated in the war. When I refused, I got to serve as a stress reliever for about 20 guards – each took his turn beating me to a pulp. They pounded me for six or eight hours. By then I was getting pretty shaky. Then they got serious. I was introduced to a bowl of water, some filthy rags and a steel rod. The guards stuffed a rag in my mouth with the rod, then, after putting another rag over my face, they slowly poured the water on it until all I was breathing was water vapour. I could feel my lungs going tight with fluid and felt like I was drowning. I thrashed in panic as darkness took over. As I passed out, thinking I was dying, I remember thanking God that we had made a stand against this kind of society.

> The pain got to the point where I truly wanted to die

At dawn two Vietnamese officers casually strolled in. I told them they might kill me, but I still wasn't interested in their propaganda. They laughed and calmly said: "It's easy to die but hard to live, and we'll show you just how hard it is to live." Indeed, the pain got to the point where I truly wanted to die. My prayers became desperate gasps. The only solution was to stop living, but ... you can't will your heart to stop beating.

Anyone trained in such affairs knows that constant torture can make captives reach a point where they can't maintain mental equilibrium; and my captors knew it, too. They could break me, and I was becoming frantic, fearing my strength would not last.

Then, they stopped. Some weeks had gone by, and perhaps they had other business. Maybe they figured I might not make it. Although they had murdered prisoners, I believe most of my colleagues who died were accidentally tortured to death. The North Vietnamese knew they could not win the war militarily, but they might succeed if they garnered world sympathy. It would be difficult for them to look good if too many POWs "died in captivity". But I came pretty close, as did many of my mates.[29]

B-52 bomb damage. The NVA took little pity on captured US airmen, using torture as a means of revenge for the attacks against the North.

CHAPTER 7
THE TET OFFENSIVE AND THE WAR ALONG THE DMZ
1967-1970

Even as US troops fought the elusive Viet Cong (VC) and North Vietnamese Army (NVA) in what was essentially a holding action, General Westmoreland and Lieutenant-General Lewis W. Walt prepared to take the war to the enemy along the Demilitarized Zone (DMZ) and in the Central Highlands. In combat operations that surpassed those of French General Henri Navarre's so-called "meat grinder tactics", Westmoreland planned to utilize his air and naval assets in support of ground troops in order to defeat decisively the VC and NVA. For the average infantryman, 1967 would be a year of hard fighting in the most decisive year of the Vietnam War. It was during this period that General Vo Nguyen Giap's forces suffered greatly at the hands of US, ARVN and allied troops.

A more mobile strategy

As recalled, 1967 was the year that US, South Vietnamese and Free World forces took the offensive. From mid-1966 to early 1967, "additional troops and other available resources enabled the scope and pace of our offensive operations to increase steadily. During this period, US strength increased from 385,000 to 486,000. The number of manoeuvre battalions available rose from 256 to 278. By year's end, 28 tactical fighter squadrons were on hand to provide close air support and assist in the interdiction campaign. More than 3000 helicopters of all types were organized into 107 units, up from 68 units the previous year. The number of B-52 sorties increased sharply from 725 to 1200."[1]

Westmoreland added that, with these larger forces, added firepower and improved mobility, "we carried the battle to the enemy on a sustained basis throughout the year. Concurrently, we planned to intensify and expand the pacification effort. The Joint Vietnamese-US Combined Campaign Plan for 1967 assigned to the Vietnamese armed forces the primary role in pacification and specified the priority areas for their employment. The same plan provided that US combat forces would carry the bulk of the offensive effort against VC and North Vietnamese main force units."[2]

The general told newspaper editors that US, South Vietnamese and Free World forces had to fight a multi-front war in Vietnam "simultaneously":

"At one and the same time, we must fight the enemy, protect the people, and help them build a nation in the pattern of their choice. The real objective of the war is the people. If the enemy could take Saigon, or the heavily populated areas of the Delta ... the war would be over without negotiation or conference. The enemy lost his chance two years ago, and I can promise you that his military tactics alone will not win him another opportunity. Yet despite his staggering combat losses, he clings to the belief that he will defeat us. And, through a clever combination of psychological and political warfare, he has gained support which gives him hope that he can win politically that which he cannot accomplish by force of arms."[3]

Westmoreland further outlined his views in a speech before a joint session of the US Congress, where he told the congressmen and senators: "The only strategy that can defeat such an organization is one of unrelenting but discriminating military,

political and psychological pressure on his whole structure at all levels".[4]

As 1967 unfolded, US, South Vietnamese and Free World forces combined efforts to deliver the VC and NVA forces a major setback. The year saw soldiers, sailors, Marines and airmen combine efforts in a massive threefold campaign that dealt Giap's strategy an enormous blow.

The first objective in Westmoreland's strategy was to attack and destroy Giap's base of operations. Both Operation Cedar Falls (8–26 January 1967) and Operation Junction City (22 February–14 May 1967) were search-and-destroy missions aimed at clearing the area north of Saigon known as the Iron Triangle.[5] In Operation Cedar Falls, soldiers from the US Army's 1st Infantry Division, 25th Division, 173rd Airborne Brigade, 11th Cavalry Regiment and ARVN units conducted a 19-day operation that killed 720 enemy and led to the capture of an additional 213. In addition, the operation yielded enemy foodstuffs, a massive interlocking tunnel system and documents that were an intelligence bonanza.

Operation Cedar Falls was followed by Operation Junction City, conducted over three months starting on 22 February. This operation was conducted by some 22 US and 4 ARVN battalions. It killed 2728 VC and NVA troops. As in Cedar Falls, allied soldiers also captured huge stores of enemy supplies. The most decisive and bloodiest battle was fought by the 1st Battalion, 26th

A dead VC soldier lies in the grounds of the US Embassy in Saigon. During the Tet Offensive of 1968, VC soldiers breached the embassy's defences, getting into the building in several places.

Infantry Regiment, over a two-day period near the end of the campaign.

The fighting around Ap Gu grew more intense as the VC refused to let up. This required the calling in of air strikes. In fact, this battle was not the usual 10-minute firefight typical of so many Vietnam confrontations, as it became apparent that the US troops were up against a major enemy force.

The intensity of Ap Gu, one of the largest single ground actions prior to the 1968 Tet Offensive, can be seen in the casualty figures. While the 26th Infantry suffered 9 killed and 32 wounded, and the soldiers from the 16th Infantry suffered 17 killed and 102 wounded, the VC and NVA suffered a confirmed figure of 609 killed and 5 captured. In an action where they were outnumbered almost six to one, the 26th Infantry and soldiers from the 1st Battalions, 2nd and 16th Infantry Regiments, inflicted casualties at a rate far in excess of their own dead and wounded.

Marines at war along the DMZ

In the northern part of I Corps Tactical Zone, Westmoreland noted in his final report that his objective was "to meet and defeat the North Vietnam invasion through the DMZ and Laos; to interdict the enemy's infiltration route in South Vietnam; and to neutralize his base areas near the coastal plain. Equally important in the southern portion of the corps zone was the protection of our base area and the lines of communication. Having largely denied to the enemy the rice-producing coastal regions of II Corps and much of Quang Nam Province of the I Corps in 1966, we intended to link those areas and expand our control into Quang Ngai and Quang Tin Provinces."[6]

Starting in June 1967, First Force Reconnaissance employed seven-man mobile strike teams that operated well to the rear of the VC and North Vietnamese, with the express purpose of calling in artillery and

THE TET OFFENSIVE

During the Tet Offensive of 1968, NVA and VC divisions assaulted South Vietnamese positions along the entire length and breadth of the country. Many of the major towns and cities, including Saigon, came under heavy attack.

air strikes against these areas. In 1968, the high point of the Stingray programme saw Marine reconnaissance teams conduct a series of 101 patrols and launch 369 artillery and 39 air strikes that killed 275 confirmed enemy troops. Regular Marine infantry teams assigned to Stingray missions had a kill ratio of 7.6 enemy to 1 friendly. Marine reconnaissance teams killed 34 enemy soldiers to 1 casualty of their own.[7]

By the end of 1967, it was becoming clear to the North Vietnamese leaders and the VC that victory against the US would be impossible if they continued with their existing strategy. The North Vietnamese were aware also that a continuation of the losses they were suffering could not be sustained. However, the North Vietnamese

had triumphed once before against a superior enemy, and so they turned to the history books and the lessons of Dien Bien Phu. Giap had masterminded the defeat of the French and, once again, the North Vietnamese needed a Dien Bien Phu to drive the latest enemy from the battlefield. The leaders in Hanoi knew this strategy would be risky, but they had reason to be hopeful.

They were aware of the growing discontent in the US for the war. They considered that a massive military defeat in an election year, with thousands of US casualties, would present US leaders with two choices – either risk fighting on but at a cost that the US people were unwilling to pay, or go to the negotiating table. The biggest problem facing the NVA and VC

Troops of the US 9th Infantry Division conduct a house-to-house search as they pick their way through the ruins of a town south of the Kinh Doi Canal.

strategists was how to prepare the number of troops needed for such a campaign without alerting the US and provoking US bombing. The NVA and VC again turned to the history books for their master plan. In 1789, Tay Son Montagnards had completely surprised and overwhelmed Chinese forces in Hanoi by attacking during the sacred holiday of Tet, the lunar new year. The VC had already negotiated a truce for Tet, and by waving the carrot of agreeing to hold talks if the US stopped bombing, the VC and NVA had set their trap and moved into position.

The campaign got off to a premature start on 30 January 1968, and the main thrust commenced on the 31st. A combined force of 84,000 VC and NVA troops began the assault on towns, cities, bases and other key positions throughout the South. The US Embassy in Saigon was attacked along with 40 other major cities and 23 bases, including Hue, Quang Tri City, Da Nang and Khe Sanh. This last place was to be under siege by

NVA forces for some 11 weeks, and was the scene of some of the bloodiest battles of the war. With determination and courage the South Vietnamese and US forces held, eventually retaking all of the captured cities at a cost of 3500 dead and 16,000 wounded. The Tet Offensive was undoubtedly a turning point in the war. Despite the fact that it was a military failure for the North (VC and NVA casualties amounted to more than 45,000 dead and 7000 taken prisoner), Hanoi gained the most from it. Despite the best efforts of the troops, it was political shenanigans in the US that made the Tet Offensive politically as well as militarily significant. The negotiations that began following Tet laid the foundations for the eventual US withdrawal, and the subsequent North Vietnamese victory in 1975.

The one group of fighting men that saw more close-in action than most were the army medics and navy corpsmen. As often occurred in Vietnam, many medics and

corpsmen performed their life-saving skills under enemy fire. Beside the corpsmen and doctors were the army, navy and air force nurses. Often just out of nursing school, these women worked in the wards day and night near the frontlines. Their bravery and dedication saved Marines, soldiers and airmen. For every 100 Marines wounded in action, 44 were treated and returned to duty. Of those admitted to hospitals, only nine would remain in Vietnam, while the rest would be evacuated to stateside naval hospitals. Only 1.5 percent of Marines wounded died as a result of their injuries.

The extensive use of the "medevac", short for medical evacuation, saved many lives. The 1st Marine Aircraft Wing in 1967–68, for example, alone conducted 57,216 medical evacuations.

OPERATION CEDAR FALLS

THE 1ST BATTALION'S COMMANDING OFFICER, LIEUTENANT-COLONEL ALEXANDER M. HAIG, JR., RECOUNTED HIS MISSION OBJECTIVE:

To find the Viet Cong headquarters, thought to be located near the bend in the Cambodian border Americans called the Fishook. Here, in the virtually roadless country west of An Loc and north of Highway 13, we were tasked to engage the VC and NVA regulars protecting it. That is the military way of saying we were the bait with which the command hoped to entice an enemy force many times our size to come out of the jungle and attack us, so that it could be destroyed in the open by American firepower.[8]

We went out and set up an NDP [night defensive position] near the village of Ap Gu ... [That night] on my watch, radio communications were intense with many positions reporting movement out in the jungle, including the guys in my platoon. I was very nervous, and it was easy to stay awake. When my shift was up I awakened one of the RTOs [radio telephone operators] to take over, and told him that all our positions were reporting movement and to be careful. I had just laid down to sleep when I remembered something I had neglected to tell the RTO. I went back to the radio, and the RTO had already gone back to sleep! I awoke him again and said: "Stay awake!" Something is gonna happen tonight."[9]

PRIVATE FIRST CLASS CLIFF ROBERTSON, MEDIC WITH THE 1ST BN., 2ND INFANTRY, RECALLED NIGHT ONE AT LZ GEORGE:

PRIVATE FIRST CLASS WOOD, 1ST BN., 26TH INFANTRY, LOST A FRIEND TO ENEMY FIRE:

We had travelled 80 metres and I had just lost sight of the point when the enemy opened fire. I stopped counting, hit the ground and tried to get my bearings. There wasn't a lot of firing; a few bursts of automatic weapons and machine guns. It was intermittent. I knew that Peterson [Private First Class William R.] was hit when [Squad Leader Sergeant Pete] Landtroop and [Private First Class Doris E.] Hand crawled back to me. Pete had been cut down by the initial burst, and Landtroop later told me that he had killed the trigger man. At the time it didn't register with me that my best friend had just been killed ... I fired at the enemy, not knowing if I got any.[10]

Fires rage as napalm is dropped onto this VC position. US troops would call in air strikes right onto their own positions if the enemy was close and in great numbers.

A CH-47 Chinook lands in the field 20km (12.5 miles) west of An Loc during Operation Cedar Falls. The CH-47 has a cargo capacity of 9091kg (20,000lb).

My two mortar tubes were still firing rounds as rapidly as possible when the radio brought a desperate plea from a recon platoon member: "Add two-five and fire for effect! Don't stop! Keep 'em coming. Six [radio call sign for Lieutenant Hill] is down ... we've got wounded ... it must be a whole company of the little bastards ... we need help."

SPECIALIST FOURTH CLASS (SPEC-4) ALBERT "BUTCH" GEARING, WHO HAD BEEN THE ACTING PLATOON LEADER OF BRAVO COMPANY'S 81MM MORTAR SECTION, RECALLED THAT:

The manoeuvre platoon of B Company, returning from a sweep of the defensive area, were closing on the battalion's perimeter when Captain Hansen was informed of the situation ... he swung his company to the north and proceeded to the assistance of the embattled platoon. With only two mortar tubes in operation, Hansen directed that all personnel not involved with the supporting fires of the weapons platoon provide additional firepower to the rifle platoons in their rescue mission.

Before I had a chance to ask for volunteers, PFCs Joe Stowers, John Day, Gary Harshbarger and Specialist Four Mike Raudenbush grabbed their weapons and gear. When contact was broken we had suffered two casualties: PFC Stowers had been killed in action, and SP4 Raudenbush severely wounded.[11]

THE INTENSE FIGHTING LASTED WELL INTO THE LATE AFTERNOON WITH NO LET-UP. PRIVATE FIRST CLASS WOOD RECALLED:

Our magazines were filled with tracers and ball rounds in a ratio of one tracer to four balls. Because the jungle growth was so dry, a fire started from the tracers ... I used the olive drab towel I carried around my neck to stamp out the flames. It finally burned up. Next I used my recon hat, a soft cowboy-style with one side flipped up ... I don't recall if its [fire] was before or after Bravo Company arrived or not, but it was clear that we were pinned down ... Somehow I was able to move away and get to a safer position.[12]

We knew we were in for a fight when the jets came in for their first strafing run and drew heavy machine-gun fire from the VC. The heavy volume of fire directed at the jets indicated not only that they were well-dug [in] well-fortified positions, but also that the unit was a large force due to the fact that it was equipped with heavy machine guns.[13]

PRIVATE FIRST CLASS LAMPMAN, A RIFLEMAN WITH THE 2ND PLATOON, BRAVO COMPANY, RECALLED THEREAFTER:

ENDLESS COMBAT

COLONEL PATRICK J. BLESSING, COMPANY COMMANDER WITH THE 3RD MARINES, RECALLED THE HEAVY FIGHTING IN AND AROUND HILLS 881 NORTH AND 881 SOUTH IN APRIL 1967:

Commanding a company [approximately 90 Marines] with three new lieutenants, moving fairly slowly into a threatening area with intelligence reporting NVA regulars in the vicinity, we moved cautiously through the area. I got a message from Battalion that we weren't moving fast enough. I responded that we were moving as fast as could be expected commensurate with the threat and I didn't want to get myself into an ambush. I was with the lead platoon, near the valley, near a river about 200 metres from my position. I stopped, and told my platoon to wait, while my left platoon, commanded by Lieutenant John Fuller, along with Staff Sergeant Charlie Webb, checked out the river bed. Told them not to go themselves but to take a squad.

They advanced while I got on the radio with the battalion commander, and suddenly gunfire erupted. One of the radio operators began yelling, "They're killing the lieutenant", not realizing that the lieutenant went with them. We started getting overhead machine-gun fire from the NVA. Then we began getting hit with white phosphorus ["Willy Pete"], and became pinned down in the valley. Right then, I began calling in both air and artillery to extricate us from the ambush. Calling for fire for effect, the artillery barrage began firing, lobbing a war-high total of 1700 rounds. Just then, an AO [air officer] came in over the net and said, "You are in a world of shit, there are NVA coming in behind you", and the AO departed, but then the air arrived and did a wonderful job. They napalmed the hills and you could hear the NVA screaming from the results of the air strikes. We couldn't get a medevac because they were still mortaring us. We received periodic air but it had no effect on the mortars. Artillery (105mm) gradually eliminated the mortaring.

Two M113s of the 11th Cavalry wait to advance against the enemy during Operation Quyet Thang.

We received six to eight CAS [close air support] missions; supporting arms really saved us. We continued to move out and got hit again, we sprung their ambush, and this is where air really helped. Artillery was slow that day, so I got on the international air net and began yelling "HELP!". Some pilot from VMFA-323 said: "I don't have much fuel but if you could mark the target I'll hit whatever is out there." So I popped smoke and the pilot came in and said: "Isn't that too close [to your position]?" "No," I said, "just dump everything you have on them."

Flying single-seat jets, they did a splendid job. If you needed air, and Marine air was nearby, they helped: even ... if they were flying another mission, they came to lend assistance.[14]

Bringing up the big guns! An M107 self-propelled gun with its crew. This massive artillery weapon could fire a 175mm shell over 32km (20 miles).

An A-1 Skyraider screams away after having dropped a napalm bomb onto an enemy position. The "Sandy" was a very effective ground-attack aircraft.

MARINE MAJOR RICHARD D. JACKSON, COMMANDING M COMPANY, 3RD BN., 4TH MARINES, 3RD MARINE DIVISION, NOTED THAT BATTLES:

were never conclusive. We located the enemy, engaged them in battle, finally they would retreat and we would chase them up to the DMZ, where they would retreat to North Vietnam. Our units returned to base; and, later, while on patrol or a sweep, we would engage the enemy, often the same enemy all over again. Win, lose, or draw, the battles seesawed back and forth, just like that, for years in this northern sector. No one really owned the terrain. Both the NVA and the Marines moved through it regularly, engaging each other and moving on. All this was followed up with frequent artillery and rocket-shelling from the NVA, their rounds dropping on our set-piece bases (fixed in position). The Marines shelled at will throughout the zone with harassment and interdiction fire, whenever and wherever enemy troops were spotted. Unfortunately, our firepower produced uncertain or undefined results much of the time.[15]

The longer the battles raged back and forth inconclusively, the more resources we committed and the more the enemy threw into the fray. The situation would continue to worsen as it escalated, even with the construction of the so-called McNamara Wall. The McNamara Wall was an invisible boundary about 15 miles long, parallelling the DMZ on the southern side. It was composed of electronic sensors planted in the ground to detect enemy troop movement through the zone. It was supported by a series of combat bases that could provide artillery and troop support to meet the threat of the NVA movement through the DMZ. This electronic wall was installed after I left this area, but, again, I believe history reflects that the results were given mixed reviews.[16]

AS CONTACT WITH THE NVA INCREASED, SO DID THE FEROCITY OF THE BATTLES. MAJOR JACKSON AGAIN:

RECONS AND STINGRAY

USMC CAPTAIN WEST RECALLED A TYPICAL FORCE RECONNAISSANCE TEAM MISSION:

Get into the bush, find the enemy and destroy him if you can. For two days we moved through the thick undergrowth, staying well-hidden, occasionally hearing the enemy chopping wood or shouting back and forth, once at mid-evening seeing lanterns bobbing down a valley floor. By the third morning we knew where their battalion bivouac area was, and called in artillery fire. To escape, the North Vietnamese had to cross a wide stream: first, a few crossed, then dozens, then scores. That was where the artillery caught and annihilated them. Chased by an NVA platoon, we left the scene at top speed. Jet fighters were scrambled and they missed the pursuit force. Following the debrief, General Walt and his G-3, Colonel John C. Chaisson, Jr., decided that such missions merited a special section in the reporting system, and chose ... the operational codename of "Stingray".[17]

MARINE MAJOR D.A. COLBY NOTED THAT, AS EARLY AS 1966:

The traditional recon role has changed ... and is indeed still changing. As we have learnt the devastating effect we can have on enemy units by taking a more aggressive role, we have moved in this direction. Whole operations resulting in appreciable destruction of enemy forces have been executed by recon. Every recon element still moves clandestinely, still observes and reports enemy activity, but is now also on the look-out for a supporting arms target. When we find it, we hit it.[18]

Captain West added that the change in the use of Marine Reconnaissance teams was significant, in that the VC and NVA were no longer the "hunters but now the hunted", and that in adopting guerrilla tactics, the Stingray teams were "becoming guerrillas in the enemy's rear".[19]

Members of a US Navy SEAL team observe the shoreline from onboard a riverine craft. SEAL teams performed dozens of successful long-range recon missions.

THE US ARMY WAS TO BE TRAINED AT NHA TRANG TO DUPLICATE THE SUCCESS OF THE STINGRAY LONG-RANGE RECONNAISSANCE TEAMS. CAPTAIN WEST DESCRIBED THE STRATEGY:

Whether the enemy is carrying on a daily routine or simply resting, he feels safe and secure in his own rear area. He then becomes the hunted by the silent teams. Like the VC, the strike teams will try to refuse contact when they don't like the situation. The size and condition of the teams makes pursuit of them fruitless and dangerous. Seven men can squirm through brush that will stop a company; in other situations, they back off into the night. For the enemy to plunge unplanned into pursuit has invited hasty ambushes and Claymore mines with delay fuses.[20]

A trooper from the US 5th Special Forces Group, accompanied by an ARVN Ranger, searches through a ricefield at My Phuc Tay following a VC attack.

OPERATION ALLENBROOK

IN OPERATION ALLENBROOK, WHERE US MARINES FOUGHT MANY NVA TROOPS, CORPORAL DEMKO RECALLED THAT:

The 2nd Battalion, 7th Marines, was built on standard tables of organization for a Marine rifle battalion, whereby each Marine company had three rifle platoons and a weapons platoon. Each weapons company had a squad of machine guns, 60mm mortars and a team of rocket launchers. Each squad had 14 Marines, and each fire team had four Marines. For the first two days [4–5 May 1968], Operation Allenbrook was boring. We had no contact with the enemy. Shortly thereafter, however, we were hit by a sizeable force of NVA regulars in what turned out later to be a regimental-sized force who were dug in and waiting for us before hitting us. They were dug into rice paddies and hedgerows. In the operation, Fox Company really took it on the cheek. We suffered the loss of 22 KIAs [killed in action] in this particular operation.

During Allenbrook, we ran into some VC during this battle who were chained to their weapons and the surrounding trees. This was because the NVA feared that the VC would run, as they were used to hit-and-run, while the NVA wanted to take us on – but on their terms. As for the ARVN, they were by and large not really good fighters. They did have some good units such as their Marines, paratroops and Rangers but, in general, I didn't have any respect for the ARVN as a fighting force.

As for when we were in the field, there was a lot of camaraderie among the Marines. There was a lot of unit cohesiveness as we all looked after each other, particularly the short-timers. After Allenbrook we participated in a "blocking operation" off Go Noi Island, after which we went to our "float phase" aboard the USS *Valley Forge* and landed on occasion along the coast in operations. The highlight of the operation was when the North Koreans seized the USS *Pueblo* in international waters. That was the first time we were ever issued live ammunition outside of landing in South Vietnam. While part of the floating battalion, we participated in a number of operations, as we were air assaulted onto land to help Marine units that found themselves in trouble. We were on a float phase [part of the US Navy's Special Landing Force] for about two months. We made a lot of enemy contact and took a lot of casualties. We went back to "Liberty Bridge" before being relieved by "Lima" Company, 26th

US infantry attack a VC position at Long Binh with the support of M113 armoured personnel carriers (APCs). APCs could provide heavy fire support with their machine guns as the troops advanced to contact.

US Marines photographed prior to taking part in Operation Allenbrook in May 1968. The Marines had a poor opinion of the ARVN.

Marines, who came in to take over Hill 22 while we took over Hill 10. We did participate in Operation Mameluke Thrust [18 May–23 October 1968], on Hill 502, looking for bunkers and a bunker complex. We had very light contact with the enemy, which was a welcome change!

As for a decrease in activity after Tet, every operation we went on had the old salts comparing the contact with Hue City, and when we would get into a firefight they would say, "You ain't seen nothing if you weren't in Tet". This changed after Operation Meade River in the "Dodge City" area, near the Go Noi area. Every time we went into that area, we suffered heavy casualties because of the heavy bunker and cave complexes and the elevated railroad grading and trestle. It was a tough operation; if you hit them before and hadn't made contact, you were in trouble. Once you got to the trestle and hadn't made contact, you were in trouble. One time, we were a blocking force, the first time I had been moved from mortars to machine guns, the first time in Vietnam I had done a regular machine-gun operation whereby the gun group is in place in what is called a machine-gun hole. We got hit by tear gas by the VC and NVA. We had more people hit from secondary fire rather than primary fire [small arms and mortars].

The VC were good fighters from the time I arrived till the time I left. In one operation, Operation Oklahoma Hills [31 March–29 May 1969], we found out that we were going up against NVA regulars and we dreaded it with a sense of foreboding, knowing all too well that it was going to be a real fight. They [the NVA and VC] had been at it for 20 some years. They were more resigned to their fate and thus fought to the death. Unlike us, who were there for a year, they were there for the duration. As for fire support, during Operation Allenbrook we went in "Cans and Vans" ["amtracs" or LVTP-5s and M48 tanks]. We also went in with the 106 recoilless rifles mounted on "Mules", and the six-barrelled 106mm Ontos, which were extremely accurate. We also had the USS *New Jersey* dropping shells that would destroy everything within sight. As for close air support, Marine pilots always put in right where you told them to put their rounds. Primarily close air support came from F-4 Phantoms that would come "screaming in" on target, dropping bombs and napalm.[21]

The spectacular effect of a napalm bomb exploding. Utterly deadly when used properly, this controversial weapon was effective but attracted criticism for the levels of non-combatant casualties it caused.

MEDICS UNDER FIRE

KNOCKED OUT BY A
GRENADE, CORPSMAN
BILLIE D. HOLMES STILL
MANAGED TO CRAWL
FORWARD TO TREAT A
WOUNDED MARINE. A
COMRADE RECALLED:

They [the enemy] were within 20 feet. Suddenly there were grenades all over. Then people started hollering. It seemed everyone got hit at the same time.

Corpsman Billie Holmes, who ignored his own wounds, supervised the other corpsmen from another Marine rifle company as they administered to the wounded leathernecks. With the firefight still going on to the front, helicopter evacuation was not possible from within the perimeter. Holmes roved back and forth, making sure that all his buddies were accounted for and taken out.[23]

We made another combat assault with choppers. We moved up a very wide trail. You could almost drive a jeep through it. We started up the trail 30 minutes maybe when they hit us with machine guns, AK-47s, RPGs. The trees were so large that it stopped most of the shrapnel. A few mild wounds. 2nd Platoon made a sweep up the left side. They [the NVA] hit us again. 1st Platoon made a sweep. I looked to my right and saw two new guys with their backs against a tree. These two said they would never drink or smoke. But both were trying to light up cigarettes while they shook. The NVA were gone again

PRIVATE FIRST CLASS
KENNETH W. MAAG
RECALLED A "SWEEP" IN
THE 4TH DIVISION'S
AREA WHEN THE CRY FOR
A MEDIC WENT OUT:

after the sweep. We made it to the top of the hill and set up a night observation post. We had a meeting at the command post. The company commander told us an NVA base camp was less than a "klick" [kilometre] away, and we were going to assault it in the morning and to make peace with your god tonight.

The next morning we moved quickly down the trail and then spread out and stopped. We could see bunkers and approached [them]. The NVA opened fire. We opened fire [and] for a moment everybody stopped firing, they were hollering "MEDIC!". The platoon leader said, "Go, Doc, we'll cover you". I went forward. They [the NVA] fired. We fired. When I got to the front they said the lead platoon medic had taken the wounded back to my left. I was next to an M60 machine gunner and he was running out of ammo. I was in between some guys from his platoon [and] threw some belts of "60" ammo. I grabbed them and gave them to the guy helping him. They called in artillery no more than 50 feet in front of us.

After the barrage everything was quiet. We made it to the top of the hill where the bunkers were. We looked around. There was a soldier with no helmet just staring at me, two guys from his platoon grabbed his arms. He was dazed. They had shot his helmet off and rung his bell. That night we set up a night observation point on a hill right across from another company with a ravine between us. The next day, on 16 August 1970, I was wounded.[24]

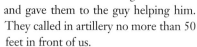

A number of emergency evacuation UH-1 Hueys are parked up waiting for the call to action. Medical personnel often saw as much action as frontline troops.

THE BEGINNING OF TET

At Qui Nhon, a depot blazes after it was attacked by VC mortars. VC sappers and mortar troops would harass US bases frequently, occasionally causing massive damage.

Me and another guy [Woodhead] were pulling security for Newport Depot just outside the gate. It started out as an ordinary night of making sure the right people got into the depot and went to the right place. We were sitting in our jeep watching some small-arms fire in the distance. I remember Woodhead commented on how crazy it was to be sitting here and watching the war go on two or three miles away. It's strange how we all could become so numbed to it. Nothing unusual, or so it seemed.

All of a sudden rockets started landing inside the depot, and the small-arms fire wasn't in the distance any more – it was just about on top of us. I felt myself go into that familiar automatic "do what you have to do" numb rush.

There was a bunker about 50 yards off to one side. I grabbed my M60 and Woodhead got the radio and we headed for it. I can still remember how long it seemed to get to safety. It was like everything was in slow motion. Just as we hit the bunker all hell broke loose. There were about eight of us in there and scared as shit as we heard the mortars and rockets continuing to land. This went on for hours. Our radio was no longer working so we had no contact with the outside at all.

I just had to get a good look at what was happening. So like a fool I got out of the bunker just far enough to see the closest thing I've seen to a vision of Hell. The sky was lit up like daytime and everywhere were dead VC. This lasted until dawn; it had to be at least eight hours we were in this "box" just waiting for the direct hit that never came. It's strange, but I can still see the eyes of the other guys in that bunker like it was yesterday. Something died in all of us that night. Our innocence.[25]

JOHN LARSON'S STORY IS NOT ABOUT GALLANTRY OR COURAGE. IT'S ABOUT THE DEATH OF INNOCENCE:

TET JOURNAL

The lights came on and I blinked. I was running down the aisle in the Triage when I heard my name being called softly. It was from a man over in the corner. I can't say it was a man, its shape was not that of a man.

"Jen, Jen," he softly called to me. I went over to him, not able to understand how anyone here might be able to recognize me. He was very young, but had no legs. His right arm was gone. His right eye was merely a bloody socket. The right side of his face seemed to have melted. He seemed filthy until I saw that he had been burned almost past recognition. He had taken direct machine-gun fire, which had severed his legs and possibly his arm. A bullet had set off the Willie Pete [a white phosphorous grenade] that had been attached to his web gear. There was obviously nothing I could do for him: he would surely die.

"Jen," he whispered again. "It's me, Jen." I looked more closely and still could not think who he might be. "I came up on the holiday to see you," he said. "Some holiday. Where's your guitar?"

There was a boot where his right arm should have been and it had a dogtag fastened to the laces. Reading the dogtag, I was struck dumb. It was Peter, my friend Mary's brother with whom I had spent so many balmy summer evenings singing songs on their front porch. Oh God.

He reached out with his left hand, charred as it was, and grasped my hand. His voice was as soft as I'd remembered it, not betraying pain at all, but serene.

JEANETTE WOLFE, A NURSE WITH THE 71ST EVAC IN PLEIKU, HAD A GUT-WRENCHING EXPERIENCE DURING THE START OF THE TET OFFENSIVE:

"Jen," he said. "It's me, Peter. Come closer, there's something I want you to do for me." As I came closer he lifted his left hand and touched my face. "God, you are so beautiful," he said, "but you're a mess. Look at all that blood on you. Are they treating you okay?" I told him I was fine, that he should rest.

"I'm going to rest soon," he said, "but first there's something I want you to do for me." I nodded, feeling as though we were isolated in a corner of the world where nobody else could possibly go. All the noises receded into the far distance and it was just Peter and me. "I'm in terrible pain," he said. "Please, Jen, give me some morphine and end it for me." How could he ask this of me? How could I bring myself to do it, even though I knew he was in pain beyond telling? His eye pleaded with me. How could I not?

"Peter," I said, "I'm right here and I won't leave you until it's time." He smiled with half his mouth. I unhitched my rubber tourniquet that I use for starting IVs and wrapped it around his left arm. It was hard to find a vein; he probably had almost no blood pressure. I was pushing in the first syrette of MS when he spoke again.

"God bless you, Jen," he said. "Please write to Mother and Mary as soon as you can. Tell them you were with me at the end. It will make them feel better to know I wasn't alone. Don't let them know how it was, Jen, they'd only grieve more. It's best they don't know."

His muscles were relaxing as I pushed the second syrette and he began to pray. I repeated the Lord's Prayer with him as I kept pushing the morphine. I could barely see, tears slipping down my face. His voice tapered off at "Forgive us our trespasses", and I finished the prayer without him as I pushed the fourth styrette into his arm and he was gone, a peaceful look on his charred face. He's only 18, I kept thinking. He shouldn't be dying.

Women also saw action in Vietnam. The nurses who got caught up in the fighting showed great bravery and courage in difficult circumstances.

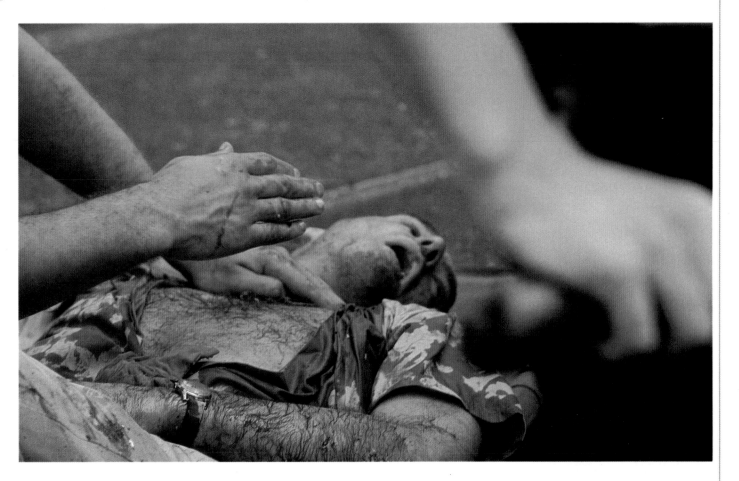

I felt so empty, just destitute. I wanted to hold him in my arms and rock him and cry until there were no more tears, but there wasn't time. People were yelling at me and I needed to get back to work. I reached for the tourniquet and when I pulled it off most of the skin on his arm came with it. I'm trying not to remember this, but I have a feeling it will haunt me clear into Heaven, should I be worthy to get there. What am I going to tell Mary and her family? God forgive me.

A badly wounded US soldier receives treatment from a medic. The absence of his uniform suggests he was off-duty when the attack took place.

Dear Ann, Dave, Mary and Family,

I know that by now you must have already received the horrible news that Peter is gone. I've no idea how the Army does these things or how long it will be until you receive his body, but I know of the magnitude of your grief.

I was with Peter when he passed on. He was very badly wounded when he came up here to visit with me for the Tet ceasefire and the fighting broke out. I'd had no idea he was coming, but just yesterday got Mary's letter telling me he was planning to come. He was brought to my EVAC when he was wounded and I took care of him. We did the very best we could for him, but his wounds were too serious.

He was not in pain and we prayed together at the end. He wanted me to write to you to ease your minds. I know this is very difficult. I mourn his loss along with you.

He was extremely brave, I want you to know that. He went to the Father peacefully, and I was right beside him. His last words were of his hope for your peace of mind and comfort, that he loves you very much and he wanted you to know he is now in Heaven.

My thoughts and prayers are with you and your family.[26]

PINNED DOWN AT KHE SANH

On the flight we learnt that we were on the way to an ominous place called Khe Sanh, an infamous on-going battle that had become the obsession of LBJ, the Brass and the worldwide media. The actions of the North Vietnamese Army had convinced the generals that this battle could be the major turning point in the war and that we must win it at all costs, (which include sacrificing my a--!). The NVA were pounding a Marine combat base located in a mountainous region at the extreme northwestern corner of the country. This was the Ho Chi Minh Trail's entry to South Vietnam and the main route that they used to infiltrate troops and supplies. The ensuing battle had become one of the fiercest of the war so the 1st Cav was sent in.

An aerial view of the US base at Khe Sanh. Situated right on the border with the North, it was beseiged for 77 days during the Tet Offensive with 6000 Marines inside.

It finally started with a vengeance about two hours later as the rockets came at us in pairs. They had perfected their aim during the day because more were now landing within our perimeter wire – within feet of our small bunker! They kept coming – pair after pair, "walking" up and down through the LZ. We could hear the screams outside as someone got torn apart by the hot metal. "Medic! Medic! My leg is gone! Medic, help me!" I desperately wanted to go out and help but I couldn't disengage myself from my helmet. The fear, the unmitigated terror, of being the target for those six-foot flying bombs propels your mind to the brink of insanity. Every time one came over we all would coil into as small a foetal position as possible and attempt to get inside our helmets. The perpetual panic of imminent death or dismemberment puts you into an out-of-body experience just to hold on to some sort of sanity. I actually felt that I was a few feet above myself watching as the explosions ripped jagged hot steel into the sandbags over my head. They kept missing but they kept coming. My body was jammed into the corner of the hole where the slide-way opened out to the night sky, and I could see the fire trail of the rockets as they kept missing us over and over again.

"Holy sh--! Here come two more!" crackled the radio, and the night turned orange with a deafening roar. The old adage is true. We never heard it coming! Suddenly the world exploded and the hole collapsed around us, half burying me in now useless sandbags and jagged steel. I was stunned and deafened by the blast. It was strange to be able to feel noise but not to be able to hear it. Sounds came back slowly and were distant, like the noises in a dream – but this was no dream! "My balls! My balls!", came a scream faintly heard somewhere behind me. "They shot off my balls!" yelled Neuy, who had also been in line with the open door

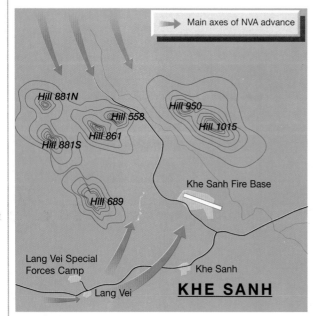

This map shows the main thrusts of NVA units as they assaulted Khe Sanh. Complete US aerial superiority over the area meant these attacks resulted in failure.

slide behind Tony. I lit a flashlight and, pushing the debris aside, crawled over to his side. There was blood gushing out between his legs and from his fingers as he covered the wound, screaming about his manhood. Someone tore open a gauze patch and tied it in the area as we tried to make him as comfortable as possible while the rockets kept pounding and pounding. I helped to push up our sandbag roof a bit so we could look at everyone else, and swung the flashlight around to count heads. It was then that I saw Tony. He was sitting blankly in the spot that I had vacated just 30 seconds before, blood oozing from every orifice on his head. He was bent over forward and on his side at the bottom of the slide, and I pushed my way over to him yelling "Tony! Tony!", and touched his arm. He moved lethargically, looking up at me with a quizzical

We yelled for the medics, but they weren't moving either

expression. "What happened? I can't hear anything," he said. The blood was dripping from his ears and I knew that the explosion and the flying shrapnel must have blown out both his drums. I pulled him back over to "my" side of the hole and away from the door slide to protect us both from the next rocket which skimmed over our heads with the now all too familiar roar. Neuy was moaning, and I could tell he was about to go into shock from loss of blood. Everyone else in the unit seemed to be OK, but we could not move to get him any help while the tempest roared outside. The radar had been blown off the air, and there was nothing to do but climb into our helmets and hopefully survive the night. We yelled for medics, but they weren't moving either.[27]

US Marines at Khe Sanh look on as a USAF F-4 Phantom makes a close air support strike on an NVA position just beyond the base's perimeter.

HOT LEAD AT KHE SANH

FIRST LIEUTENANT BRUCE M. GEIGER, 1ST BATTALION, 44TH ARTILLERY, 108TH ARTILLERY GROUP, RECALLED THE INTENSITY OF ENEMY FIRE:

I was a platoon leader responsible for up to eight "Dusters" – M42A1 self-propelled light tank (M41 Walker Bulldog) with a twin 40mm antiaircraft gun system mounted in an open turret. Each "Duster" was manned by a crew of four to six men including the driver, and fired 40mm point-detonating explosive rounds up to 4000 metres at a rate of 240 rounds per minute. This was devastating firepower used against enemy personnel and hard targets.

Our mission at Khe Sanh was to defend the northern perimeter (blue sector), which ran parallel to the airstrip (approx. three quarters of a mile), and was manned by one company of Marines (C 1/26), one Marine "Ontos" crew and ourselves. Other duties included direct fire support for Marine infantry operations, minesweep, supply and tactical convoy escort along contested highways to break up ambushes, and defensive perimeter security at forward fire bases throughout "Leatherneck Square" along the DMZ.

When the siege began on 21 January 1968, the Marines were ill-prepared for a static defence of the base, and engineers hurriedly began to dig trenches and lay additional rows of concertina wire around the perimeter. Trenching machines were flown in to cut into the rock-hard surface before the attacks reached a peak in late January through mid-March 1968. Bad weather in February and early March often left the combat base shrouded in fog for hours or even days at a time. With the fog providing cover from NVA snipers and artillery spotters, we seized the opportunity to drive the Quad 50 trucks or the Dusters for water, ammunition and C-rations.

I remember moving cautiously through the trenchline one clear morning when a careless young Marine stood up and walked across an open stretch of ground between unconnected trenches. In an instant he was struck in the side of his face by a sniper round. Fortunately the round went through his cheek and out of his mouth, knocking out a few teeth, but otherwise leaving him in a relatively good condition. The incident reinforced my resolve to crawl when moving across open ground in clear weather.

NVA gunners had the airstrip zeroed in, and few fixed-wing aircraft were able to land without being hit or destroyed. My bunker was only a few yards off the edge of the runway, and every landing and take-off was a nerve-wracking adventure. One quiet morning, I had my 35mm camera in hand as a C-130 Hercules landed and rolled towards the turnaround ramp at the west end of the runway. As I watched in horror, incoming rounds slammed into the runway and apparently struck the C-130's left main landing gear, causing the aircraft to swerve and smash into a forklift waiting nearby to unload the cargo. The wing tanks burst into flames that quickly engulfed the aircraft. Runway personnel rescued the crew, who escaped with only minor injuries, but the aircraft and its cargo were totally destroyed.[28]

A USMC KC-130 smoulders on the runway after it was hit by an NVA mortar whilst landing. Eight people were killed and three others injured in the attack.

CHARLIE: I SEE YOU IN MY DREAMS...

As a member of the 377th Combat Security Police at Tan Son Nhut, Vietnam, during Tet 1968, I worked a bunker several towers down from the 051 Bunker at Gate 051. The Tan Son Nhut gates were numbered 051, 055, 057, etc. It's Tet '68, and my combat experience was zip, and Charlie wanted to kick ass right into my bunker.

The night of the Tet Offensive was a shocker for everyone. I couldn't believe that it was happening! This was Saigon, Paris of the Orient. From my first new-guy-day they told me we would never get hit at Tan Son Nhut. This must be somebody's idea of a sick joke, I had thought. Doesn't Charlie know he's supposed to be in the jungle, or a nice rice paddy, or somewhere else? Right? WRONG!

The attack started as I watched from my bunker in Alpha Sector. First, rockets hit Bravo Sector. Then a Freedom Bird started lifting off the runway. As he climbed over the fence line in Echo Sector, I saw a curtain of red and green tracers rise from the ground to the Freedom Bird. Thousands of tracers told me just how many VC and NVA were kicking at our door. I heard on the radio that the fence line was penetrated, and positions in

Scared? You bet! My knees were knocking like a jackhammer

Echo and Alpha Sectors were overrun. 051 Bunker was hit hard and fighting to repel the attackers. Then my radio croaked and died and I was cut off from the world. I didn't learn until later that 051 Bunker was overrun and Sergeants Cyr, Fisher, Hebron and Mills were killed in a valiant defence of their post.

Scared? You bet! My knees were knocking louder than a jackhammer, and my teeth were chattering so hard it's a wonder they didn't shatter. I didn't lose my cookies, but my bladder and bowels were taking on a life of their own. It didn't matter that the 377th Combat Security Police Squadron was at 100 percent alert; the 25th Division and the 199th Infantry Brigade were taking names, and many more units were engaging the enemy.[29]

NVA dead lay strewn along Plantation Road in Tan Son Nhut after a vicious battle with US forces during the 1968 Tet Offensive.

AN AIR CAVALRYMAN AT WAR

FIRST LIEUTENANT GARY F. BIRKENMEIER RECALLED BEING SENT TO THE FAMOUS "1ST CAV" IN NOVEMBER 1970:

I was sent to Vietnam in November 1970. I was given command of the 2nd Platoon of C Company, 1st Battalion, 8th Cavalry, of the 1st Cavalry Division. The draft was in effect, so the vast majority of troops were not volunteers and were highly reluctant to serve in Vietnam. Effective leadership at the platoon and company levels required providing a soldiering example as well as technical competence in map reading, tactics, calls for fire support, organization, and in issuing clear and reasonable orders. Even among the draftees, the 1st Cav was considered a "good unit". In June of 1970, the division had been sent into Cambodia to disrupt NVA staging areas in that country. Morale was still high from the success of that mission. In November 1970, our brigade headquarters was near Son Be, and our division rear was in Bien Hoa. Our battalion's area of operations (AO) was a free fire zone (i.e. "friendlies" had been evacuated so we were allowed to shoot on sight). Our battalion had recently changed tactics from moving in company size units to patrolling independently by platoons. The platoons were usually no closer than one day's march except on resupply day, which occurred every three to four days. Patrols lasted for two to three weeks, after which the company was rotated to the battalion fire bases to provide base security and reinforcement for field units if necessary. On patrols, our packs, weapons and accessories weighed from 80 to 120 pounds.

About three days into our rotation on the battalion fire base, two Vietnamese families appeared at the edge of the fire base. The perimeter guards signalled the families to approach. They were fed and the headmen were interrogated. They were from a village that was being forced to grow rice for the VC and NVA. They told us that there was one NVA officer and 10 to 20 VC controlling their village. They said that when they escaped they had to take their entire families with them. Any members left behind would have been tortured and killed to discourage further escapes. A possible location for the village was determined. The mission of C Company (with the battalion Recon platoon attached) was to rescue the villagers and destroy the VC/NVA force.

It was decided that C Company's CP [command post], my platoon and another platoon would proceed directly to the village during a night march with two headmen as volunteer guides. The Recon platoon and our remaining platoon would take a different route to set up a blocking position approximately 300 metres opposite us on the other side of the village. At dawn we were to demand that the VC/NVA surrender the village. Our hope was that they would run, leaving the villagers behind, and stumble into our ambush. The morale was high – we were actually going to help people.

We departed the fire base just as it was getting dark. Everyone was nervous because of the possibility of a trap. We had to rest every 30 minutes due to the heavy packs. This created a problem because it was so dark. Our closeness made us an easy target for an ambush. Moreover, a trooper might fall asleep and be left behind when movement resumed. We travelled until about 04:00 hours, when the headmen told us that we would not reach the village for quite some time. The decision was made to form a perimeter and sleep.

We arrived in the late morning at an abandoned village that never had been spotted by helicopter or patrols. The villagers would be forced to move from village to village so as not to destroy the natural camouflage and to grow as much rice as possible. The two headmen reported to me. I informed them that if I thought they had led us into an ambush I would shoot them. They understood and continued as guides. In the afternoon we were fired upon by a sniper. I did not have my rifleman return fire but told the M60 machine gunner to spray the area to our front with 100 rounds. I then reported the situation to the CO.

First Lieutenant Gary F. Birkenmeier (far right) sits outside a cleared village with the platoon M60 machine gunner, "Ratso", and his assistant.

After receiving no more in-coming fire for several minutes, I took five men and moved to our flank to try and encircle the sniper. We found the position abandoned. So now the enemy knew we were coming. After patrolling several hundred metres forward and securing the area, I reported to the CO and warned him of punji stakes placed on the route. We set up for the night after moving out of the punji stakes area.

We were nearing the limit of our artillery coverage and were required to remain in a static position on this day. I took the squad out approximately 500 metres along the trail to set up an ambush. Three VC entered the killing zone. One was killed outright, one was wounded, and the third was able to escape. We carried the wounded man to a point where a helicopter inserted a "jungle penetrator" to extract him.

The headmen informed us that we were within a day's march of the village. It turned out that the village was nowhere near where we had originally thought. Our plan was that the CP and the other platoons would move directly into the village while my platoon took the VC/NVA camp. After a very cautious approach we found the camp abandoned. In their haste, the enemy had left a map. We then joined the CP and other platoons at the village, which was also abandoned. The trail continued beyond our division's boundary but we could proceed no farther.

Hot food, water and other supplies arrived. The battalion commander congratulated us on what we had accomplished. Although we had destroyed some of the enemy, captured documents and disrupted the enemy's food supply, we regretted not being able to free the villagers. The headmen were rejoined with their families and together they were evacuated to a safe area. I am very proud of the performance of my platoon on this mission.[22]

CHAPTER 8
THE ARMY OF THE REPUBLIC OF VIETNAM 1961-1975

In the wake of North Vietnam's stunning victory over South Vietnam, many of the "voices" of the Army of the Republic of Vietnam (ARVN) have been ignored and forgotten. While history has downplayed its contribution to the war, the ARVN's role was just as important as that played by US servicemen and North Vietnamese Army (NVA) soldiers. This is the ARVN's story.

Background

The ARVN had its roots in French General Jean de Lattre de Tassigny's decision to create a Vietnamese National Army. Trained and staffed by French officers and noncommissioned officers, the army from the start took on a conventional appearance. After the US replaced France as the guarantor of South Vietnamese independence, it continued to build upon the structure that had been in place before the arrival of the US military mission under Brigadier-General Trapnell in 1952.

From 1954 to its defeat in April 1975, the South Vietnamese troops trained, recruited and fought as a distinctively conventional force. By 1965, the ARVN had been organized on the "triangular" model used by the US Army. Infantry divisions had been organized into three regiments of three rifle battalions each, two artillery battalions (one 105mm howitzer battalion and one 4.2in mortar battalion), support units (engineer battalion, plus administrative, reconnaissance, signal, medical, quartermaster, ordnance and transportation companies) and a military police detachment. There were exceptions, such as the 23rd Division whose tactical area of responsibility lay concentrated in a "special zone"

headquarters that controlled an area smaller than that of a normal infantry division.[1]

Prior to the arrival of US ground troops in March 1965, the ARVN's inventory of armoured vehicles consisted of five tank troops equipped with the World War II-era light M24 Chaffee tank, while three scout troops possessed M8 armoured cars. South Vietnamese mechanized infantry had fairly modern equipment in the form of the 21 rifle troops who had M113 armoured personnel carriers. The South Vietnamese High Command had organized its 29 existing troops into six armoured cavalry squadrons under the direct control of the corps commanders.[2]

Insofar as artillery was concerned, the ARVN enjoyed a distinct advantage over its northern rival. Supplementing the 18 divisional 4.2in mortar and 105mm howitzer battalions were 10 separate artillery battalions. These included six heavy battalions of 155mm howitzers under direct corps control, and several 75mm and 105mm batteries of the general reserve.

The ARVN Ranger battalions operated under the direct command of the corps commanders spread throughout South Vietnam. Organized as a light infantry force, specially uniformed in tiger-striped uniforms, the Ranger battalions specialized in counter-guerrilla operations. Eventually the Ranger units, plagued by internal political and discipline problems, were eclipsed by the South Vietnamese Special Forces units organized by the US Green Berets and other special forces outfits.

The Vietnamese Marine Corps (VNMC), one of the South's élite fighting forces and the most dependable during the

war, was organized in October 1954 as a separate component of the Vietnamese Navy. From a force of 1137 officers and enlisted men, the VNMC expanded steadily throughout the next decade from a brigade of 8000 men to that of a full division organized along the lines of a US Marine Corps division. Because of its ability to move quickly from one trouble spot to another, the VNMC became known as the "fire brigade" during the war.[3]

From 1965, the VNMC was, as Major-General Nguyen Khang noted, "committed increasingly to I and II Corps Tactical Zones. During the spring of 1965, two battalions under the command of a task force headquarters remained in II Corps near Bong Son in Binh Dinh Province for nearly four months. The Viet Cong [VC] paid dearly for that deployment, as the Marines killed 444 and captured another 150. For their conduct during that campaign, and especially at the battle of An Thai Hamlet on 7–8 April, the 2nd Battalion of the Vietnamese Marine Brigade was cited by the Republic of Vietnam and was recommended for the Presidential Unit Citation by the US."[4]

The South Vietnamese infantryman was armed with a variety of American World War II weapons such as M1 Garands, M1 carbines, Browning Automatic Rifles (BARs), air-cooled .30- and .50-calibre machine guns, augmented by 60mm and 81mm mortars, and 2.36in and 3.5in rocket launchers. Territorial forces were armed with

An ARVN infantryman stands on the alert at a forward position during an operation against the Viet Cong. Note the grenade attached to the barrel of his rifle.

The South Vietnamese National Defence College in Saigon, which produced some of the South's finest military personnel.

a variety of American and French weapons, most notably the US M1 carbine and 12-gauge shotguns. Due to the diminutive size and weight of the South Vietnamese soldier, the weight and recoil of the M1 Garand made it difficult to handle or match the volume of fire put out by the AK-47 Kalashnikov that was used by VC and North Vietnamese units. The uniforms and "steel pot" helmet the ARVN wore into battle were of American origin, though the territorial forces wore the traditional black pajamas that made it difficult to distinguish them from the Vietnamese peasant or VC.[5]

Heavy and specialized equipment was primarily all of US manufacture. While observers have criticized the US for not supplying its South Vietnamese ally with modern equipment, the level of sophistication was such that US officials organized and trained the ARVN at first as a predominantly light infantry force. South Vietnamese General Tran Van Don noted that the US organized the ARVN as if it were going to fight a Korean War-type conflict. Tran, in fact, stated that the US Military Advisory and Assistance Group (MAAG) organized the South Vietnamese Army into "four field divisions of about 8000 men and six light divisions having only 5000. In addition, thousands of combat, logistical and administrative support troops were authorized by General O'Daniel and his successor General Williams."[6]

As for manpower, the situation can best be described as chaotic. Reliance upon a military draft in a country where men shared common names and widespread corruption made it all but impossible to determine eligibility and just how many young men were, in fact, available for military service. Obligatory military service in Vietnam, at least on paper, began at

20 years of age and lasted to 33. Enlisted men served for three years while reserve officers and noncommissioned officers served for four years. Recruitment was done at the provincial level, where induction centres then transported the draftees to one of five national training centres or to the Thu Duc Infantry School.[7]

The ARVN at war, 1965–75

Tran noted that one of several problems that hampered the ARVN during the war was that the entire effort was uncoordinated. This permitted many mistakes. Tran stated that when the Civil Guard was finally placed under control of the ARVN High Command it was too late, as much ground had been lost forever to the VC. Tran stated that "starting with Kennedy's introduction of American support troops, such as aviation companies, the character of the Vietnamese war changed. With the addition of each American, we Vietnamese lost more and more ability to direct the conduct of the war. Until the Americans pulled out in 1973, the war progressively was waged with American direction and tactics and for American objectives."[8]

Saigon was the main target of the enemy during Tet. The majority of forces in and around Saigon were from the ARVN (army,

airborne, Ranger, artillery and Marines). The Military Assistance Command, Vietnam (MACV) and South Vietnam's Joint General Staff placed the ARVN in charge of the clearing operations after 31 January 1968. Here, the five airborne battalions, five marine battalions, five Ranger battalions, one artillery battalion, two military police battalions and two service battalions conducted a search-and-destroy operation. This eventually cleared every pocket of enemy resistance in and around Saigon in a series of firefights that resulted in the complete destruction of the VC. In one of the last battles in Saigon, and with the support of a US unit, ARVN Rangers completely wiped out a 30-man, high-level enemy command post that resulted in the capture of important documents and other intelligence-related materials.[9]

Often, battlefield effectiveness depended on the type of unit, the number of US advisors and the availability of proper fire support during an operation. During the South Vietnamese invasion of Laos' Plain of Jars between February and March 1970 (known as Lam Son 719), ARVN performance once again showed marked signs of improvement. "In Lam Son 719 the ARVN for the first time … conducted a multi-division offensive without the assistance of US advisors; most command and control fell upon the ARVN commanders and their staffs," said Lieutenant-General James W. Sutherland, commanding general of XXIV Corps. "While the ARVN performance had been uneven, most US commanders insisted that the overall results gave encouraging evidence that the Vietnamese were learning how to fight their own war." [10]

Despite the ARVN's success during Lam Son 719, its dependence on US helicopters and fixed-wing aircraft pointed to some glaring operational deficiencies. As the 1972 Easter Offensive and eventual fall of South Vietnam demonstrated, the ARVN was not able to correct the deficiencies of Lam Son 719 in time to meet the onslaught by the heavily armed

and heavily mechanized North Vietnamese Army units.

As for an over-dependence on air power and close air support, as well as on the helicopter, Tran admitted that the South Vietnamese Army had become "unduly dependent on them for everything. It really was too rich for our blood, in a land where one usually walks from one place to another carrying one's goods by backpack. The NLF [National Liberation Front], our adversary, performed all his supply and tactical operations by using foot traffic. Until practically the end of the war, he never exposed his trucks, tanks and artillery to counterfire. He kept things simple; we should have, too."[11]

In the end, what doomed the ARVN was not its inability to fight but how it was

organized and trained. Tran summarized the ARVN's problems as "America's unwillingness to depart from conventional views and methods when dealing with an unconventional situation like that in Vietnam".[12] Tran, however, overlooked two important points. The first was the failure of President Thieu and his military staff to order their armies in Military Regions 1 and 2 to stand and fight instead of withdrawing. The second occurred at the start of the communist offensive in January 1975, and centred on the ARVN's over-reliance on the hope that the US would intervene at the last minute.

A US military advisor instructs a South Vietnamese recruit in the use of the Browning Automatic Rifle.

A MISGUIDED STRATEGY

GENERAL TRAN BELIEVED THAT THE US NEVER HAD A CLEAR STRATEGY OR OBJECTIVE FOR WINNING THE WAR IN VIETNAM:

What I am saying is that the pouring of more and more men into the country without some clearly defined plan for military victory was a useless endeavour. Operations for the greater part were conducted against NLF units within the boundaries of our country south of the 17th Parallel. Except for some small clandestine work, American and Vietnamese major units never hit the communist sanctuaries in Cambodia and Laos, but by this time many valuable chances had been lost. We Vietnamese had trouble understanding why this vast and highly competent force did not come in and really get down to the business of winning the war. It seemed to serve more as an instrument of intimidation and reinforcement of policy rather than as a genuine war machine. The powerful air and naval forces were never used to their full potential since air strikes could never be extended beyond predetermined and pre-announced limits of time and territory.

Two fully equipped ARVN soldiers enjoy a smoke as their unit takes a break during an operation in Hau Nghai Province, west of Saigon.

The "computer strategy" of Secretary of Defense Robert McNamara ended as a semi-failure because it robbed the bombing of its elements of surprise and lessened its effectiveness. The communists were able to anticipate American bombing raids and have their missiles and other antiaircraft defences ready to take a heavy toll of American planes. So deadly was this fire that pilots often missed their targets altogether, dropping their bombs outside the target area, thus causing terrible loss of civilian life and destruction of property and installations of no particular strategic or tactical value. Protests and condemnations of this type of bombing from Vietnam, the US and elsewhere increased pressure for de-escalation and compromise, to the enemy's advantage. It appeared to us that military decisions, properly the job of local commanders, were being made in Washington by politicians who could not hope to understand the complexities of this strange type of war.

In Vietnam, the American commander had a hopeless task since he had two contradictory missions to perform, one to make war on the enemy force and the other to pacify the countryside from enemy subversion. His strategy and tactics could not be standard and wound up, not being appropriate to either mission.

Robert McNamara, the United States Defense Secretary during Vietnam. Considered an able and intelligent man, he was influential in formulating the US war strategy.

Generally, air raids were preferred over ground combat, so most ground actions were fought by Vietnamese troops. Operations ordinarily were not carried out jointly: the too limited participation of Vietnamese troops in US operations greatly decreased their impact.

The all-important counter-guerrilla campaign could not ever be waged effectively by the Americans. They needed large bodies of enemy troops to engage in conventional warfare. In guerrilla warfare, where there are no lines or rear areas and where the enemy is everywhere, a strong national army is required, possessing several key attributes: the same language and customs as the people; familiarity with the land and climate; the ability to adapt readily to local conditions; and, above all, the ability to gain ready information from its own countrymen.

During the time of the big US build-up, Vietnamese forces were not used on important missions. Such a disunified approach never won a war anywhere. With the conditions we were operating under, no further build-up of American forces was required. They probably had more than they needed.

What was required was true Vietnamese participation in all phases of planning and operations. In effect, we were fighting at least two separate wars against a common enemy, one of the reasons for our common military defeat.

We should have had a single allied commander charged with detailed coordination of all forces, as in the Korean War. Supplies would have arrived where intended and in proper quantity, corruption could have been detected and suppressed, tactical support such as air operations would have been better coordinated, and tragic errors involving needless loss of life could have been avoided.

We were fighting at least two separate wars against a common enemy

Another regrettable condition that prevented real unity of purpose was obsessive American mistrust of the Vietnamese Army and unjustified fear that we might some day attack North Vietnam. For this reason we were never provided with the latest weapons normally issued to American forces, despite the fact that our common enemy received the best the communist arsenals could procure.

By the time the US was ready to leave, enormous quantities of all manner of heavy equipment were being poured into Vietnam in an effort finally to "Vietnamese" the war. All of this was without adequate planning or sufficient time for us to assimilate it. It was a question of too much, too late.[13]

In the sweltering Mekong Delta, ARVN troops on M113 armoured personnel carriers (APCs) patrol the swampy area in search of communist units. Corruption among ARVN officers weakened its military effectiveness.

155

DEFEATING THE VC

Having just been dropped off by troop carrier, South Vietnamese Marines prepare themselves in the village of Nha Ve before heading off on a sweep of the area.

THE VIETNAMESE MARINES PERFORMED SUPERBLY DURING THE BATTLE FOR AN THAI HAMLET, SAID GENERAL KHANG:

In that battle, the 2nd Battalion, in defensive positions around An Thai, withstood an attack by a numerically superior Viet Cong force. The 2nd Battalion repulsed six different assaults in a night-long battle fought entirely with organic infantry weapons.

With superb fire discipline and leadership, each small unit of the 2nd Battalion held its ground and fought as a team. When overrun and bypassed by enemy forces, the Marines turned in their fox-holes and shot down the VC from the other direction. After being slowly pushed back at dawn in a seventh attack, the Marine forces rallied and counterattacked to regain their positions and force the withdrawal of the Viet Cong. When the battle subsided, 205 enemy dead littered the battlefield, and 59 of the bodies were within the 2nd Battalion's perimeter.

This victory had special significance in the war because it clearly demonstrated to our allies that a trained, disciplined Vietnamese unit with determination and leadership could defeat hard-core Viet Cong units of superior numbers. The victory was also an inspiring and stimulating page in our history.[14]

THE TEST OF COMBAT

In the III Corps area, on 27 October an ARVN battalion successfully held back an attack by an NVA regiment at Song Be in Phuoc Long Province near the Cambodian border. Two days later, a regiment of the enemy 9th Division struck against the district town of Loc Ninh in Binh Long Province. The enemy penetrated the district headquarters area and gained control of about half of it, but was finally repulsed by the defenders, who were reinforced by elements of the 18th ARVN Division and strongly supported by US tactical air [power]. Despite this, fighting spread into the adjacent plantation areas and did not abate until several days later, after the intervention by a brigade of the US 1st Infantry Division. During this battle, the enemy lost in excess of 800 men.

In mid-November, another major battle took place in Dak To, northwest of Kontum City in II Corps area, pitting four enemy regiments against four ARVN battalions and two infantry brigades. The engagement lasted 22 days and eventually compelled the US command to bring in the US 173rd Airborne Brigade from the coastal zone as a reinforcement, which increased the total friendly commitment to division size. When the enemy finally broke contact, he had left behind over 1400 dead, inflicted to a large extent by B-52 ["arc light"] strikes.[15]

Most RF (and ARVN) battalions performed unexpectedly well, fighting courageously in defence and counterattacking with enthusiastic vigour, aided by US infantry units, armour, artillery and gunships. As a result, targets temporarily overrun by the enemy at the beginning of the attack were all retaken within a short time.[16]

ARVN Airborne Division troops lay down fire against VC soldiers on the southwest perimeter of Tan Son Nhut during the Tet Offensive.

LAM SON 719

US GENERAL SUTHERLAND
HAD THIS TO SAY ABOUT
THE ARVN DURING
OPERATION LAM SON 719:

The forces that participated in Lam Son 719 proved that the Republic of Vietnam possess[es] a viable military organization that is significantly more capable, cohesive and better led than the military organization that existed … only three years ago. The overall results of Lam Son 719 indicate that Vietnamization is progressing well in MR [Military Region] 1.[17]

The advance of ARVN troops to Tchepone [deep inside Laos] was considered excellent. While the NVA had greatly outnumbered us in antiaircraft weapons and also in troops … there were no major contacts between combined troops and NVA units, only scattered engagements with the enemy when ARVN troops moved to Tchepone.

ARVN Rangers seemed to perform best of all, pushing the enemy back at each engagement. They seized more than 500 assorted weapons in their first contact with an NVA unit, but two days later the communists launched a counterattack on a hill previously seized by ARVN Rangers. It might have been the communists' tactical purpose to let the ARVN troops move easily into Laotian territory, but then the communist forces began their attack.

CAPTAIN LU VAN THAN,
WHO SERVED AS AN ARVN
TRANSLATOR WITH THE US
MARINES AND XXIV CORPS
IN VIETNAM, NOTED THAT
DURING LAM SON 719:

In the fiercest fighting throughout the night, the NVA finally succeeded in eliminating the whole ARVN Ranger battalion. We received that bad news from the field without much surprise. The command ordered a step-by-step withdrawal from Tchepone. Although at least one regiment provided security for each withdrawing battalion, ARVN troops were besieged by NVA units with modern weapons supplied by China and the Soviet Union, weapons that inflicted heavy casualties on the ARVN troops. US air support was unable to provide much help against these ground forces.

The step-by-step withdrawal [as ordered by the ARVN High Command] was fatal. It was my opinion that Lam Son 719 was a total defeat; the ARVN suffered heavy casualties and enemy losses were unknown.[18]

Weapons captured from the VC during Operation Coburg are put on display. The communist forces received a great deal of help from the Soviet Union and China in procuring all sorts of weapons, including small arms.

During the Lam Son 719 campaign at A Luoi base in lower Laos, I witnessed hundreds of deaths – deaths that were tragic and unjust. With our troops surrounded, our commanders decided to withdraw along the path of a spring, hoping to get back to Route 9 and Dong Ha. Bordered on two sides by walls

South Vietnamese M113s patrol along a road during Operation Lam Son 719. Incursions by VC troops from across the Cambodian border were common.

of mountain rock, the spring became our death march. Guessing our move, the enemy had placed a heavy machine gun above, aiming at our path. We knew that we'd suffer high casualties, but didn't have a choice. The alternative would be the wiping out of complete units. Soldiers elbowed each other, pushing and stepping on each other to rush forward, under the barrage of machine-gun fire. Screams. Cries. Sounds of bodies tumbling into the water. Fallen bodies piled on top of each other. The spring ran with blood.

KHANH TRUONG JOINED THE ARVN AS A PARATROOPER IN 1966:

At about the same time, on the hills of A Luoi, the enemy had overrun us, and artillery was called to fire on our own position. Men seriously wounded were left behind, becoming targets for artillery fire. The lightly wounded rushed to open ground, waiting for airlift by helicopters. There were too many soldiers; they fought each other to get on to the helicopter, to hold on to the skids. When the helicopter reached altitude, men fell to the ground like ripe fruits.

These images sometimes re-appear in my dreams. I hate war.

I detest war.[19]

Fallen bodies piled on top of each other; the spring ran with blood

CHAPTER 9
THE END OF THE SECOND INDO-CHINESE WAR 1971-1975

Even as US forces began an incremental withdrawal, the war in the countryside continued. As 1971 began, the Vietnam War progressed in all of its ferocity. Within four years, the stage was set for the last act – the North Vietnamese invasion that culminated in the collapse of the South and the reunification of Vietnam. For those participating in the war's final years, the end in April 1975 signalled the conclusion of America's longest and most bitter conflict.

As US forces continued their phased withdrawal, the Army of the Republic of Vietnam (ARVN) prepared to go it alone. The I Corps Combined Operation Campaign Plan issued by the Military Assistance Command, Vietnam (MACV) stated that: "President Richard M. Nixon's reduction of American forces, now into its second full year, had been based on a periodic assessment of the level of North Vietnamese infiltration into South Vietnam; the ability of the South Vietnamese to fight their own war; and, finally, progress in the Paris negotiations."[1]

Offensively, the Marines and US Army maintained pressure. In the Que Son Mountains, the 7th Marines continued to hunt down the enemy. Throughout the first half of 1970, the 7th Marines accounted for about half the division's total contacts with the enemy. The 7th killed 1160 enemy soldiers, took 44 prisoners and captured 291 weapons. Throughout the 1st Marine Division's tactical area of responsibility (TAOR), the Marines accounted for 3995 North Vietnamese Army (NVA) and Viet Cong (VC) killed while taking 826 prisoners.

By March 1973, all US ground elements had departed Vietnam while NVA forces remained in South Vietnam. Most South Vietnamese commanders realized that, with the withdrawal of the US, it was now but a matter of time before the NVA would act. Despite the fact that the ARVN had held its own during the North's Easter offensive of March–June 1972, only with US air power could the South Vietnamese push back the NVA. As the events of 1975 indicated, the refusal of the US to intervene doomed South Vietnam and its infant republic to the tanks and guns of the NVA. The NVA waited for the signal to strike south in what it thought would be a two-year campaign. Much to its surprise, the conquest took just four months.

The fall of Saigon

The seizure of the provincial capital of Phuoc Long on 6 January 1975 signalled the beginning of the end. Located north of Saigon, Phuoc Long was considered by the ARVN to be "untenable in case of a heavy attack due to its geographical position". It was isolated and practically encircled by enemy forces for months before its capture. Supplies had to be flown in or road convoys escorted. Phuoc Long was considered by ARVN commanders to be "weakly defended" and "offered little resistance".[2]

The NVA's seizure of Phuoc Long was designed to test the will of the South's armed forces and to gauge the reaction of the US. The loss of Phuoc Long was the first time in the Vietnam War that an entire province had been lost to the communists. It was obviously a flagrant violation of the ceasefire agreement by the communists. Yet ARVN forces chose not to react militarily, while the US made no significant move to deter the communists. In the words of South Vietnamese President Nguyen Van Thieu, while it was not "impossible to reoccupy Phuoc Long", from a military standpoint "it was not worthwhile" as it would have drained troops from other critical areas.[3]

Following Phuoc Long, city after city fell. Only the battle at Xuan Loc, considered to be the high point of South Vietnamese resistance during the last days of the war, offered any hope. Here, several ARVN divisions stood their ground and consistently fought well and according to the lessons taught by US advisors during the American advisory era.[4]

As the resistance at Xuan Loc ended, NVA tanks headed towards Saigon. The US Seventh Fleet had already been alerted to the likelihood of an evacuation of US citizens and their dependants. The US Marines would perform yet another rescue mission.

The end of a long war

Vietnam's war for independence lasted nearly 30 years. In that time, French, North and South Vietnamese, Americans, Japanese, Chinese, Australians, Canadians, South Koreans, Filipinos and others battled in the jungles and swamps of the country. The NVA and the VC did not defeat the US military on the field of battle. What they couldn't win militarily was won psychologically. The "voices" of those who fought in this long and bloody war have faded, but their bravery and loyalty will never be forgotten.

In the South China Sea, Vietnamese refugees disembark from USS *Durham*, an amphibious cargo ship, onto a waiting smaller landing craft.

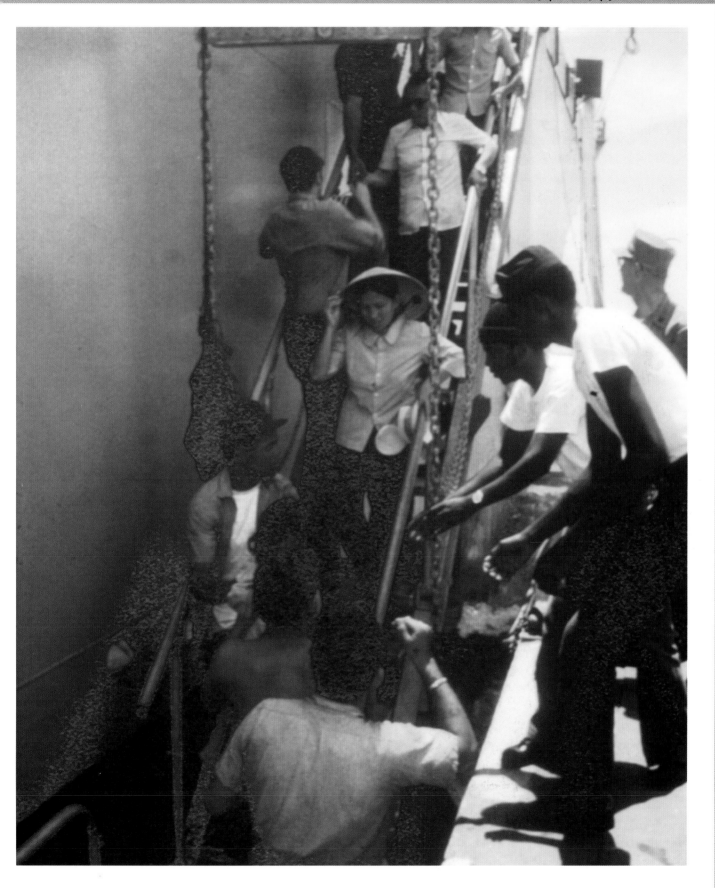

A FIGHTING WITHDRAWAL

reacted by pulling squads off the more secure part of our sector of the perimeter and pushing them down head-on into the penetration area and getting it secured and then pursuing with small teams out to the wire to actually kill the enemy as he was running.[5]

Fire Base Apollo 16km (10 miles) northeast of Lai Khe. Even as US involvement in the war drew to a close, US troops still attacked the enemy.

After we landed on Hill 800 and walked down on the southeast side, we stayed down there for a couple of days checking out the area. We didn't find anything of significance – a couple of bodies that had been buried approximately a month. Then we got word to move out in search of a comms [communications] centre and having almost reached this comms centre we found that the Chieu Hoi had decided that it wasn't in this place and he gave us another coordinate on the other side of the mountain. So my platoon was placed in the lead to go back and find our way over the mountain. As we started moving over the mountain we came to an enemy base camp, started seeing bunkers, well fortified, well positioned. We moved on and up, found this cave complex, checked it out, found a considerable amount of ordnance, gear, no weapons. Next day we moved on over Hill 845, started down on the northwest side. After staying there for a couple of days [we] started to move out. My platoon again found another complex. This time they found 12 SKSs, several light submachine guns, one light machine gun, approximately 1000 pounds of corn, 750 pounds of potatoes, lots of documents. There were also some graves in this area. We found some mortar rounds that were booby-trapped in these caves. We … destroyed all this as we left.[6]

US FIRST LIEUTENANT WALLACE L. WILSON, JR., COMMANDING I COMPANY'S 1ST PLATOON, RECALLED THE SEARCH FOR THE ENEMY:

A US soldier opens up on the enemy with his jeep-mounted M60 machine gun. The stability of the jeep mounting allowed for excellent accuracy.

THE NORTH'S STRATEGY

THE 1972 OFFENSIVE

The Spring Offensive of 1972. NVA and VC formations launched a three-pronged invasion of South Vietnam following the withdrawal of US fighting strength.

BY EARLY 1970, THE NORTH VIETNAMESE BEGAN TO CHANGE THEIR STRATEGY, AS NOTED BY US MARINE LIEUTENANT-GENERAL JOHN R. CHAISSON:

For the past five years the enemy has employed a mixed strategy, which may be defined as the sum of violence perpetrated against a variety of [Southern] and US targets by a spectrum of enemy forces with distinct organizational characteristics, intended purposes and doctrines. The enemy's strategy is also "mixed" in a geographic sense, with the level (as well as the causes) of violence differing markedly from one locale to another. In a given area, he is liable within the same short time frame to strike at hamlet officials, PF [Popular Forces] outposts, ARVN forces on sweeps, and US fire bases. He exploited weakness or carelessness by attacking. And while his directives stressed some target categories (such as combined action platoons) more than others, his actual attacks reflected tactical opportunism. That in different areas of the country we have seen different enemy styles and targets should not be attributed to his deliberate choice. In various areas he may not have the wide range of strategic options we have attributed to him. He may be impeded by the US/GVN actions, or by command-and-control problems, or by the decentralized, localized nature of the war.[7]

ARVN personnel gaze at North Vietnamese dead during the 1972 offensive. US air power ensured that Hanoi's attempt to crush the South ended in failure.

THE SOUTH FIGHTS ALONE

THE 1975 OFFENSIVE

The North's 1975 offensive split the South in two. Victory was made easy by the absence of US air power.

CAPTAIN LU, ARVN, REMEMBERED WATCHING THE LAST AMERICAN TROOPS LEAVE SOUTH VIETNAM:

As the planes left, I stood motionless, watching, until the last plane full of US troops took off. The US involvement in South Vietnam – from the first advisors in the 1960s until 27 March 1973 when the troops pulled out – had ended, and this finally became real when the last plane disappeared in a clear sky that day. Even then I was worrying about the future of my country without the presence of US troops. The ARVN troops could hardly provide security for all parts of the country. The departure of the allied forces, especially the US troops, had left a big gap in providing security for the vast part of MR [Military Region] 1 from the DMZ down. In those days I felt that sooner or later something would happen to my country. The malicious smile of the NVA representative when he had supervised the withdrawal of US forces, and the words of Mr Brown [the US Consul General to South Vietnam] before he left Vietnam for the US, at times kept coming back to my mind. The ever-increasing bureaucracy, corruption and bribery seen in every corner of the government institutions were among the main causes of the dissatisfaction of the people; the lack of allied support both in aid and in manpower discouraged most RVN military commanders.[8]

A Senior NCO addresses US troops before they board a "freedom bird" to take them home. Many were pleased to be leaving, but found life hard once they got back.

THE BATTLE OF XUAN LOC

THE BATTLE OF XUAN LOC WAS THE LAST MAJOR ACTION OF THE VIETNAM WAR, IN WHICH COLONEL DO NGOC NHAN, ARVN, TOOK PART:

During the 14 days of fighting at Xuan Loc, ARVN troops received more than 20,000 rockets and artillery shells, but they destroyed 37 communist T-54 tanks and killed more than 5000 communist attackers.

From the psychological point of view, the Xuan Loc resistance was a great help to relieve the extremely agitated mental state of the people and soldiers. It brought back the courage and self-confidence in military commanders whose guilt complex was torturing them after the rout from the Central Highlands. The heroic resistance at Xuan Loc revived everyone's hope that finally the South Vietnamese troops could stop the enemy aggression and thwart the enemy offensive, as they had done in 1968 and 1972.[9]

Tanks of the victorious NVA enter the gates of the Presidential Palace in Saigon in 1975 following the defeat of the ARVN outside the city.

FREQUENT WIND

STAFF SERGEANT SABANSKI DESCRIBED OPERATION FREQUENT WIND AND THE EVACUATION OF US CITIZENS FROM SAIGON:

We made another high-speed run from Subic Bay. This time other ships were also under way from ports throughout the Pacific. Ships of the US Seventh Fleet were ordered to our area to assist and/or defend us. Aircraft carriers to tugboats came from all over with just one thought in mind: evacuate Saigon and our friends who had fought side by side with us for almost a decade. One night the sea was clear as the sun sank beyond the horizon. The next time the first rays poked into the brightening blue skies, a vast armada had gathered. The possibility of enemy ships or aircraft attacking was no longer a joking matter for us. Sailors and Marine volunteers stood watch, scanning the skies and the sea for the sighting of hostile forces. Live ammunition was made ready as gun mounts and missile launchers were tested.

The endless rounds of planning, briefings and rehearsals were once more going on. Everything and everybody connected with the landing was checked. The feverish activity aboard the ship began to abate. Slowly, the Marines of the battalion and sailors of the fleet settled down to wait.

The delay in sending troops ashore could be traced directly to the American Ambassador in Saigon. Why he chose to adopt the wait-and-see attitude is open to conjecture. Days passed and we got no word and gradually the keen fighting edge of the landing force eroded. Tempers grew short and flared amongst the crew members and embarked passengers. The officers of the ship, working with the COs of the battalion and air group, got together to discuss ways and means of relieving the mounting tension.

While awaiting the ambassador's decision, the ships were cruising in a five-mile circle just outside the sight of land. Day melted into night and then back into day again. New faces started arriving aboard our ship as reinforcements were flown in from Okinawa. Others disappeared, as they were transferred back to the "Rock", their 12-month overseas tour completed. Soon we noticed that some of our "key" people were getting special briefings, changing into civilian clothes and leaving the ship. Our ambassador had asked for some Marines to be filtered into Saigon in civilian clothes to assist the embassy Marines. Part of their duties was to help process the thousands of applications to leave Vietnam. Another, more important task was to locate suitable landing sites for the helicopters, once the mission was officially started.

New planning meetings were held daily. Communications strategy for the landing force was updated constantly. When word for the operation to start finally came, the radio plan was presented

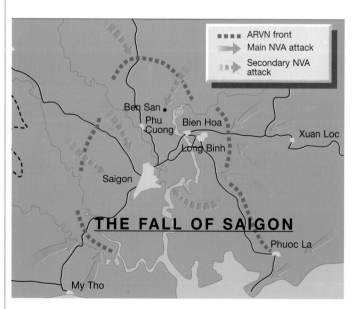

THE FALL OF SAIGON

- ▪▪▪▪ ARVN front
- ➡ Main NVA attack
- ⇢ Secondary NVA attack

Ben San
Phu Cuong
Bien Hoa
Xuan Loc
Long Binh
Saigon
Phuoc La
My Tho

The fall of Siagon. By 29 April 1975, the forces of communism had overrun the ARVN and had taken Saigon, the capital of the South.

US Marines aboard the amphibious assault ship USS *Blue Ridge* prepare ammunition before flying into Saigon on an evacuation mission.

to the Bn. CO and other staff officers. The ambassador finally realized that the ARVN could not hold back the tide and the call went out, "Send in the Marines". By this time, we were a reinforced battalion complete with a commanding general. The air group on our ship was also reinforced by the arrival of the aircraft carrier USS *Boxer*.

At first light, "land the landing force" echoed from the ship's speakers. Again US Marines would land in a hostile country to bring to safety thousands of people. The "whump" of helicopter blades would be heard in all the ships involved. Jet fighters would be on station over the fleet, the landing areas and the routes in between. The fleet itself had started to move closer to the shore.

The first helicopter to land on our ship was that of the VNAF. Out of this craft came the families of the pilot and co-pilot, who also left the helicopter. More VNAF-marked "birds" started to arrive. There was no room for our 'copters to land so the word went out to push all non-American aircraft over the side. A string of war-weary helicopters went to a watery grave in the South China Sea. Below decks, where I was stationed, the flow of humanity began. We quickly gathered up two Vietnamese women wearing the uniform of their air force and pressed them into service to help search our new women passengers.

A string of war-weary helicopters went to a watery grave

As the line of passengers grew, we encountered former rulers of their nation. Some were demanding that they were important and could not wait in line. Others quietly endured the process. Everyone was treated according to the way they approached our station. The cooperative ones were politely handled and quickly processed. The outspoken ones were gone over slowly and carefully.

The flow of refugees turned to a trickle and I was ordered to move to the hangar deck. This allowed the compartment to be used by refugees. Once on the hangar deck, we were amazed to see that night was upon us. Still the helicopters continued the ferry service. Some of the pilots never got out of their planes all day long. Meals were eaten on the run.

The trickle of refugees finally dried up and the last planes from Saigon lifted the guards from the roof of the now empty embassy. Frequent Wind was the final operation of an unpopular war. Loaded with humanity that had lost everything, the ships turned their bows and headed towards Subic Bay. [10]

A DETERMINED FOE

MARSHALL DARLING, 1ST AIR CAVALRY, FORMED A LASTING IMPRESSION OF THE ENEMY AND WHY THE US WOULD NEVER WIN IN VIETNAM:

Suddenly a running figure appeared out of the middle of the inferno and the cheer stopped as if a radio were turned off. The man was burning from head to toe. It was an NVA soldier who had been in the tunnel complex and now was totally engulfed in the napalm hellfire. We all stopped whatever we were doing and watched a man die.

He must not have been a normal man because he fought the inevitable with all his strength. The jet had done a short vertical loop and was coming in to drop another "egg", when the pilot must have seen him and began to lay down a line of machine-gun fire that chewed up the ground in a direct line towards the running figure. The all-encompassing flames were sucking the life from his soul when suddenly he stopped, turned and faced his attacker. I was completely flabbergasted at what I saw next – he raised an angry blazing arm and "shot the bird" at the oncoming jet just as the bullets caught up with him and his body exploded into smouldering fragments. At that moment I knew there was no way that we could possibly win in Vietnam.

I had heard of the dedication and focus of the enemy at all levels but to actually see it and finally to be shocked by an event on the battlefield was more then a "mind blower". It was the moment in time that solidified my opposition to the position that the Old Men in the government had put us in. We had no prayer of doing anything positive in that country because the enemy was everyone – everyone either hated us or just wanted to be left alone to grow their rice.[11]

VC and NVA troops earned a grudging respect from US soldiers due to their spirit and will to fight. It was this spirit that kept them in the war against all odds.

WHY THE NORTH WON

Young women of the NVA train their sights on the skies above Hanoi. The US bombers, however, had gone home.

North Vietnamese workers begin to repair the Trung-Long water reservoir. It was bombed 200 times by US aircraft and totally destroyed.

Vietnamese people have an independent spirit, stubborn people, I suppose, who do things the Vietnamese way. So now the plan is to mobilize the entire population in the fight against backwardness and misery. While there are the problems of war and the problems of peace, there are also concrete laws, social laws, great laws, which retain their value whether in peace or war. You have to be realistic. You have to have a goal. You have to be a realist and use reality as a means of analyzing the object laws which govern things. To win, you have to act according to these laws. If you do the opposite, you're being subjective and you're bound to lose. So, we learn from the experience, both good and bad, of Capitalism. But, we have our own Vietnamese idea on things. I'd like to add that we are still for independence, that we still follow the path shown us by Ho Chi Minh, the path of independence and Socialism. I'm still a Socialist but what is Socialism? It's independence and unity for the country. It's the freedom and well-being of the people who live there. And, it's peace and friendship between all men.[12]

VO NGUYEN GIAP MASTERMINDED THE NORTH'S VICTORY AND WROTE A MANUAL OF GUERRILLA WARFARE:

PARTING THOUGHTS

DAVID HACKWORTH SPENT FIVE YEARS IN VIETNAM. HE EARNED MANY MEDALS DURING HIS 26-YEAR ARMY CAREER, INCLUDING EIGHT PURPLE HEARTS:

In 1965, America began to dispatch a conventional army to Vietnam. Pound for pound those airmen, Marines, sailors and soldiers were the finest warriors we had ever sent to war. In the beginning, they were highly trained regular volunteers, who had long been indoctrinated to kill a "Commy for Mommy".

But the Americans were trained to fight the Soviet Union. Their doctrine, tactics and equipment were designed to engage a communist enemy on a European battlefield, not an Asian opponent in the jungle. The training and mindset of their generals and admirals were to fight great air, land and sea battles not unlike those that brought us victory in World War II.

There was another problem. Their Vietnamese opponent refused to be sucked into a war of attrition or to fight an American-style war. He had over the centuries defeated the Chinese, Japanese and the French not by fighting by conventional rules but by following the strategic and tactical doctrine of Sun Tzu, written two-and-a-half-thousand years before: enemy attacks, we retreat; enemy digs in, we harass; enemy exhausted, we attack; enemy retreats, we pursue.

For eight years, the powerful US war machine mostly attacked shadows and mainly bombed an invisible enemy. It was seldom able to lock its opponent into the classical big battle, where it could bring to bear its overwhelming firepower and technological advantage over its Third World foe. The enemy fought battle for battle mainly on his terms and almost always played the tune. He acted, we reacted. When the fight was over he danced away to fight another day, almost always leaving the ground bloody from American casualties. He took his lumps, too, but they weren't shown on the Vietnamese nightly TV news. And he was prepared to pay any human price to wear down his American opponent.

Sadly, from "The Iron Triangle" to "Hamburger Hill" – always in search of the big battle, the big victory, the big knockout – the American leadership never learnt. What worked in World War II was the standard. In their haste to recreate a Guadalcanal or a Normandy KO, the top brass failed the basic lessons of war-fighting: to understand your enemy and know cold the nature of the war.

Despite a massive technological advantage, the US armed forces were simply not geared towards fighting a cunning and elusive enemy in a non-conventional conflict.

The men of the US armed forces fought hard with all their ability, but ultimately it was poor political and strategic decisions that cost them dear.

For eight years, America fought the same battles on the same terrain using the same obsolete tactics. There was no clear-cut military plan, nor was there an institutional memory. Frontline unit leaders were shifted every few months, and the division and corps commanders – whose tenure was much longer – were totally out of touch with what went on down at the pointy end of the bayonet. The mistakes that were made in 1965 were repeated each year, as each annual crop of American cannon fodder was fed unto the field until 1973, when we withdrew.

The valiant men well understood the enemy's game. How he would dart in, make them bleed and run away. How he was into making the Second Vietnamese War a protracted affair that would frustrate America's leaders and wear down the American people, who from the beginning of the conflict questioned the morality of the war, wondered how our country's national security was even remotely at risk in the far-away jungles of Southeast Asia, and saw the wrongheadedness of our being there.

Virtually no senior commanders spent time with the grunts to learn the true nature of the war. Most were isolated from the fighting men – not unlike the French, British and German senior brass of World War I. Similarly, they lived in royal comfort, complete with white-coated servants and sparkling china-set tables, safely away from the killing fields. When a battle did rage, they whirled above it in helicopters making decisions that may have worked in another war, but didn't make sense to the men on the ground. These sky-borne leaders became bitterly known to the men who did the dying as "The Great Squad Leaders in the Sky".

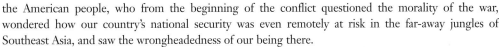

The war was a disaster from its bad beginning until its tragic end

The Vietnam War was a disaster from its bad beginning until its tragic end. It killed four million Vietnamese and over 58,000 Americans. Millions more, Vietnamese and Americans, were wounded by shell or shock, and the war came close to ripping our country asunder. With the exception of the Civil War, no war wrought such long-range damage to the American soul.

Did our military establishment learn from the tragic lesson of Vietnam? The mistakes were all buried. No autopsy was conducted. In 1993, in Somalia, the US Army made exactly the same mistakes that were made in Vietnam. Again, mainly young Americans paid the supreme sacrifice.

Unless we learn from the past we will again face dark days ahead.[13]

CHAPTER NOTES

Chapter 1

1 Bernard B. Fall, *Hell in a Very Small Place: The Siege of Dien Bien Phu* (J.B. Lippincott Company: Philadelphia, 1967), p.35.
2 Stanley Karnow, *Vietnam: A History* (Penguin Books: New York, 1984), p.150. Hereafter cited as Karnow, *Vietnam*.
3 Ibid, pp.150–1.
4 Ibid, p.156.
5 Ibid.
6 Ibid, p.157.
7 Ibid.
8 See Ho Chi Minh, *Appeal by Ho Chi Minh to the Compatriots to Carry out Destruction, To Wage Resistance War, 6 February, 1947,* in Gareth Porter, et al, *Vietnam: The Definitive Documentation of Human Decisions* (Earl M. Coleman Enterprises, Inc.: New York, 1979), pp.140–1. Hereafter cited as Porter, *The Definitive Documentation.*
9 Ronald H. Spector, *The United States Army in Vietnam: Advice and Support: The Early Years 1941–1960* (Center of Military History, U.S. Army: Washington, D.C., 1985), pp.85–6. Hereafter cited as Spector, *Advice and Support.*
10 Ibid, p.86.
11 Ibid, p.87.
12 Ibid, p.89.
13 Ibid, pp.89–90.
14 Ibid, p.90.
15 Ibid, p.125.
16 Ibid.
17 Ibid, p.126.
18 Ibid.
19 Ibid, p.142.
20 Ibid, p.161.
21 See Bernard B. Fall, *Indochina – The Last Year of the War – The Navarre Plan*, Military Review, U.S. Army Command and Genera Staff College, Ft. Leavenworth, KS, reprinted in U.S. Army, *Selected Readings in Guerrilla And Counterguerrilla Operations* (Fort Benning, GA., U.S. Army Infantry School, August 1966), p.174. Hereafter cited as Fall, *Indochina – The Last Year of the War.*
22 Ibid, p.187.
23 See George Armstrong Kelly, *Lost Soldiers: The French Army and Empire in Crisis, 1947–1962* (Massachusetts Institute of Technology Press: Cambridge, 1965), p.71. Hereafter cited as Kelly, *Lost Soldiers.*
24 Paul-Marie De La Gorce, *The French Army: A Military-Political History* (Weidenfeld and Nicolson: London, 1963), p.394. Hereafter cited as Gorce, *French Army.*
25 Ibid, p.400.
26 Peter Scholl-Latour, *Death in the Ricefields: Thirty Years of War in Indochina* (Orbis Publishing Co.: London 1979), p.60.
27 Ibid, pp.61–3.
28 www.pbs.org/wgbh/peoplescentury
29 www.dienbienphu.org
30 Ibid.
31 Ibid.
32 www.pbs.org/wgbh/amex/vietnam/reflect
33 www.pbs.org/wgbh/peoplescentury

Chapter 2

1 Spector, *Advice and Support*, pp.103–4.
2 Ibid, p.222.
3 Ibid, p.224.
4 Ibid, p.240.
5 Interview with former Marine Sergeant Leo Daugherty Jr., with author, 9 May 2002, Cleveland, Ohio.
6 Spector, *Advice and Support*, pp.293–4.
7 Ibid, p.295.
8 Ibid.
9 Robert F. Futrell and Martin Blumenson, *United States Air Force in Southeast Asia: The Advisory Years to 1965* (Office of Air Force History, USAF: Washington, D.C., 1981), pp.49–50. Hereafter cited as Futrell and Blumenson, *USAF In Vietnam: The Advisory Years.*
10 Ibid, p.55.
11 Edward J. Marolda and Oscar P. Fitzgerald, *The United States Navy and the Vietnam Conflict* (Naval Historical Center, Department of the Navy: Washington, D.C., 1986), pp.100–1. Hereafter cited as Marolda and Fitzgerald, *The US Navy and the Vietnam Conflict.*
12 See Lieutenant-Colonel Archie J. Clapp, USMC, *Shu Fly Diary*, United States Naval Institute Proceedings, October 1963, No. 10, reprinted in *The Marines in Vietnam: 1954–1973: An Anthology and Annotated Bibliography* (History and Museums Division, HQMC: Washington, D.C., 1985), pp.12–23.
13 Marolda and Fitzgerald, *The US Navy and the Vietnam Conflict*, p.175.
14 Ibid, p.214.
15 Ibid.
16 Ibid, p.229.
17 Porter, *The Definitive Documentation*, p.420.
18 Spector, *Advice and Support*, p.229.
19 Ibid, p.274.
20 Ibid, p.287.
21 Ibid, p.288.
22 Marolda and Fitzgerald, *The US Navy and the Vietnam Conflict*, p.216.
23 Spector, *Advice and Support*, p.352.
24 Lieutenant-Colonel Clapp, *Shu Fly Diary.*
25 Marolda and Fitzgerald, *The US Navy and the Vietnam Conflict*, p.64.
26 Ibid, p.228.
27 Ibid, p.217.
28 Master Sergeant W. V. "Bill" East, USMC (Retired), to Leo J. Daugherty III. Letter dated 11 February 2002. Letter in possession of the author.

Chapter 3

1 Lieutenant-General Phillip B. Davidson, Jr., US Army (Ret.), *Vietnam At War: The History, 1946-1975* (Oxford University Press: New York, 1988), p.317. Hereafter cited as Davidson, *Vietnam At War.*
2 Ibid, p.318.
3 Ibid, p.320.
4 Jack Shulimson and Major Charles Johnson, USMC, *Marines in Vietnam: 1965: The Landing and Buildup.* Unpublished Working Draft in possession of author. (History and Museums Division: Washington, D.C., July 1977), pp.3–4. Hereafter cited as Shulimson and Johnson, *Marines in Vietnam: 1965.*
5 Shulimson and Johnson, *Marines in Vietnam: The Landing and Buildup: 1965* (History and Museums Division, HQMC: Washington, D.C., 1978), pp.6–7. Hereafter cited as Shulimson and Johnson, *The Landing and Buildup: 1965.*
6 Ibid, pp.6–7.
7 Ibid, p.7.
8 Ibid, p.15.
9 Ibid, p.27.
10 Ibid, p.278.
11 General William C. Westmoreland, US Army (Retired), *A Soldier Reports* (Dell Publishing Co.: New York, 1980), p.174. Hereafter cited as Westmoreland, *A Soldier Reports.*
12 Ibid.
13 USMC Museum.
14 Shulimson and Johnson, *The Landing and Buildup*, p.51.
15 Brigadier-General Edwin H. Simmons, USMC, *Marine Corps Operations in Vietnam, 1965–1966*, as reprinted in *The Marines in Vietnam, 1954–1973. An Anthology and Annotated Bibliography* (History and Museums Division, HQMC: Washington, D.C., 1985), pp.51–2. Hereafter cited as Simmons, *The Marines in Vietnam, 1954–1973.*
16 Shulimson and Johnson, *The Landing and Buildup: 1965*, pp.134–5.
17 Jack Shulimson, *U.S. Marines in Vietnam: An Expanding War: 1966* (History and Museums Division, HQMC: Washington, D.C., 1982), p.13. Hereafter cited as Shulimson, *An Expanding War: 1966.*
18 Ibid, p.13.
19 Admiral Ulysses S. G. Sharp and General William C. Westmoreland, *Report on the War in Vietnam (As of 30 June 1968): Section I: Report on the Air and Naval Campaigns Against North Vietnam and Pacific Command-Wide Support of the War: June 1964–July 1968 by Admiral Sharp; Section II: Report on Operations in South Vietnam January 1964–June 1968 by General Westmoreland* (Government Printing Office: Washington, D.C., 1968), p.115. Hereafter cited as Sharp and Westmoreland, *Report on the War in Vietnam.*
20 John M. Carland, *Stemming the Tide: May 1965 to October 1966. The United States Army in Vietnam* (Center for Military History,

Headquarters, U.S. Army: Washington, D.C., 2000), p.363. Hereafter cited as Carland, *Stemming the Tide*.
21 Ibid.
22 Marolda and Fitzgerald, *The US Navy and the Vietnam Conflict*, p.457.
23 Ibid, p.457.
24 Ibid, p.466.
25 Ibid.
26 Westmoreland, *A Soldier Reports*, p.144.
27 Ibid, p.132.
28 Ibid.
29 Truong Nhu Tang, *A Viet Cong Memoir: An Inside Account of the Vietnam War and its Aftermath* (Vintage Books: New York, 1985), p.91. Hereafter cited as Tang, *Viet Cong Memoir*.
30 Shulimson and Johnson, *The Landing and Buildup: 1965*, p.11.
31 Philip J. Caputo, *A Rumor of War* (Ballantine Books: New York, 1990), pp.50–5. Hereafter cited as Caputo, *A Rumor of War*.
32 Shulimson and Johnson, *The Landing and Buildup: 1965*, p.29.
33 Caputo, *A Rumor of War*, pp.80–1.
34 Shulimson and Johnson, *The Landing and Buildup:1965*, p.51.
35 Ibid, p.52.
36 www.pbs.org/wgbh/peoplescentury/episodes/guerrillawars
37 www.mishalov.com/death_ia_drang_valley
38 www.first-air-cavalry-division-airmobile-in-vietnam-1965-1972.com
39 Sharp and Westmoreland, *Report on the War in Vietnam*, p.110.
40 "Boondock" in US Marine terminology refers to the jungle or countryside.
41 Shulimson and Johnson, *The Landing and Buildup:1965*, pp.134–5.
42 Ibid, p.133.
43 Shulimson, *An Expanding War: 1966*, p.13.
44 Ibid, p.171.
45 Ibid.
46 www.frankandtepo.com/attleboro/chap3-1
47 Sharp and Westmoreland, *Report on the War in Vietnam*, Section II, pp.114–6.

Chapter 4

1 Bill Adler, *Letters From Vietnam* (E.P. Dutton: New York, 1967), p.92. Hereafter cited as Adler, *Letters From Vietnam*.
2 Ibid, pp.26–27.
3 Westmoreland, *A Soldier Reports*, pp.205–6.
4 Adler, *Letters From Vietnam*, pp.139–44.
5 Ibid, pp.28–9.
6 www.home.att.net/~vietnam67
7 Adler, *Letters From Vietnam*, pp.37–8.
8 Ibid, pp.40–1.
9 Ibid, pp.43–4.
10 Ibid, p.43.
11 Ibid, pp.47–8.
12 Captain Francis J. West, Jr., USMCR, *Small Unit Action in Vietnam. Summer 1966* (History and Museums Division: Washington,

D.C., 1977), p.p.3–14. Hereafter cited as West, *Small Unit Action*.
13 Adler, *Letters From Vietnam*, pp.18–25.
14 Ibid, pp.89–90.
15 Ibid, pp.91–2.
16 www.mystae.com/reflections/vietnam
17 www.greene.xtn.net/~wingman/stories
18 www.lcompanyranger.com
19 www.pbs.org/wgbh/amex/vietnam/reflect/heinemann
20 www.8th-4th-arty.com/pucker
21 www.greene.xtn.net/~wingman/stories
22 www.grunt.space.swri.edu/loutplei.htm
23 www.1stcavmedic.com/june_2.html
24 www.vietvet.org/wid-vil

Chapter 5

1 Ho Chi Minh, *Report by Ho Chi Minh to the Fourth Conference of the Party Central Committee, 25–30 January 1953*, printed in Committee to Research Army History, Political Directorate, *Viet-Nam People's Army*, (Quan Doi Nhan Dan: Hanoi, 1974), pp.511–13, reprinted in Porter, *The Definitive Documentation*, pp.422–3.
2 Le Ly Hayslip, *When Heaven and Earth Changed Places. A Vietnamese Woman's Journey From War to Peace* (Doubleday: New York, 1989), pp.39–40. Hereafter cited as Hayslip, *Heaven and Earth*.
3 Wilfred G. Burchett, *Vietnam: Inside Story of the Guerrilla War* (International Publishers: New York, 1965), p.82. Hereafter cited as Burchett, *Vietnam: Guerrilla War*.
4 See Ho Chi Minh, *Appeal to the Entire People to Wage the Resistance War (20 December, 1946)*, in Bernard B. Fall, et al, *Ho Chi Minh on Revolution: Selected Writings, 1920–1966* (Frederick A. Praeger: New York, 1967), p.172. Hereafter cited as Fall, et al, *Ho Chi Minh on Revolution*.
5 Porter, *The Definitive Documentation*, pp.422–3.
6 Vo Nguyen Giap, *Directive by Commander in Chief Vo Nguyen Giap on Guerrilla Warfare*, dated 14 November 1947 (Extract). *Activating Guerrilla Warfare, the fundamental military task in the present phase*, excerpted in *Vo Nguyen Giap, Dan Quan Tu-Ve [Self-Defence Militia]* (Su That: Hanoi, 1974), pp.16–21, reprinted in Porter, *The Definitive Documentation*, pp.169–71.
7 Hayslip, *Heaven and Earth*, p.18.
8 Ibid, p.23.
9 Ibid, pp.39–40.
10 Burchett, *Vietnam: Guerrilla War*, p.82.
11 Ibid, pp.86–9.
12 Ibid, p.88.
13 Hayslip, *Heaven and Earth*, p.41.
14 Ibid.
15 John M. Carland, *United States Army in Vietnam: Combat Operations: Stemming the Tide: May 1965 to October 1966* (Center of Military History: Washington, D.C., 2000),

p.171. Hereafter cited as Carland, *Stemming the Tide*.
16 Presidium, Central Committee, South Vietnam National Front for Liberation, *Crush the Forthcoming Enemy Counteroffensive, Score Big Victories in the Winter 1966–Spring 1967 Campaign in South Vietnam: Initial Failures of the U.S. "Limited War"* (Foreign Languages Publishing House: Hanoi, 1967), pp.18–19. Hereafter cited as N.F.L, *Failures of the U.S. Limited War*.
17 General Van Tien Dung, *South Vietnam: U.S. Defeat Inevitable* (Foreign Languages Publishing House: Hanoi, 1967), pp.35–36.
18 General Vo Nguyen Giap, *How We Won the War* (RECON Publications: Philadelphia, 1976), pp.26–31.

Chapter 6

1 John Schlight, *The United States Air Force in Southeast Asia. The War in South Vietnam:The Years of the Offensive, 1965–1968* (Office of Air Force History, HQUSAF: Washington, D.C., 1988), p.3. Hereafter cited as Schlight, *Years of the Offensive*.
2 Earl H. Tilford, Jr., *Set Up: What the Air Force Did in Vietnam and Why* (Air University Press: Montgomery, Ala., June 1991), p.62. Hereafter cited as Tilford, *Set Up*.
3 Ibid, p.64.
4 Schlight, *Years of the Offensive*, pp.11–2.
5 General William W. Momyer, USAF, *Airpower in Three Wars (World War II, Korea, and Vietnam)* (Government Printing Office: Washington, D.C., 1978), p.15. Hereafter cited as Momyer, *Airpower in Three Wars*.
6 Ibid, p.17.
7 Ibid, p18.
8 William Buckingham, Jr., Ph.D., *Operation Ranch Hand: Herbicides in Southeast Asia, 1961–1971*, at http://cpcug.org/user/billb/ranchhand/ranchhand.html, p.2.
9 Miss Erin Keating. Oral Interview with Sergeant John J. Keating, USMC, reprinted in *Agent Orange and its Effects*, an unpublished research paper at The Ohio State University at Lima, dated 11 June 2002, in possession of the author.
10 Momyer, *Airpower in Three Wars*, p.237.
11 Ibid, pp241–2.
12 Ibid, pp.242–3.
13 Tilford, *Set Up*, p.62.
14 Momyer, *Airpower in Three Wars*, p.18.
15 Ibid, p.14.
16 See Admiral U.S.G. Sharp, USN, to the Joint Chiefs of Staff, dated 11 May 1965, in David C. Humphrey, Ronald D. Landa, Louis J. Smith and Glenn W. LaFantasie, *Foreign Relations of the United States, 1964–1968. Volume II Vietnam: January–June 1965* (U.S. Government Printing Office: Washington, D.C., 1996), p.641.
17 Momyer, *Airpower in Three Wars*, p.23.
18 Ibid, p.22.

CHAPTER NOTES

19 Adler, *Letters from Vietnam*, Major Theodore J. Shorack, Jr., USAF, dated 30 November 1965, pp.31–2.
20 Ibid, p.33.
21 Ibid.
22 Colonel Darrell D. Whitcomb, USAF Reserve (Ret.), "Brave Jolly Green", at www.vwam.com/vets/jogreen.html.
23 Seaman (E-4) Dennis Barr, USN, at www.vwam.com/vets/carrierwar/carrierwar.html, pp.1–2.
24 www.popasmoke.com/story20.html
25 www.vietvet.org
26 www.wildweasels.org
27 www.js-net.com/~phantom/
28 www.vwip.org/articles/h/HumphriesJr James_SpectreInTheNightSkyMeansTrouble OnTheTrail.htm
29 www.nd.edu/~ndmag/moew95.html

Chapter 7
1 General William C. Westmoreland, *Report on the War in Vietnam, Report on Operations in South Vietnam: January 1964–June 1968*, p.131. Hereafter cited as Westmoreland, *Report on the War in Vietnam*.
2 Ibid.
3 Ibid.
4 Ibid, p.132.
5 Ibid, p.133.
6 Ibid, p.133.
7 Lieutenant Commander Ray W. Stubbe, USN, *First Force Reconnaissance: A History*. Unpublished Manuscript in possession of the author (History and Museums Division, HQMC: Washington, D.C., 1975), p.176. Hereafter cited as Stubbe, *First Force Reconnaissance*.
8 David H. Puckett, Sr., *The Blue Spaders at the Battle of Ap Gu, 31 March–1 April 1967* (Cantigny First Division Foundation: Wheaton, Il, 1997), pp.5–6.
9 Ibid, p.7.
10 Ibid, p.8
11 Ibid, p.9.
12 Ibid, p.11.
13 Ibid.
14 Westmoreland, *Report on the War in Vietnam*, p131.
15 Major Richard D. Jackson, USMC (Ret.), *Yesterdays Are Forever, A Memoir. A Rite of Passage Through the Marine Corps and Vietnam War*. Revised Edition (Protea Publishing Co.: Atlanta. 2002), p.124.
16 Ibid, pp.124–5.
17 Stubbe, *First Force Reconnaissance*, p175.
18 Ibid, pp.177–8.
19 Ibid, p.178.
20 Ibid.
21 Corporal J. Michael Demko, USMC, Golf Company, 2nd Battalion, 7th Marines, 1st Marine Division, interview with Leo J. Daugherty III, Ohio Dominican College, Columbus, Ohio, 10 April, 1990. Tape in

possession of the author.
22 Professor (Captain) Gary F. Birkenmeier, *Mission of Mercy, Personal Reminiscences*, Typescript to Leo J. Daugherty, III, dated 24 June 2002, in possession of author.
23 West, *Small Unit Action in Vietnam*, pp.26–7.
24 Oral History Manuscript of Private First Class Kenneth W. Maag, U.S. Army, 3rd Platoon, Charlie Company, 4th Battalion, 3rd Infantry, 11th Brigade, "Americal" 23rd Light Infantry Division, to the author, Leo J. Daugherty dated 22 July 2002, in possession of author, pp.7–8.
25 www. greene.xtn.net/~wingman /stories/tet68.htm
26 www.illyria.com/women/vnwnamvet7.html
27 www.military.com/Content/MoreContent? file=darling01
28 www.war-stories.com
29 www.vspa.com/heavens-door.htm

Chapter 8
1 Jeffrey J. Clarke, *United States Army in Vietnam: Advice and Support: The Final Years, 1965–1973* (Center for Military History: Washington, D.C., 1988), p.34. Hereafter cited as Clarke, *Advice and Support: The Final Years*.
2 Ibid.
3 Major-General L. Nguyen Khang, VNMC, "Republic of Viet Nam Marine Corps", *Marine Corps Gazette*, November 1966, Vol. 50, pp.66–7.
4 Ibid, p.67.
5 Ibid, pp.38–9.
6 General Tran Van Don, *Our Endless War: Inside Vietnam* (Presidio Press: San Rafael, 1978), p.151. Hereafter cited as General Tran, *Our Endless War*.
7 Ibid, p.41.
8 Ibid, p154.
9 Colonel Hoang Ngoc Lung, "The General Offensives of 1968–1969", *U.S. Army Indochina Monograph Series* (U.S. Army Center of Military History: Washington, D.C., 1981), pp.72–4.
10 Graham A. Cosmas and Lieutenant-Colonel Terrence P. Murray, USMC, *U.S. Marines in Vietnam: Vietnamization and Redeployment, 1970–1971* (History and Museums Division, HQMC: Washington, D.C., 1986), p.210.
11 General Tran, *Our Endless War*, p.160.
12 Ibid.
13 Ibid, pp.156–8.
14 Major-General L. Nguyen Khang, VNMC, "Republic of Viet Nam Marine Corps", *Marine Corps Gazette*, November 1966, Vol. 50, p.67.
15 Colonel Hoang Ngoc Lung, "The General Offensives of 1968–1969", *U.S. Army Indochina Monograph Series* (U. S. Army Center of Military History: Washington,

D.C., 1981), p.9.
16 Ibid.
17 Graham A. Cosmas and Lieutenant-Colonel Terrence P. Murray, USMC, *U.S. Marines in Vietnam: Vietnamization and Redeployment, 1970–1971* (History and Museums Division, HQMC: Washington, D.C., 1986), p.210.
18 Captain Lu Van Thanh, *The Inviting Calls of Wondering Souls: Memoir of an ARVN Liaison Officer to United States Forces in Vietnam* (North Carolina: Jefferson, 1994), pp.20–1.
19 www.pbs.org/wgbh/amex/vietnam/reflect/ truong.html

Chapter 9
1 Graham A. Cosmas and Lieutenant-Colonel Terrence P. Murray, USMC, *U.S. Marines in Vietnam: Vietnamization and Redeployment, 1970–1971* (History and Museums Division: Washington, D.C., 1986), p.11. Hereafter cited as Cosmas and Murray, *U.S. Marines in Vietnam, 1970–71*.
2 Stephen T. Hosmer, Konrad Kellen and Brian M. Jenkins, *The Fall of South Vietnam: Statements by Vietnamese Military and Civilian Leaders* (Crane, Russak & Company, Inc.: New York, 1980), pp.160–1.
3 Ibid, p.161.
4 Ibid, pp.242–3.
5 Cosmas and Murray, *U.S. Marines in Vietnam, 1970–71*, p.49.
6 Ibid, p.53.
7 Ibid, p.85.
8 Captain Lu Van Thanh, *Memoir of An ARVN Liaison Officer*, p.25.
9 Stephen T. Hosmer, Konrad Kellen and Brian M. Jenkins, *The Fall of South Vietnam: Statements by Vietnamese Military and Civilian Leaders* (Crane, Russak & Company, Inc.: New York, 1980), pp.242–3.
10 Staff Sergeant Thomas J. Sabanski, USMC. Unpublished Oral History Memoir Manuscript in possession of the author. Interview conducted at Camp Joseph H. Pendleton, California, 1 March 1988, pp.75–81.
11 www.military.com/Content/MoreContent? file=darling01
12 www.pbs.org/wgbh/peoplescentury/ episodes/guerrillawars/giaptranscript.html
13 www.pbs.org/wgbh/amex/vietnam/reflect/ hackworth.html

The Brown Reference Group plc has made every effort to contact and acknowledge the creators and copyright holders of all extracts reproduced in this book. We apologize for any omissions. Any person who wishes to be credited in any reprints should contact The Brown Reference Group plc in writing: The Brown Reference Group plc, 8 Chapel Place, Rivington Street London EC2A 3DQ, U.K.

INDEX